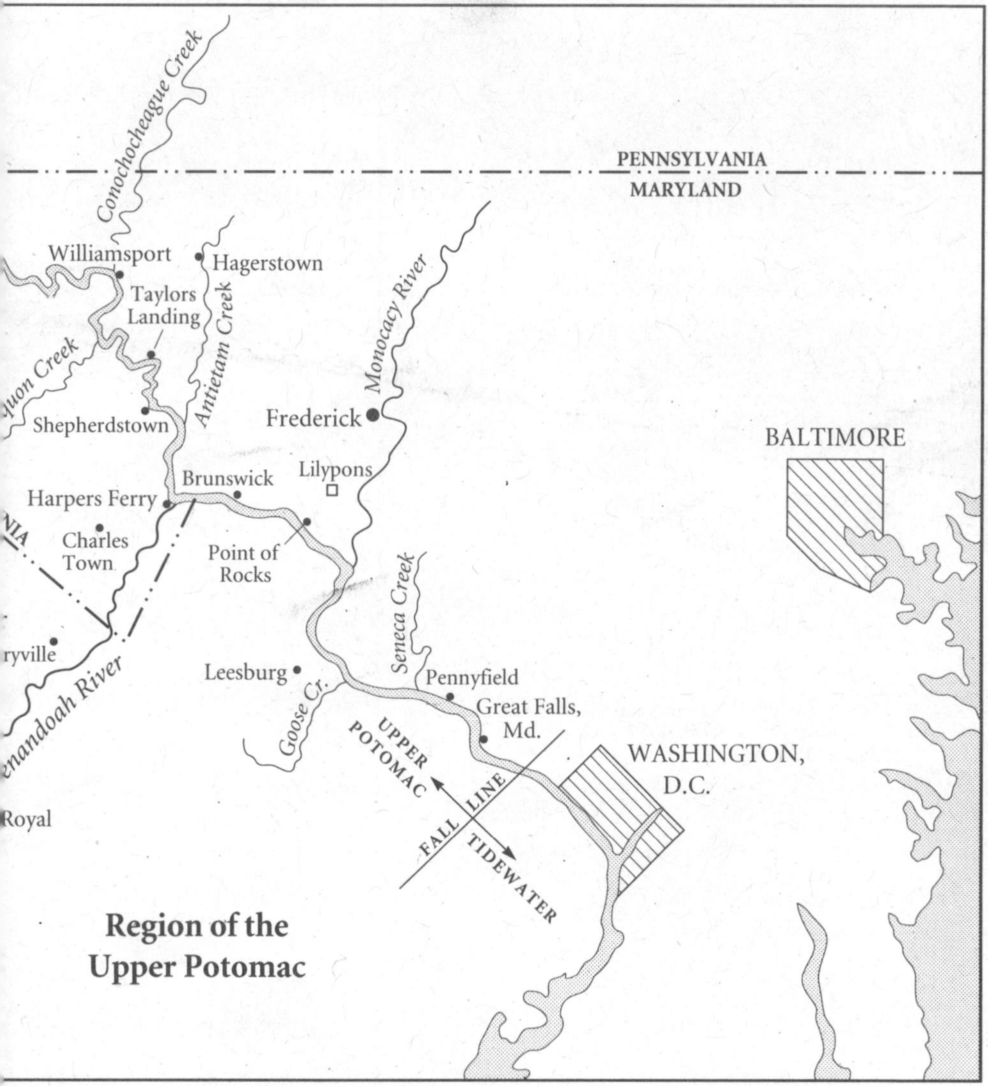


**Region of the Upper Potomac**

# LEANING SYCAMORES

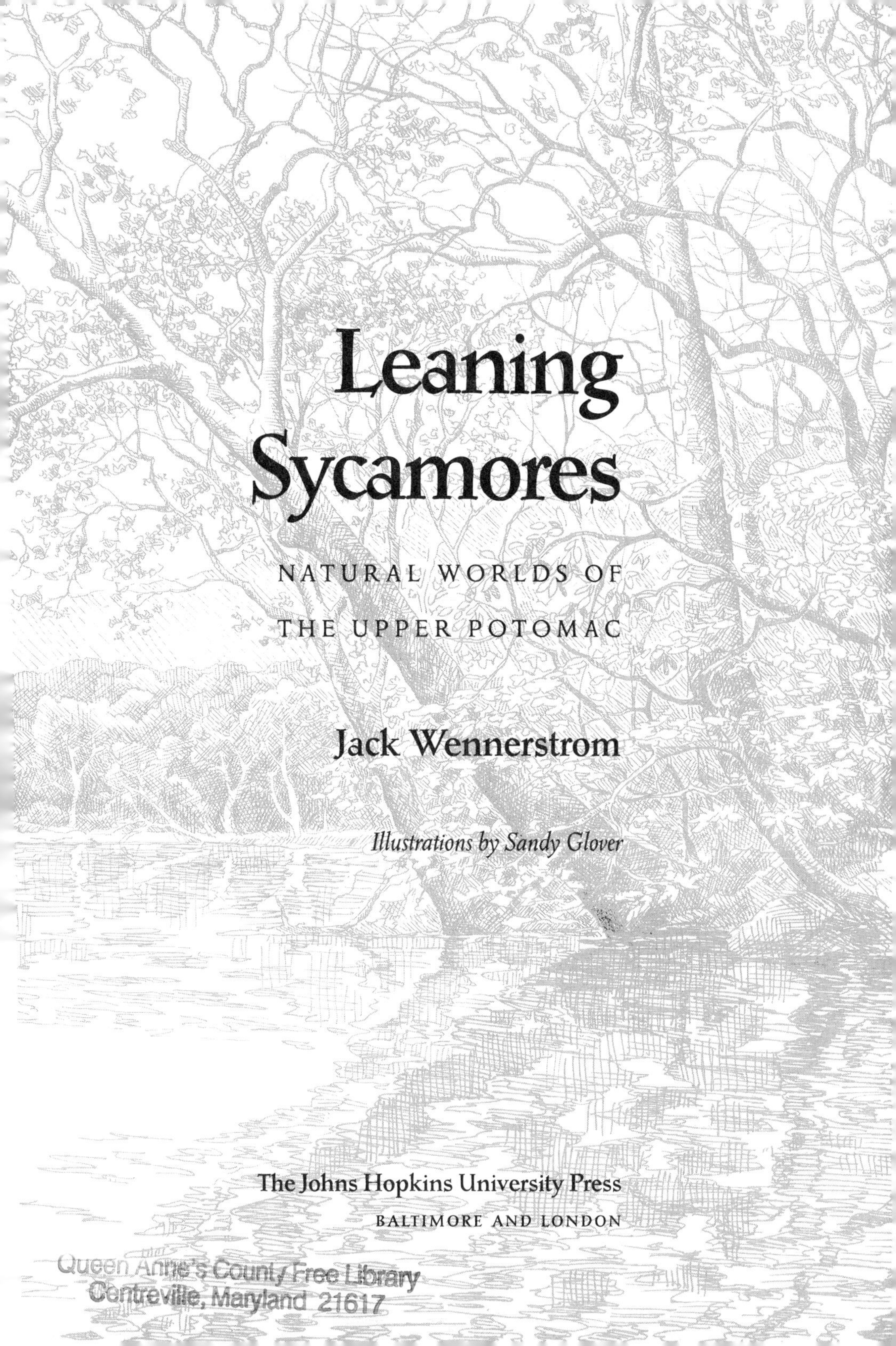

# Leaning Sycamores

NATURAL WORLDS OF THE UPPER POTOMAC

Jack Wennerstrom

*Illustrations by Sandy Glover*

The Johns Hopkins University Press
BALTIMORE AND LONDON

Printed in the United States of America on acid-free paper
05 04 03 02 01 00 99 98 97 96 5 4 3 2 1

The Johns Hopkins University Press
2715 North Charles Street
Baltimore, Maryland 21218-4319
The Johns Hopkins Press Ltd., London

ISBN 0-8018-5189-0

Library of Congress Cataloging-in-Publication Data
will be found at the end of this book.
A catalog record for this book is available from the
British Library.

*To Donna, as always*

I was for that time lifted above earth;
And possest joyes not promis'd in my birth.

—IZAAK WALTON

Wherever the trees and skies are reflected, there is more than Atlantic depth, and no danger of fancy running aground.

—HENRY DAVID THOREAU

# Contents

# Preface

In water there is fascination. I have always found it to be so. As a small boy exploring the margins of depleted, remnant prairies in the upper Midwest, I was charmed by potholes and tiny ponds, flooded fields, channels of snowmelt, seasonal wet spots, rivulets and creeks. Large lakes delighted me and were the scenes of my first fishing forays. My earliest sight of a true river, a polluted but luxuriant arm of the languid Des Plaines, where a single mallard bobbed against the current, is forever etched in my memory. To the stock intrigue of water's liquid mystery, rivers add music and motion and the distinct sense—as with time, destiny, and life itself—of steady yet fickle progress. In such features, too, lie the powers of hypnosis.

I eventually learned that "river reverence" was no mere province of childhood or adolescence. Adults were at least as susceptible as kids. One of my first essays for a birding magazine was received by an editor whose coprofession was ornithology. But his hobby turned out to be fly-fishing. Of the half-dozen or so editors on a renowned New York City magazine whose name is synonymous with birds and who bought another of my early pieces, fully four were avid stream anglers. Indeed, while I've known my share of country folk smitten by the lure of the banksides, people with addresses in the city, and especially editors and publishers, seem particularly prone to the affliction. In the metro regions of New York, Baltimore, and Washington, D.C., an inordinate number are linked by their love of rivers.

There are two in particular I'd like to thank. Nick Lyons of Lyons and Burford was the first to encourage my early struggles with this book and offer advice and direction. And Jack Goellner, the longtime director of the Johns Hopkins University Press, championed the manuscript from its beginnings and was a source of steady reassurance through the many stages of its completion. Besides being accomplished fishermen, both are advocates for rivers and the living things maintained by them, not only in the regions where they live and work but in places around the globe.

Others who have helped me are a diverse lot. Warren Steiner of the Smithsonian Institution, who likes nothing better than to wade barefoot in a creek or stream in search of aquatic invertebrates, was, along with his wife, Jil Swearingen Steiner, an early source of moral and technical support, as was Warren's colleague at the Smithsonian, Paul Spangler. Ann Walston, yet another adroit angler who is also connected with publishing, was particularly cooperative in her role as a book designer at the Johns Hopkins University Press. And my wife, Donna Shoemaker, an editor and writer herself, was my greatest advocate by far, offering unmatched love and support throughout the book's evolution.

At various times technical or research-related questions were willingly answered by a broad array of professionals, including Stuart Schwartz, Sally Bowen, Ken Pavol, Bruce Michael, Victor Kennedy, Ed Thompson, William Martin, Ed Enamait, Peter Jayne, Ed Golden, William McShea, Meheret Woubeshet, Chris Lea, Melvin Brown, Deidre Murphy, and Tom Tapley.

At least as important have been the many "nonexperts" I've met during many years of discovery along the upper Potomac, people who, in their frequent contact with the river and its surroundings, are knowledgeable in ways that no expert can fathom. These have been too numerous to recall fully or mention, but prominent among them are Kay and Bill Miller, Nick and Joanie Blanton, Ron and Pete Leggett, Jeanne House, Fred Swain, Louis Wesley, Alan Himes, and Donna Huffer.

If there is a human fabric to the river, it is surely made up of all the people I have mentioned and more, of their threads of character and destiny, their work, their play, their thoughts and conversations, their hopes and fears and lifelong tenacious strivings.

# LEANING SYCAMORES

# Prologue

The upper Potomac River, from its headwaters in West Virginia, to the fall line near Washington, D.C., winds 281 miles. Its landscape, despite some three hundred years of disturbance and exploitation, is today essentially a wild one. A city and a few small towns intrude, some industry and a man-made lake, but now—thanks largely to much of its floodplain being preserved as parkland—its character and substance are shaped by wild nature. The persistent theme of that wild nature is water and trees, and, among the latter, the recurring signposts of gnarled and woody glory are the sycamores, which lean along the banks like static titans, stiff and flaking dinosaurs from a greater natural age, old ghosts and behemoth shades of the way things were before white men, great flawed and broken windmills to be tilted at by madmen. I am one of those madmen.

The upper Potomac has been written about before but never in the way I shall write of it. Mine is a new story and an old one together, a meld of ancient and modern, science and philosophy, hard fact and informed speculation. It is not about movers and shakers, the future of enterprise in the river's valleys and hills, or my prowess in a canoe. It is, you might say, a story about shadows and the strange living things that throw them: above the river's banks and feeder streams, below its bluffs and caves, in its pools and rapids, along its bars and islands. It is a story about that which lurks, about mystery and minutiae, about the quiet and unsung, about the shy natives of the river, past and present, who have gained the least attention. It is an underdog's story, a tale of the slighted and ignored, the snubbed, the subdued, and the seldom pondered.

Nothing lurks quite so persistently and mysteriously as a fish in flowing water. So my story concerns fish as well. And the easiest way to unveil their mystery is to draw them up out of darkness, to lure them from their shadowed lairs—where they devour or are devoured—and bare them, shimmering, to the light. Some people call this fishing. I call it the revelation of enigma, an ancient and holy calling. To probe a deep pool, to plumb some pocket in the earth with the message of a sinking line—a predatory false tapping in the dark—and to receive an answering tug or violent thrash of response from a creature beyond sight of men, is a thing to make one muse. I have mused on the river for almost twenty years. What follows is the result.

Writing about a river, any river, tempts one to the tricky brink of literary precedent and cliché. In the verbal abyss below lies not only the strewn, stupendous body of all things once spoken on the subject, of every epic and allegory, every tested wisdom, every mythic adventure drawn out in the time-flood of words, but all the cheap devices of cornball yarn or purple prose, the striving machines of inflated deeds, the wrecked vehicles of sportsmen and heroes who loomed against every salmon dusk or stretched in the rosy dawns. They extolled the well-known virtues and unveiled blatant truths. Some backed their pickups to the brink at night, while critics slumbered, and dumped the trash of ten million words in the valleys of the endless streams. The best of it sublime, the worst stinking, the whole of this flotsam dulls and corrodes below, broken by the rocks of ages, occasionally winking like porcelain or chrome, beneath the feet of the brinksman. It is a hard panorama to absorb, a slippery glory to compress.

In these times one tries to add something fresh and nonpolluting. One is moved and wishes to respond. One teeters on the edge and looks down, daunted and hopeful both. Here one brings something young, to be made old by time and immensity—one's forged reflections, things shiny that will someday also dull. Here one must dump cracked magic, spill one's poor porcelain and chrome.

CHAPTER ONE

# Beginnings

There are several beginnings to my story about the upper Potomac River. One beginning unfolds in spring, in the mountains, in the distant past. It could unfold as far back as six hundred million years ago, in the Cambrian epoch of the Paleozoic, among the ancient spreading seas or among the great upliftings of sandstone or the Carboniferous forests half again as young, with their coal-making *Lepidodendrons* and hawk-sized flying insects. But I prefer the witness of mankind, the periods—beginning some twelve thousand years ago—marked by human presence.

Native peoples called the upper river by several names. One was Wappacomo. In that spring of man's time on this continent, when the ice had pulled north and nomads pressed into its valleys, they deemed it a separate river. Today it is called the South Branch and is thought of as a tributary.

The South Branch of the Potomac begins in mountains, in the Alleghenies, and flows from south to north, its own principle branches shaped like a frontier meat fork: long and three pronged, and forged too, out of hardness. Today they are named, west to east, both illogically and windily: North Fork of the South Branch, South Branch River (the middle fork), and South Fork of the South Branch. If Indian names seem unwieldy, one may dote here on Wappacomo, a relative model of simplicity.

The valley of the South Branch drains millions of acres, nearly all in today's West Virginia, though the headsprings well up in Virginia by a matter of several miles. This is the loftiest land in a very lofty state. Spruce Knob is the state's highest point, at just under 5,000 feet, and it watches over the North Fork from a distance of less than three miles—which says much about the valley's steepness. The sandstone is cut so sheerly here that ridges fall away as cliffs. Some become isolated blades, sculpted phantasmagorically and once held sacred by the Seneca, westernmost tribe of the Iroquois nation, who camped at their wooded bases and basked in their alien aura.

Here in early spring the gray-brown slopes and ridges tinge faintest green and are stippled throughout by the shadbush in bloom, whose white petals cluster round their pistillate cores like Keats's starry fays, or like the snowflakes so near in memory they are often no memory at all but come with the April winds. The creeks flow loudly in the bright light, bulging, and with no surrounding foliage to drink off their rackety tunes. Thawed mats of last year's leaves reek like winter silage, but with vernal perfumes added from a hundred vague sources, atomized on the breeze, while the pinks and whites of hepatica and trillium lay sprinkled on the woodland loam. The first sweaty clouds of the season rush by overhead, the waterthrush bobs on wet stump or rock, and phoebes dip by the trails.

Along such trails came Iroquois warriors, in elk-skin leggings and mocassins, bare limbs and chests striped red and pitch, with shaved heads and blackened eyes and feathers in their locks. They toted their weapons and their small sacks of corn, traveling light through the mountains to the south, 25 miles a day, rockahominy and maple sugar for their meal at night in some cave beneath the ridge brows. They repeated this twenty days and, in darkness on the twenty-first, surprised the Catawbas in their camps, captured or killed them outright, in the foothills of the Smoky Mountains. The attackers sang and suffered on the way and showed enemies little mercy, not because they were evil but because, by the rules of their order, compassion was fatal frailty, and frailty singled you out and marked your families for death. Cruelty overawed foes, who then might leave you in peace. The mountains were cruel, the falcon was cruel, the spring frost was cruel, and all were everlasting, and great, and unencumbered by pity.

When white men arrived in the 1600s they were caught up in these cruelties, as early records attest. Cadwalader Jones, a Virginia trader, wrote Lord Baltimore in 1681: "This year the Indians will need Roanoke [bead money] and I have considerable trade with them. Through it I learned six weeks since of the Seneca Indians about 300 miles S.S.W. from here. They took from an Indian town 35 [people], and 4 or 5 from several small towns under the mountains near 500 miles. They have so far oppressed these Indians that they have made no corn this year. They are now in full body returning home. By reckoning they may be in your country [Maryland] on their return, when the turkeys gobble, by information of those that were here."

This last was no mere aside but a warning that armed bands of warriors would soon be among the settlements.

But an earlier period on the upper Potomac predates this roving warfare and suggests a quieter existence. The North Branch of the Potomac, called by natives of old Cohongoronta, was, beginning a millennium ago, a place of stockaded villages and 10-acre fields by the river, where squash, corn, and beans were grown in alluvial soils, while deer, elk, and turkey were steamed or roasted in pits. The people who lived here, linked to a westerly culture—that of the so-called Monongahela—had crossed from the Ohio Valley to settle in these bankside towns and to bury their dead on the ridges.

Traces of Monongahela life along the upper Potomac and elsewhere have but recently been dissected. Their preference for terraced bottomlands near major streams, their circular houses in settlements not exceeding one hundred souls, their distinctive shell- or limestone-tempered pottery adorned with line-filled triangles and oblique slashes, even the percentage of meat, fish, and plants in their varied diet, are noted by archaeologists as proof of a common culture and as clues to imagining their lives.

But clues are all that remain. The full scope of their cultural perspective may forever elude understanding. A unique vision died with the virgin wilderness. For the natural world they knew, a world of towering hemlock and spruce and plentiful fish and game, was a world in which awe and wonder were not things touted abstractedly but the stuff of daily life. One lived briefly, by modern measure, but lived in the grip of nature unreduced, vividly, overarched by its fluxing forces, its palpable demons and gods. One did not seek out wildness, as some do today, but was part of it, in its thrall body and soul. The same spellbinding vista, some long view eastward on a jutting ridge, which inspired the living man, was the same on which he was buried, in a stone-heaped tomb over four feet high, companioned by the natural magic—bird bone, goose feather, shell bead; pendant of blue chert, crystal quartz, or cannel coal—which brought solace to his time on earth.

My story might also begin in autumn, when the leaning sycamores of the banksides have lost many of their leaves and stretch, before winter's long sleep, in every twisted posture and arthritic pose, stripped beside the bath of the river, half-naked in tones of ochre and buff and gray.

In most autumns they loom dryly above the heaped confetti of fallen leaves. A fruity odor pervades. Fog obscures the dawns and haze the twilights. Pawpaws ripen, pokeberries plump, mushrooms engorge and rot. The bluejays call through the arid whisper of tickling branches and discharging boughs, through the remnant signals of doomed crickets, above the river's shrinking pools.

Unless, that is, the rain clouds come in the mountains from some wayward tropical storm or hurricane pushed up from the Gulf and are squeezed out on ridges by the cold hands of the highlands. Then the bath rises to meet these trees, rushing past their roots or climbing above their knees and thrashing out its torrent in the brown floodplain tangles. The flotsam of leaves, stems, and rootlets lodges in the forks of low branches, silt suffocates sassafras and spicebush and tarnishes their gold, and snags show up with tires and drums, overnight, settled down like weary squatters as the coffee waters recede.

And a flaking giant will here and there have indeed taken its bath, undercut for the last time and collapsed into the stream. The floodplain will set to rotting in the pale presolstice light, the ridges will shake down their last freight of color in the foothills further west, and the wind will howl on the headwaters peaks, bending down the hemlock and spruce, stiffening sap till spring, and displacing the night-black ravens, who will sheer away like burnt bits of paper toward the shelter of the lower slopes.

In this season on the river, in the 1700s, Thomas Lewis, that forgotten knight of Lord Fairfax, reached his goal along the North Branch. A surveyor, he was hired in 1746 by the sixth Lord Fairfax to find "the first or most distant fountain of the Potomac." Fairfax wished to confirm the extent of his "Northern Neck" holding, a vast tract of inherited Virginia wilderness whose boundaries were still in dispute.

With a few picked men, including Peter Jefferson, father of our second president, Lewis traversed mostly highlands. He set out in September, running the "Fairfax Line" from the head of the Rappahannock to a faint effusion on a hillside near present-day Kempton, Maryland. It was a straight-line distance of 76 miles. By modern standards it was hardly more than a toddle; in Lewis's day it was a life-threatening odyssey. There was fear mixed with the solace men found in prejourney drinking. Lewis's pocket-sized notebook, leather-bound and quill-scratched, tells the quaint tale best: "Tuesday [September] 16th: Spent the day in preparing for our journey and in the evening retired to our camp where we spent our hours with a great deal of pleasure and merriment. Was taken ill in the night. Violent vomiting."

Steeped in tales of frontier heroism, we often assume these stout pioneers were beyond giving in to mere dread. Quite the contrary—in a world in which death was sudden and commonplace, most clung to life sensibly, choosing prudence without much shame: "Saturday 20th: The mountains made such a dismal appearance that John Thomas, one of our men, took sick on the same, and so returned home."

A more concise statement about frontier reality could hardly be wished for. Men knew the risk of such ventures, and the thought could make them sick. The best hands might be drawn from the ranks of what Walt Whitman called, in a later era—and with affection but a shake of the head—"thoughtless youths." Imagination and sensitivity kept one in the towns.

While illness and hunger were their frequent companions, these were just for openers. The virgin Allegheny slopes were a literal jungle of green. Tough mountain laurel and big rhododendron were hell for bushwhacking parties proceeding in beeline fashion up hill and down, with horses and bulky stores. The wood of mountain laurel is hard and strong, so tough it was used for briar pipes. Known as "ivy" by old-time Southerners, it, along with robust big rhododendron, called "laurel" by the hill folk, embowered whole slopes from their bases to 4,000 feet. Both the foliage and flowers of the former are toxic to grazing mammals. The Lewis party often cursed its way on a path directly through it:

> Tueday [October] 14th: . . . no place for our horses to feed, and to prevent their eating of laurel, tied them all up, least they should be poisoned. . . . This river was called "Styx" from the dismal appearance of the place, being sufficient to strike terror in any human creature, ye laurels, ivy, and spruce pine so extremely thick. . . .
>
> Wednesday 15th: The laurel and ivy as thick as they can well grow, whose branches growing of an extraordinary length are so well woven together that without cutting away it would be impossible to force through them. Fell into clefts and cavities without seeing the danger before we felt the effects of it. Frequently we

had the roots to cut and the rocks to break to free our horses, of whom four or five might have been seen engaged at a time.

Trees that stood on the survey's true line, between the two head-springs, were marked with blazes or initials, and their regular mention in the journal serves as survey of the forest species then present in that country: chestnut, white and red oak, birch, pine, spruce, maple, black locust, beech, walnut, chestnut oak, dogwood, poplar, cottonwood, ash, hickory, black gum, arborvitae, and our old friend the sycamore. Nearly all grew untouched by humans. Lewis made note of the cherry trees: "the most and finest I ever saw, some 3 or 4 foot diameter, thirty or forty foot without a branch."

Amid this vast arboreal garden it was beech and spruce that signaled their final success, marked with initials by the party of 1736, whose imperfect survey had preceded them. Thus, on October 22, 1746, finding they had reached the Potomac headspring, Lewis remarked, "We dined on loin roasted venison, about 3 o'clock, at the spring-head; drank His Majesty's health."

A stone was set at the spot and marked "FX," the so-called Fairfax Stone, replaced no less than four times in the long period since. The Lewis survey satisfied Fairfax and His Majesty's Council, but not the resulting states of the later-formed nation, who fought over jurisdiction in the region for well over a century. Not until 1911 were boundary matters, inextricably linked to the Stone, settled between Maryland and West Virginia. Additionally, some still dispute that the North Branch—and not the South Branch, whose forks wind much further through the highlands and are the true "most *distant* fountains"—was the rightful head of the great river Potomac.

Meanwhile, the looming forests were stripped of their ample glory. In the headwaters country great tracts of red spruce and hemlock were reduced to barren knobs, slowly at first by settlers and pensioned Revolutionary veterans, then swiftly and surely by the railroads and mines, whose hirelings clear-cut with no second thoughts and left not a virgin mile. Even the tough rhododendrons lost out on many of the slopes, and erosion left hillsides barren for thousands of contiguous acres. But that is still another story, a nineteenth-century one, that begins in the heat of summer.

Inauspicious starts may mark the affairs of men but are often overcome. So when the sixth president of the United States, John Quincy Adams, attempted, on July 4, 1828, to sink his shovel and turn the first clod of dirt in the building of a great canal, and failed—not once but three times—there was yet little cause for concern among the crowd gathered west of Georgetown for the ceremony. A buried tree stump prevented his success until the fourth plunge, when the dirt finally flew and the crowd cheered. It was perhaps the last heartfelt hurrah the Chesapeake and Ohio Canal would get in its long history of troubles.

At almost the same time, near Baltimore, the aging Charles Carroll of Carrollton was helping to set the cornerstone for another speculative transport venture, the Baltimore and Ohio Railroad. Charles Carroll was patriarch of a distinguished Maryland family, was a former U.S. senator, and had signed the Declaration of Independence. He was noted for the boldness of his commitments, having vainly but stubbornly sought Canada's aid against the British during the Revolution. His commitment to the B & O was to be no less zealous.

The expansion boom was on along the upper Potomac and beyond, where cheapness of transport would be king. Both companies hoped especially to capture the lucrative Ohio Valley trade routes, and both risked heavily. Railroading of the day was a dicey experiment in crude steam power, dabbled in mostly by the British, and the time when Peter Cooper's "Tom Thumb" locomotive would puff gingerly a few miles out from Baltimore at a top speed of 18 miles per hour, was still over two years away. Canalling, though a far older concept, wasn't much better. Its routes were slaves to adjacent rivers, causing frequent destruction by flood, and construction was labor intensive in extremes, forcing prolonged hardship on unwilling navvies, overworked engineers, and skittish financial backers.

George Washington's Patowmack Company canals were the first along the river, preceding those of the C & O by several decades. Begun in the 1780s, in existence nearly fifty years, and major achievements for their day, they were yet little more than a series of "skirting" canals designed to augment, not eliminate, risky riverboat travel. The difficulty of their construction and maintenance discouraged even the brilliant James Rumsey, true father of the steamboat, who, despite much success, resigned from the Potowmack Company's "Matildaville" project at Great Falls after serving only a year. Yet if canal building had drained men and budgets, it had also seen triumph. The success of the Erie Canal, completed in 1825, was warm in the mind of entrepeneurs and, perhaps more than any one factor, urged the C & O stockholders forward.

Though most of their conflicts are forgotten, the railroad and canal companies feuded from the start. The canal had the backing of the federal government and the railroad of powerful Marylanders, in whose state jurisdiction the proposed routes lay. No sooner had the Erie Canal's chief engineer, Benjamin Wright, been hired by the C & O in the same capacity, than the State of Maryland, on behalf of the B & O, sued to prevent construction of the canal beyond Point of Rocks, some 50 miles upstream from Georgetown. The narrow passage there between the river and Catoctin Mountain was not, to use the well-worn parlance of town bullies in the Old West, "big enough for the both of 'em." Each fought viciously in court for the right of way, and canal construction was stymied for almost four years. And old Charles Carroll must have chuckled as he laid the B & O cornerstone, for his trump card against the C & O was an estate he owned on the canal company's route and which he refused to sell through years of bitter litigation.

Other of the difficulties are more well-known: labor disputes, lack of skilled workers, and excessive costs for both canal and railroad as well as, for the C & O, repeated outbreaks of cholera and the infamous Paw Paw Tunnel, a canal company "shortcut" projected as a two-year job but which actually ate up twelve.

The impact of all this construction on the river landscape was great. Hillsides above the Potomac were quarried for granite, sandstone, and limestone, and, while most of the riparian hardwoods had already fallen to homesteaders, timberjacks, charcoalers, and iron mongers, the needs of canal and railroad finished off pockets of resistance and left the floodplain a sparsely treed shambles of shantytowns, rubble heaps, wagon roads, makeshift gardens and stock pens, and every manner of jerry-built office, hovel, sutler's hut, tavern, lockhouse, blacksmith's or peddler's station. Some scaly sycamores survived, leaning over the river and out of harm's way, and a scattering of maples for shade, with patchy islands of bramble, box elder, and sassafras. Few were shocked by such vistas. Indeed, they were not so far from the contemporary ideal of busy, well-used land shaped by man's divine impulse toward industry and progress.

In the end the B & O Railroad not only won the race, reaching Cumberland, Maryland, in 1842, eight years ahead of the C & O, but proved the superior technology, soon pushing on to Wheeling, (West) Virginia and the Ohio River and carrying all manner of goods at unheard-of speeds. The canallers were left to carry bulky nonperishables—coal, iron, flour, and limestone by-products—and to contemplate their limited range, flood-prone locations, and mule's pace.

For wild nature the larger significance of these two new enterprises was the opportunity they provided for natural exploitation on a grand scale. Previously, men cut wood for their homes and mills and for modest local industries. Now the market for lumber and coal had expanded exponentially—had become, in fact, worldwide—and the rising entrepreneurs could not get enough of the timbered slopes and underground veins in the river's upper reaches. The big grab was on, and the concept of limitations was grasped only in terms of what investors would bear. "Should you?" was not an issue. Only "Could you?": Could you scare up the capital? Could you gather and hold the work crews? Could you outduel competitors for markets near and far?

The once-modest George's Creek coal industry of western Maryland wound its tentacles ever more efficiently into each placid valley and gouged out what it needed. And men like Henry Gassaway Davis, a piedmont native who moved west with the railroad, became Horatio Algers of the region. Davis rose through the B & O ranks, later testing the waters of resource development as a dealer in coal and lumber and pressing into banking and politics. When the Civil War came, Davis supplied the Union army with coal for its locomotives and timber for ties and bridges and bought thousands of acres on Great Backbone Mountain, from which much of the North Branch springs. Virgin conifer woodlands, underlain with coal, he bought for a half-buck an acre. He became a senator, railroad magnate, and candidate for president, and he clear-cut the headwaters giants into virtual extinction. In the 1880s his own railroad company reported that "the coal and iron ore lands are covered with a primeval forest of black walnut, cherry, white spruce, ash, hemlock, maple, and poplar." Some areas were "a thick forest almost covered with spruce and hemlock, the trees being of enormous size and good quality."

Subsequently, every acre of headwaters country was leveled but for a small "picnic grove" for workers, a place of shaggy hemlocks which still stands today, an unintended reminder of its preserver's lack of foresight. The remaining moonscape of naked hillsides and highland "balds" led to topsoil erosion and flash floods, lifeless creeks tinctured with mill, tannery, and mining wastes, and unsightly watercourse buildups of sawdust, bark, and iron sulfide crustings known locally as "yellow-boy."

The legacy and perspective of men like Davis carried well into this century. Though virgin timber was exhausted, paper milling of lesser trees was expanded and refined. Deep mining for coal was augmented or replaced by strip-mining, and shafts that finally shut down leached chemicals into streams and groundwater for decades after, and indeed, to this day. New words and phrases entered the vocabulary of freshwater consumers: *erosion, siltation, polluted aquifer, leachate, dioxin, PCB, acid-mine drainage, parts-per-million.*

The United States had grown vigorously into the twentieth century like no nation in history, and the upper Potomac had helped it do so. It had jumped, as no human society had ever jumped before, to a million rich tunes played by a million mad pipers. The dance was wild and uplifting, the liquor plentiful and heady, but, as the night of indulgence wore on and yet another new century loomed, the pipers presented their bills.

It is winter on the Potomac when this last story begins. The spring of early man is a pale facet in the artifacts of museums, the autumn hardships of past explorers are a humus of old books and papers, and the fat summer of exploitation beside the banks and in the hills is a gout that will never quite heal. In winter one best views the facets, smells the humus, muses on the many scars. And in winter, too, one sees the fresh promise, the newest hope that the seasons will circle and replenish with time and wisdom what centuries of stress removed. In winter the masks are laid bare, the structure of bone is revealed, and the chance for a fair reconstruction is apparent in the face of the land.

Prominent again are the water and trees, to the exclusion, indeed, of man's dreams, for wildness has returned to the river in these last days of our century, and human structures are rare. There is quiet on the modern towpath, where pools reflect gray sky. The floodplain is once more a forest, carpeted shaggily with leaves in this region beside the canal bed, which sometimes holds dark water, sometimes a rubble of stonework, and sometimes solemn walls or locks, hoary with moss and memories. The river gurgles, the pools gleam, the aged sycamores lean.

Winter is a time to take stock here, in the late twentieth century, and to ponder what remains. For the lover of wild nature what remains is a lot indeed. It is not so much a remains as a rebirth. That large and graceful mammal, the white-tail deer, is here in great numbers, beyond those even of its earliest golden age. It has prospered near a new human culture that procures its meat from stockyards, leaves waste corn in its fields, and values graceful neighbors. Birds are here in plenty, not as many as before Europeans but in numbers and species greater than when men gouged out the canal and laid the iron rails. Reptiles and amphibians, a secretive lot, have held their own, with notable exceptions; fishes, though fewer and different in species, are balanced in the waters of a river that has not been so clean in a century. Insects, a hard group to gauge, are yet plentiful past common need and less varied past common notice. Plants have suffered upheaval huge, sweeping, and irreversible. But they are used to upheaval, and on it some even depend. Though entire communities have vanished, or have been so badly disturbed that alignments are permanently shattered, the newcomers carry on, and old lines linger in pockets or return where habitats renew.

Most critically, for all these, the river and the land beside it have been granted a kind of reprieve. The environs of the upper Potomac, at least in one narrow corridor, one vital strip beside the waters, have been given their first real stability in over three hundred years. Those other natural components, *humans,* have taken their business elsewhere and declared this land a "park." They have stopped demanding too much and now only ask for one thing, a thing called "recreation." The traces of their deeds remain and, indeed, are part of the bargain. They come to view them and to ponder. And they come to share the wildness with their fellow keepers of the land.

The trees are bare in this season, in this season of hope and reflection. Frail sunlight pours to the forest floor and onto the glinting river. But it strengthens with every day. I sit now by the river, in the growing light of late winter. I sit beneath the sycamore that leans above the water. I view the river and the trees, and I think of all I have seen here and all I still wish to see. A breeze blows off the water and behind me toward the floodplain forest, toward the wet bed of the canal, toward hills and mountains beyond. I detect a sweatiness in it, a subtle vernal warmth. The time of renewal grows near. Let us go, then, and explore this kingdom, and dote on its secret treasures, and see what people have seen for all time or have never seen before.

CHAPTER TWO

# Moving Water

In rivers, the water you touch is the last of what has passed and the first of that which comes. So with time present." This simple profundity, penned by Leonardo da Vinci some five hundred years ago, gets at the heart of both time and the river as has no description since. A river is moving water, and its nature changes with time.

Thus, what the upper Potomac or any river really is, from any number of viewpoints—biologic, hydrologic, hydraulic, limnologic, ecologic—cannot be accurately fathomed without the bedrock admission that it is a medium not only in flux but in flux in different ways and at different points, both in time and along its spatial course.

Amid this flux and variance, however, a river can be said to have two fundamental features: the motion of water and its transport. Not only are rivers in motion—a motion variable in both speed and direction and at points along its length—but in motion variably from bank to bank and from top to bottom as well. Currents that are swift a short way from the bank may languish at midstream or boil near the opposite shore, while top-water drift may slacken a few feet under the surface, then grow or subside at the bottom.

In addition, river water transports not only its own chemical bulk of pure hydrogen and oxygen but also mineral sediments acquired from terrestrial runoff and riverbed scouring, and the matter of the living and dead, the organisms or their by-products constantly adrift there—from tiny algae known as phytoplankton, to the zooplankton that feed on them, to insect larvae, small mollusks, crustaceans, fish, other higher animals, and both flowering and nonflowering plants.

The shoreline of the river is also in flux, changing from dry to wet or wet to dry, the alluvial habitats of untold species dependent on its variable moisture.

Thus the medium of river water is as plastic and diverse as any in nature, being different meter to meter, mile to mile, right or left, up or down, in drought, in flood, or in between. Rivers are, in some sense, a *form* of motion, of "hydraulic flow," classified by scientists and engineers according to momentum, energy, inertia, and viscosity and expressed through equations and formulas. The momentum of flowing water, for instance, is the product of its mass and velocity and, measured "per unit time of water passing a given point," is expressed as "density times discharge times velocity." One expert on hydraulics has gone so far as to define rivers themselves in the following single sentence: "Concepts resting on geomorphological theories of minimum variance and minimization of work, simplified for biologists by the statement that one cannot maximize both efficiency and stability in biological systems."

But the moving water of my story is a good deal greater than this. What of the upper Potomac's flow? Amid all these features of analysis comes a need to define it as more. One longs to perceive it in a much larger sense, to be near it, upon it, even *in* it, but not to reduce it by formula or summary. I cherish my own concept of its motion, my own brands of measurement, my own devotion to its flux. I had watched it from the banks long enough before applying such detailed scrutiny. I had watched it as hiker, birder, botanizer, and bankside fisher, or as casual Sunday stroller. Then, somewhere along the line, my mode of engaging it changed.

It began, I suppose, on a whim. On a whim I entered a surplus store on a hot August dog day to admire the commercial flotsam of outdoor recreation, to wonder at it mostly, and in part just to dodge the heat. My eye caught an object in a corner, suspended oddly from the ceiling. It was gaudy blue and yellow, made of plasticized rubber, bulbous, curvaceous, quaint. It was an old inflatable boat, what most call a rubber raft.

But it somehow seemed more than a raft to me as I slowly walked beneath it. I got it down with the manager's help and carefully looked it over. Brass-fitted air valves, swivel oarlocks, 400-pound capacity, with room, supposedly, for two, though it looked like one man would fill it. It was the last of its kind in the store, Japanese-made, and superseded by cheaper ones that were stacked along one wall, made in Taiwan or the Philippines, and without brass fittings or swivel locks. It had hung in the shop for years, it seemed, and had trouble holding its air. I asked if it were on sale. No, said the manager, and, though it was obviously shop-worn, he refused to lower the price.

I then pondered a place near Pennyfield Lock, a place that was on my mind of late, a stretch of upper Potomac where I'd seen several bass from the bank on a mellow autumn day. I thought of the deep holes beyond, out past the shallows, which I'd stood on tiptoes to fathom, on stumps and in tree forks, but ultimately failed to probe. And I heard in my mind the rustling of leaves, dry in the sycamores above me, saw the whitish flicker and flash of the maple leaf backsides downstream, caught in the wind near some rapids. I thought about mid-September, the cicadas droning through the floodplain, the swallows dipping to the river pools, and the anglers in their lithe canoes, drifting down with the tawny current, beyond me and out of sight. I blocked out the old boat's cost, its flaws and ludicrous posture, its impossible size and color. And I bought it on the spot.

*To drift.* The verb is fraught with paradox. It suggests both movement and immobility, sloth and adventure, quiet and excitement, the simple and the complex. Its very objective meanings invite subjective thought.

Of the former, the dictionary provides some half-dozen: "to be carried along by currents"; "to proceed without resistance or move unhurriedly and slowly"; "to move from place to place without regular employment and with no particular goal"; "to wander from a set course"; "to oscillate randomly about a fixed setting"; and, finally, "to be piled up in heaps by the force of a current." All might apply to my first experience in that small inflatable boat. None are the sum of that experience and, even less, of its parts.

I could not resist my new toy and wasted no time launching it. I purchased both oars and hand pump, drove west to Pennyfield Lock, inflated the device near my car, and walked it down to the riverbank in the sweltering late-day heat.

The upper Potomac in August, if the weather has been typically dry, as it had been that summer, is a shallow welter of transparent pools, tinted faintly with tannic seep or sediment, adrift with phosphatic foam flecks or limp wracks of pondweed, and raggedly parqueted on its surface by alternate sun glare and shadow. The rank, dusty canopy of hardwoods above each bank looms clifflike against the glare, and the heavy bulges of cumulus move like slothful conchs on some tedious inverted sandbar, in the hazy lagoon of the sky.

I pushed off with one muddy sneaker and became that first definition: "carried along by currents." So, too, did I "proceed without resistance" and "move unhurriedly and slowly," for, once away from shore, I checked my temptation to grab the oars and merely floated free. Certainly, I was "without regular employment" and "had no particular goal," and the "set course" I wandered from was that of a beeline boatman or canoeist, for my course was as drunken as a fly's. Had I cared much at the time, I might also have noticed I was "oscillating randomly about a fixed setting," turning in gentle circles against the frozen backdrop of the shoreline, the static walls of green, and the constant skyward glare. But I cared only for drifting, and fresh subjective senses craved little of objective meanings.

I moved in the present, amid spontaneous impressions. What perhaps impressed me most, and impresses me still today, was the sense of slow revelation, constant and incremental, which the shallow Potomac affords. Assisted by polarized lenses I peered into recessed cavelike realms and otherwise hidden grottoes. I was taken, in effect, on a private tour by the whimsical guide of the current, and the visions provided were half-limpid peeps, faintly clouded disclosures of a world maybe one meter deep, easily accessed by the eye and mind yet tinctured with the gauze of dreamland—slow-motion, resin-pale, magnified realms that were just beyond arm's length and perhaps just that far past reason and the rational world of the landsman.

True to the paradox of drifting, there is—moment to moment in the changing flow—not just a sense of disclosure but of disclosure swiftly thwarted, of epiphany strangled at the threshold, of coalesced meaning that dissolves the instant before it is grasped, as in some haunting dream one wakes from a second too soon. A perception is beautifully gathered, its strands of image and emotion, of analysis and memory, are briefly pinched for the knot, then all of it fades or becomes something else, kaleidoscopes forward or back and away, and the strands give out or are pulled too late and fail to be sensibly woven. They are somehow pleasant, these teasing threads, and in fact impose fascination, in the way that one learns to love longing and to be most inspired by promise. Each is the fragment of a puzzle, the ragged clue of some mystery that begs investigation.

The upper Potomac is nowhere deep. It averages 2 to 4 feet in the low flow of summer dry spells, with pools or deep holes running 5 to 8 and the noted "chasms" of 80-foot depth, near Chain Bridge and Three Sisters Island, being just below the fall line and thus part of that quite different place, the tidal, or lower, river.

The flow of the upper river is measured in gallons per day and the speed of the river's flow in cubic feet per second per day. They are both really measurements of flow, one computed as volume and the other as speed or velocity. The average flow, measured through the last several decades at a place called Little Falls, is 7 billion gallons per day. Its extremes are worth noting. A drought in 1966 brought a late-summer reading of just 388 million gallons a day, while the all-time recorded high, during the massive flooding of March 1936, was 313 *billion.*

Flood highs vary widely as well and, because of their fearsome nature, get the most statistical attention. Some floods barely jump the banks and go all but unnoticed, as the one of February 1984, at some 102 billion gallons. Others are thoroughly infamous. A record disaster such as the 1936 flood, with its 313 billion gallons, produced also the highest velocity, 484,000 cubic feet ps/pd, and the highest crest ever at Hancock, Maryland, of just under 48 feet, which is 18 feet above flood stage. Yet the record high crest on the river, once solely held by the 1936 flood, was tied in 1985, when November rains in the mountains brought the level at Paw Paw, West Virginia, to a devastating 54 feet, some 29 feet above flood stage.

Statistics, of course, do not really tell the story. Whole communities, human and nonhuman alike, are wiped out by such events, and some do not recover. In 1852 the Potomac rose 64 feet at Great Falls and brought damage of $100,000, a huge sum for its day. The flood of 1924 left the C & O Canal in ruins and forced its final closure after nearly a hundred years. Among other appalling losses, the 1936 flood took out every bridge save one along the upper length of the river. And Harpers Ferry, which rests beside the triple threat of a major confluence, deep rock gorges, and steep river gradients, has been badly damaged a dozen times in the last hundred or so years, with, on average, the river rising 5 feet over the towpath every five years, and twice wildly swamping it to a depth of 21 feet.

But, if seven billion gallons is average flow, in summer the flow is much lighter, perhaps one or two billion gallons a day in a month without much rain. On that August afternoon when I first launched my boat it was likely within that range. The current and visibility produced by such low volume offer ideal visual scanning of the variable bottom contours, composed, in the Pennyfield region, mostly of quartzite and schist, with brief plains of sand or silt and gravel broken down from the rock types. Overall, these much resemble a landscape, especially one hilly or mountainous, and drifting above them is like floating along in some silent hot-air balloon. Here I examined the ledges once invisible from shore and learned what existed both fore and aft of protruding crags and boulders, especially those that, from a distance, are merely V's in the surface glaze or trailing lines of foam.

Here, too, I first met the water-starwort, in its secret submarine garden, and distinguished the various pondweeds of the genus *Potogamon,* in their undulate riverbed "forests." Water celery, the river's version of eelgrass, waved from its quiet anchorage like so many graceful tapeworms, and fish in small schools, especially white suckers, appeared in openings like farm beasts might from some peaceful balloon elevation. Other fish—squat redbreast sunfish and tiny smallmouth bass—could be glimpsed to the side or out ahead, fleeing my looming shadow.

It was smallmouth bass that I focused on, and soon I cut short my drifting and tied up to a snag. I assembled the rod and reel that I'd brought along from the trunk, tied on a plastic lure, slipped anchorage, and began plugging the pools. In the hottest part of a summer's day I didn't expect much action, but before long I had a strike.

Here is a subtle glory that escapes the grasp of those who don't fish, and even many who do. Less than an hour before I was in some stale building, hiding from the city heat, from the noise, the glare, the traffic, yet now I was floating on liquid glass, surrounded by quiet and sunlight and green, by the fust of the floodplain sand and silt, the reek of the torpid trees. And below me, as I turned in the wash of a quartzite ledge, over the shaft of a drop-off, some creature was making my rod throb, trying to take my tackle, darting across the current.

One must make nonfishers see this, take some time to explain, to outline part of the excitement. The possibility exists, indeed it is more than likely, that an individual fish of whatever actual species, rare or common, fresh or salt, has never been seen by a human being from the instant it was hatched until the moment one draws it from the water. Of what else can this be said in a world long scoured by science and reduced by endless scrutiny?

Thus did I soon gaze fully on a creature of exquisite detail which shone and shimmered like the numen of a dream, which pulsed with an alien energy that, in its individual expression, I was the first to view, of all men on the planet. The horns were honking on River Road, the stink of a hundred buses and a hundred thousand cars was fogging the streets somewhere near, but I alone viewed the channel cat, a species of pearl gray flank and fin, of salmon-dotted sides, of fleshy whiskers and gargoyle eyes and ancient croaking voice.

Indeed, it croaked when I grasped it, as these catfish often do, then twisted in my grip like an angry pup and vaulted from my hand to my lap. I soon released it, held it over the side and let it shimmy out from the gunnel, let it disappear like some watery sylph and return, like a sinking ingot, to its place of perpetual mystery.

I remained adrift for less than two hours, though it seemed like a full afternoon. I had uncanny first-timer's luck, at least at the task of fishing. I caught three more channel catfish, two redbreast sunfish, and, to my utter and blissful shock, a 13-inch smallmouth bass. The heat abated not a wit; the shadows grew imperceptibly; the sun's glare dimmed but a notch. I was guided, dumb with delight, over many more air balloon landscapes, preserved in their fossil resin but supple and gracefully alive.

At last I reentered the well-defined realm of the landsman. I fulfilled my objective destiny, that final dictionary meaning, "piled up"—as I was at last, in a "heap" of satisfied pleasure, plasticized rubber, teasing visions, and oozing river silt—by the gentle force of the current, against the Potomac bankside.

Other driftings on the upper Potomac are far more important than my own. They comprise the aquatic food chains that sustain the river's life. Tiny floating algae, known as phytoplankton, are fed upon by almost equally small aquatic animals called zooplankton, which include such families as Cyclopids, Calanoids, and Cladocerans. Both algaes and zooplankton are in turn eaten by aquatic insects, of which over one hundred species exist in the headwater streams alone, with at least another two hundred species in the mid-reaches of the main upper stem. Prominent among these are the orders of Ephemeroptera (mayflies), Trichoptera (caddisflies), and Plecoptera (stoneflies). Then, in the more familiar elevations of the food chain, small fish devour aquatic insects, and big fish eat little ones.

All these organisms make up the links of at least two recognized food chains, which at times are intertwined. One is called the "grazing" food chain and the other the "detritus" food chain. In the former, green plants are consumed directly, while in the latter, the consumption by assorted organisms is of organic debris.

The larvae of the caddisfly, for example, are part of the grazing chain due to their preference for gleaning small aquatic organisms from the river or stream current. Yet some species of caddisfly also consume detritus in the form of leaf and twig litter that finds its way into the current, in varied stages of decay, from the bankside vegetation. So, caddisfly larvae may be part of two chains at once.

Both the grazing chain and the detritus chain depend on drift. The ebb and flow of single-celled diatoms and multicelled rotifers, of filamentous green and blue-green algaes and the wee critters that devour them, the swaying larvae of aquatic insects whose feeding often depends on a fixed position in the flow, and the constant load of organic particles and nutrients sloughed off by the living and dead from both water and land, is a complex dance of swirl and twist played out on the stages of the currents and largely invisible to humans. The creatures that lurk in these food chains have limited mobility and habitat tolerance, but all depend on the perpetual opportunism afforded by moving water.

For a large grazer like myself, however, mere drifting does not suffice. To fish effectively on the upper Potomac one must deftly handle oars, row against currents, anticipate hazards, and stay alert and mobile, for the river is nothing if not full of fluxing tricks. The best way to gauge those tricks is to know the river "stages," which are measured daily at a number of Potomac "gauging points" for over 200 miles. A recording announces these levels, in feet of depth, and a simple phone call alerts one to this vital information.

Little Falls, just west of Georgetown, is a major river gauging point and the first one I learned to keep track of. In the dry days of summer, 2.9 to 3.2 feet is a typical Little Falls reading range. But there is no standard measurement to which gauging points relate. Even with uniform conditions there is variance, for the depth of the pools in which the measurements are made is different at each location. When Little Falls measures 3.2, Paw Paw, far upstream, may read 4.3 and Point of Rocks 1.8, though rain may have ceased in the watershed for a period of several weeks. A local storm in the valleys or hills brings further variation, so the game is to study the ranges over time, know the average levels in periods of typical dryness, and factor in cloudbursts and rain fronts. Little Falls readings above 5 feet (and, say, 7 at Paw Paw and 4 at Point of Rocks) are considered, as the phone message puts it, "unsafe for recreation."

To know that my craft is "nonstandard" (and to some eyes less than that) is to understand my caution. It is all of five feet long, carries no motor or power source, is stuck together with epoxy and thread, and boasts millimeter fractions of bottom ply between river water and occupant.

I named it after a turtle. Or a terrapin, really. The University of Maryland, where my wife once both worked and studied, has a terrapin for a mascot. Its name is Testudo. Thus I dubbed my tube-ringed rubber boat *Testubo* in its honor.

*Testubo* got her acid test on a day in late September. The Little Falls reading was 4.6—still safe for most excursions but a bit of a strain for lightweights like mine, especially if the object is fishing. The moment I reached the main current I knew it would not be our day. *Testubo* and I careened past the holes at a pace that frustrated casting, and the drag on the line with my diving plug was enough to bow the rod. I soon saw this was futile and rowed for a brush-free place near the bank which offered suitable takeout. But I made no headway in the current and was swept at a sharp cross-angle a number of yards downstream. I persisted and bucked the flow. That's when one of the oar blades snapped like a piece of stale praline. I managed to slide in the shoreline current to some semblance of a landing, using the oar shaft like a push pole and grabbing at sycamore rootlets. I soaked one leg to the knee and then stumbled in poison ivy. After that I bought some stronger oars, but I'd learned our limitations. When Little Falls reads above 4.5 I do not take *Testubo* on the river.

In just about all other ways, however, I consider *Testubo* a superior craft for exploring the upper river. She easily fits, deflated, in a car trunk, and inflates in a matter of minutes. She is almost completely silent, gently sighing or hissing over ledges and coughing against the odd rock. Canoes I have known (especially of metal) are like noisy kids, banging and grating loudly and echoing every commotion on board with nerve-tweaking mockery.

*Testubo* rides high, peacefully drifts, responds at once to the oars, and is so compact one can jack her about, goose and slide and pivot her, as if moving one's own lower body with a pair of muscular arms. The oars, in fact—thanks to swivel locks—are easily and neatly shipped, so that nothing dangles in the water when one sneaks up on a pool or prepares to drop through a chute. She can also slip a haystack with grace, flex and give in the rapids, or undulate over washboards. The chief problem with her losing air, I quickly learned, was that the rubber gaskets around her valve fittings had badly eroded. In a hardware store I found the right O-rings, jammed them into place, and she ceased to leak in the slightest.

Perhaps best of all, *Testubo* is portable. No involved portage or shuffling of cars at pickup points is required at any time. She is made for the solo explorer, compacting well when deflated, neatly filling her tote sack, and easily backpacking miles to the car on the long return trail of the towpath. And she is that rare combination most vehicles are not: quiet and utterly simple. In this she is like the experience I court, for I come to the river for its quiet and, despite its multiplicities, for the simpleness of its rhythm and pulse, the essentially unrefined breath it exhales from the complex corpus of its workings.

That which the drifter feels least, the wader feels most. Resistance—the life of the current throbbing against one's unmoving legs or, most inconveniently, pushing, punching, and swiping at those legs as one tries to make some progress—is the river's commonest reaction to the creatures it meets from land.

I am not so addicted to floating that I don't sometimes wade the Potomac. When I do so it is usually to fish, but I also collect plants and insects, mollusks and crustaceans, and the odd stranded lure. And my greeting from the river is always the same, this steady fluid embrace that borders on aggression. The river knows not shyness or constraint but presses its uneasy welcome, till the visitor from terra firma grows tired, makes his or her excuses, and leaves feeling rudely handled.

Besides being much too chummy, the river has sticky fingers. Its current makes off with whatever rises or falls or is not securely tethered. In the case of its taste for risings, these are mostly silts and shoreside muds that ascend in billows when one steps from the bank and soon are kneaded by the flow, which prods and pokes their chocolate bulge, then devours them with dilution, till nothing remains but some fleeing crumbs, 20 yards downstream.

The things that fall are from waste or mistake, and fair game for the current, though the issue is often disputed. Water peels from the lips of deer, mud and old hair from their graceful but dirty ankles. None of it is contested as the river makes its claim and sweeps this cargo downstream. Thermos cups slosh in the cold hands of men and deliver whiskied coffee drops to the pools and gentle riffles; sandwiches crumble in those same numb fists and release unchallenged freight. But if popping bug or crawfish plug should happen to slip its moorings where the clumsy wader is stationed, or a hat or treasured visor, then the scramble is on, the deal is undone, and the river's rights are contested.

These are the forms of resistance which the upper Potomac musters against those that invade it directly. Sometimes it goes too far. Sometimes it gets so persistent, so slaphappy touchy-feely, that it literally knocks its visitor down and tries to take him with it. One makes a cautious sideways step—harmless and quite polite, one thinks—or attempts some motion forward, and the river responds with a rude shove or suck and trips one onto its flooring. If recovery is not both agile and swift, one finds oneself being transported, a few feet or a few yards, depending on the river's depth of mood and one's own reaction to the insult.

This brings to mind yet another way one communes with Potomac currents. The concept is called immersion. Perpetual as are its energies, the upper Potomac on balance is a friendly place when treated with respect. In the low flow of summer the river is often a maze of small islands formed by feeder streams and sweeping bends, which pile up sandbars and gravel bars that soon support vegetation. Between these islands, and usually near the shore, are narrow channels with rocky pools, chutes and riffles, ledges and logjams, all overhung with verdure and reflecting filtered rays. The deepest pools are but neck high, clear and wavy with light and shade, protective of sunfish, catfish, and bass, cool and quiet and inviting.

Indeed, it is hard to wade this place—on hot summer days, in cutoffs and ragged sneakers—and not feel the urge to merge with its flow, to sink oneself in its bosom. To lie on your back in a riffle or wash and let the knotty hands of the current work coolness into your shoulders is splendid summer therapy. To feel your arms and kidneys lift as you float in a limpid hole or to squish sandy silt through once-cramped toes and to watch this curious process from the leaning perch of log or ledge, from the distance of the length of your body, is a primitive affirmation.

During such baptisms you cavort with your fellow drifters and grazers. The one-celled algae called diatoms, who huddle nearby in colonial millions, are of myriad shapes and sizes, appearing together on microscope slides—disks and diamonds and ovals, with intricate stellar innards—like the contents of a seamstress' button box spilled on a pane of glass. That tumble you took from a slippery rock could be blamed on these fellow bathers, whose colonies form slimy coatings on most things hard and submerged. The tiny multicelled rotifers, lost to the naked eye but surely present around you, charge about in the current, spinning nutrients inward with their comic pinwheel cilia. Minute green algaes, elongate but single celled, cling to rocks in the swiftest runs with the aid of special holdfast cells, while other algae smear crayfish and snails and darken them almost to black.

One is circled by living mysteries here, immersed in invisible realms, feebly observing but a fraction of the dramas that swirl nearby. Even the larger players lead lives you can only guess at: a school of tiny dace are attracted by the windfall disturbance of your silt-sifting toes, an opportunistic sunfish eyes the maddened dace, the shadow of a fleeing sucker crosses the path of some freshwater snails, whose progress along a submerged slab of rock is discernible only with effort. For a change you stare straight up at the sky, at its buttressed framework of sycamore boughs, at the light-tickling silver maples, and always there is the current's pulse, its subtlest or rudest greetings, its liquid language of resistance speaking wordlessly through your limbs.

Immersion in current is an intimate act. It connects us with things elemental, with things we profess to love, and it banishes fear and neurotic care without extinguishing caution. Merging completely with the river, at the proper time and place, is the best way to cherish its nature and to know its subtle strength.

Yet to seek this communion these days is to break the law, for "swimming" is not permitted. Fishing, however, is, and fishers often slip. Which is not the same as making mistakes, a confusion that afflicts the righteous. Fools will always misjudge water and find a way to drown. But the standard measure of wisdom that the best of us have in tow is nourished by all things intimate and is natively shy of transgression. To such worlds as the upper Potomac and its infinite riddle of parts our attention is a kind of reading. It is up to us to wonder and watch and to read the message plain. Again, it is quiet and simple, a message that any fool can see but only the sage can make sense of. Come along, says the river, and measure my strength—watch me, touch me, ride me, breast me, enter in my complete, but only in my season. There is for each a season, and you will know them when you know me, though I am mystery itself.

CHAPTER THREE

# Trees, Man, and the River

Once there was a forest on the west coast of that region we now call Greenland. It was part of a much larger woodland that surrounded the northern pole in a nearly continuous arc. From the remains of this Greenland forest came, one hundred million years later, our first fossil records of the hardwood trees now common in the eastern United States. These records suggest that the dominant tree of Greenland's Upper Cretaceous woodlands was, for several million years, the sycamore.

During this reign the sycamore was gradually joined by other familiar hardwoods of our time, such as tulip tree, hawthorne, hornbeam, hickory, and walnut. The ancient sycamores mingled, too, with trees that we temperate zone dwellers think of as utterly strange: moonseed, breadfruit, and cinnamon. For the polar region of old was much warmer, was washed by currents from the south that could carry buoyant seeds, and was connected to Asia, and perhaps other continents, by land bridges useful for migrations.

Indeed, according to one theory, present western China and northeast India were long ago the birthplace of our mid-Atlantic deciduous trees, which got here by moving gradually eastward across the Aleutian land bridge. In modern Yunnan Province, for example, grow maples closely related to our own as well as tree species native to our Southeast but to almost nowhere else: hackberry, locust, sweet gum, and persimmon. Subsequent ages of ice killed off the less-hardy varieties, but many species common here today escaped by edging south from those first subarctic strongholds.

The next place in the fossil record that the sycamore shows up is along the Potomac River. From evidence collected in the lower Potomac Valley we know that ninety-five million years ago—just five million years after the dominant sycamores of Greenland and in a time when dinosaurs still roamed the earth—*Platanus occidentalis,* our American sycamore, grew along the river. But here it was far from dominant, forming, with willow, poplar, oak, elm, and sassafras, a mere quarter of that ancient forest so long ruled by palmlike cycads, gingkos, giant ferns, and those ancestors of pine, the *Auracaria. Homo sapiens* was still nearly ninety-five million years away from its bipedal debut, and the Rocky Mountains were a bump somewhere on the landscape to the west, awaiting gigantic upthrust.

By the time Europeans arrived here, virtually yesterday in geologic and evolutionary terms, the sycamore was one of some one thousand two hundred modern North American tree species (a number exceeded elsewhere on the globe only by the species of India) covering some 900 million undisturbed acres. Settlers found it, with its distinctive peeling bark, ruling the riverbanks and bottomlands and notable especially for its girth. In the late eighteenth century the French botanist André Michaux came upon an Ohio River sycamore measuring 40 feet around and 13 feet through the middle, while his son beat this record years later, meeting one monster with a 47-foot circumference. Such stoutness, combined with recorded heights of 200 feet, make sycamores the biggest deciduous trees on the continent. Pioneers stabled livestock in the hollowed core that evolves in such giants and even sheltered their families inside until they could build proper cabins.

On the upper Potomac sycamores rule to this day, and, considering the ravaged landscape nearby, their persistence is no less astounding than their size. I have measured a few fully 18 feet around, and 25 feet in circumference is not unheard of today. This puts the age of some beyond a century and a half and means such trees were growing when the canals and railroads were built. What saved them? Probably their small stature at the time, and perhaps deformity or a queer location. The wood makes a weak beam or column relative to other hardwoods, and it easily decays. But it is very difficult to split. Butcher blocks are thus often fashioned from sycamore. In pioneer days men got bins and barrels ready-made from crosscut sections of the hollow trunks, in need only of bottoms. In like fashion they made lard pails, buckets, and washtubs from the hollow boughs and limbs, and unhollow trunks could be cross-sectioned, too, to form solid wheels for oxcarts.

But the sycamore's glory and importance is not in human utility. The upper Potomac bankside is virtually defined by its presence. For long stretches of river two out of three trees within 50 feet of the water and more than 40 feet tall are sycamores. Thus, two-thirds of the canopy sunlight in such spots is absorbed by sycamores, much of the deepest streamside earth is held in place by their roots, and the bulk of the broad-leaved detritus and woody deadfall, both near and in the water, comes from this species. A large percentage of the "leaf-mining" insects—moths, beetles, and flies whose eggs and larvae develop within leaves—must be sycamore linked or compatible, as must the fungi, yeasts, and bacteria in their billions which break the leaves down further. Though the lives of few higher animals are sycamore specific, dozens of species, from the larger invertebrates to reptiles and amphibians, birds, and mammals, depend in some way on the sycamore's myriad parts for food, shelter, and successful breeding, as do the fishes of the river.

The sycamore is no mere symbol, then, but a major force and essential link in the upper Potomac's biology. It manages also to inspire: human beings watch the gnarled giants from river or towpath, see their peeled columns and blistered boughs shine coolly through summer verdure or etch their moonbeam paleness against a dark winter sky, and respond to their simple spectacle. Hikers crush the furry fruits, pick up the scrolls of curled bark—shed as if from some reptile, one side warty and greenish with mold, the other like dried human flesh—or mark where it catches in the box elder branches, hung out like drying laundry. Nothing about the sycamore is quite settled or expected, despite its venerable age. Its seeds are queer, its stature when grandest is gouty, its oldest leaves tenderly peach-fuzzed. It does not flame in autumn but understates its tones, defers instead to its oracle of limbs, its cream and buff and pewter skin that whispers with shadow and bursts with change, failing to suffer growth seamlessly like most of its placid neighbors. It is something like our own mother earth, ancient but erupting through its surface for all the force it mantles. It is the callow giant of the Greenland woods, one hundred million years young, bursting and writhing like an imperfect youth still adjusting to the hulk it has become.

From the Potomac floodplain's largest tree, consider now its smallest. Both are in many ways each other's opposite. Where the sycamore is stout and soaring, this tree is spindly and short, averaging just 20 feet tall and several inches around. Where the sycamore maintains elbow room, this tree is fond of groups and is quick to colonize openings or fields in weedy, gregarious stands. Where the sycamore's leaves are drab, this tree blazes in autumn with brilliant yellows and reds. And, where man made humble use of the sycamore and rarely touted its practical merits, this tree was a legend of utility, was valued to the point of myth and sought out like precious ore.

*Sassafras albidum* is its Latin name, known simply as sassafras to most, though the common name of ague tree hints well at its former reputation. For it was once thought a cure-all by Europeans, a remedy not only for ague, or influenza, but for just about everything else in the late sixteenth and early seventeenth centuries. The first written account of its powers came out in 1574, when a physician named Nicholas Monardes proclaimed it a sovereign remedy for malaria, fevers, frailness, headaches, chest colds, tertian agues, lameness, lust, and complaints of the stomach and liver. A Europe beset by baffling diseases embraced it as a panacea, and by 1602 it was bringing over 300 pounds sterling per ton on the English import market. Expeditions went forth solely to collect sassafras, from New England (the northern limit of its natural range) to the Carolinas. It ranked with Arabian spices as a precious commodity and was demanded of the Jamestown Colony, like tribute, as a condition of their charter.

Today it is astonishing that something so humble as sassafras should have caused such a stir. Along the upper Potomac it is chiefly a sapling of the understory, fighting for fragmented light with a half-dozen skinny competitor species and thus rarely attaining its ideal height of 50 or 60 feet. In summer here it seems little more than a stout weed. Its confusion of three different leaf shapes—two-lobed in the well-known mitten design but also elliptical and three-lobed—appearing all on one tree in varying size and prominence, and similar to those of red mulberry, only make it harder to recognize.

Yet in two ways it stands out. As noted, its fall foliage is dramatic, a preponderance of yellow and orange which is shaded and blotched with pinks or vermilions, garnets, roses, and ochres. Then it takes its place beside spicebush—which, curiously, shares both its yellow fall tones and fragrant essence—as the glory of the floodplain understory. Its little mitten flags are hung out smartly above and betwixt the honeysuckle mazes, suffused with sunlight to a gold or pomegranate brightness, dangling limp-stemmed in sanguine bits like lost shards from stained-glass windows. Other small trees or vines, their chlorophyll likewise having broken down to show carotenoids and xanthophylls and the sugar-built anthocyanins, compete at this place on the spectrum. Poison ivy and Virginia creeper form isolated sprays of scarlet, the odd black gum or dogwood drifts more red through the middle elevations, and spicebush spreads golden thickets under dangling, frondlike pawpaw leaves and unpretty box elder scaffoldings. Sassafras holds its low ground, unmistakable now in petite scarecrow postures beside the towpath and the dry canal, stitched with saffron patches.

But it was odor, not color, which brought the sassafras fame. The oily sap present in its leaves, twigs, bark, and roots is highly aromatic. Centuries ago both Old and New World consensus had it that fresh or pungent fragrance purged evil and, by extension, disease, since illness, it was believed, sprang from evil. Aromatic spices and herbs were therefore highly valued. When sassafras failed to cure most afflictions, as it once was expected to do, its curative aura lingered. It was still added to medicines, soaps, soups, perfumes, candies, soft drinks, and teas and was used for bedposts and floorboards to promote bug-free interiors.

Even in this century and, indeed, up to the present, well-known naturopaths list its properties as stimulant, alterative, diaphoretic, and diuretic. It is said to "purify the blood" and "cleanse the system," to act as a tonic on bowels and stomach, to relieve gas and remedy spasms, and to be good for inflamed eyes, toothache, colic, skin disease, varicose ulcers, and troubles of the throat, chest, bladder, and kidneys. In some quarters, it seems, the more things change, the more they stay the same.

There may be some truth to its merit, even for shameless cynics. When something becomes legendary it acquires the influence of an icon, and icons can affect human spirit. The power of suggestion is strong, and symbolic good or evil can alter mood, even thought, through the path of autosuggestion. A cup of sassafras tea, with its clean and spicy flavor and smell, can lift the spirit of a head cold sufferer and relieve a scratchy throat. And the hiker is cheered, on some thirsty march, by the sight of that old friend sassafras, whose familiar mitten extends in greeting and which, if plucked and chewed, promotes a pleasant salivation and sense of mental refreshment far out of proportion to the chemical reality of that single sticky leaf.

How does one praise a giant whose chief distinction seems one of confused identity and bland anonymity? Often as large as the sycamore, and nearly as numerous at bankside, this large maple not only gets no respect along the upper Potomac but goes virtually unrecognized. "Willow" is what I have heard it called by some anglers, or simply "that big tree over the water." This last is closer to the truth, for *Acer saccharinum,* the silver maple, hangs huge over the bank, often dangling its lower branches nearly to the river surface. It does, like the willow, favor watery locations, as its other names suggest: water maple, river maple, creek maple, swamp maple.

But people often clutch at impressions while ignoring obvious details. This tree's toothed, deeply five-lobed leaves are clearly those of a maple and as unlike the blades of a willow as can be. Yet, due to their very long stems, they shiver willowlike in wind, twist their massed pale undersides and pendulate branches, and broadcast a soughing music. The old trunks, too, are fat and shaggy, like those of aged willows, and the foliage in fall, quite un-maple-like, goes bland rather than brilliant. No one paying close attention would ever call them willows, but a distant impression based on just such misleading clues might tempt one in that direction.

Their outline is unlovely. The silver maple crown is jagged and broken, the larger limbs twisted, irregular, and scarred with the stumps of breakage, and the trunk base full of flaky bark and weedy sprouts. Their wood is brittle. Though they quickly reach good size, they are relatively short-lived trees, drop a mess of winged key fruits in springtime, and are prey to insect pests, which mar the leaves and twigs. Midwestern settlers made a superior syrup from their sap but found the flow too meager. Along the upper Potomac their lowest drooping branches, upturned at their tips candelabra-style, hang with unsightly wads of debris, stuck there during high water, dark and matted like foul, discarded wigs.

The tree has its fine points, some already suggested. Its silver flash of underleaves, its tickling windsong, and a speedy growth rate make it a popular transplant. And it has some use in industry, for furniture and boxes. But it is clearly a floodplain underdog. A certain kind of pragmatist will never see it as lovely.

I view it as a companion, an accepted presence on the river. For utility one has its ready roots at bankside, big furrowed shelves of muscular wood, ideal as tie-up or take-out points. The up-curved talons of its branches, which stoop out over the water sometimes 30 feet from shore, make useful places to tether one's craft while fishing a deep hole or trough.

In aesthetics I am a maverick, seeing loveliness in wood-rot and visions in the dark glass of puddles. So, I have no trouble loving the silver maple. Bland old giant it may be, but blandness in things large and strong is itself a virtue when malice so rules our world. Many of my shoreside lunches, my hasty snacks and rest stops, are taken beside these old friends, and I am nothing if not welcomed, sometimes by a brooding silence, sometimes by a midday song and dance of sighing and shimmying leaves. At dawn these maples are graceful clouded apparitions, breathing dimly with a fog whose frailest banners lift from the water and entwine the pale reaching fingers that curl above the current. Orioles whistle in their crowns; woodpeckers beat their flanks. All the while one floats beside them, rolls a cast beneath them, accepts a slap from their outstretched limbs, or kneads a hung lure from their grip. They scintillate when the wind rises—boldly in autumn, flailing with light and life; shyly in summertime heat, their leaves turning over like pale restless fish, shoaling in a torpid dream. They invite the imagination, like any good work of nature. Their impact is essentially implicit; it hinges on the user and the tools he may bring to bear, though those tools be nothing but a mind's eye and a keenly whetted ear.

On September 18, 1806, along the lower Missouri River, Lewis and Clark wrote in their famous journal: "Our whole stock of provisions is one biscuit for each person; but as there is an abundance of pawpaws, the men are perfectly contented." No doubt Hernando de Soto's conquistadores, the first Europeans to find the pawpaw and its fruits nearly three hundred years earlier, were similarly pleased; at times it was their only food. Native peoples loved pawpaw and, indeed, planted it widely—no small endorsement from the members of an unsettled culture. And pioneers from Maryland to Missouri ate the fruits raw or cooked through the course of several centuries. A few even named their towns for this widespread riparian species.

*Asimina triloba,* commonly called pawpaw, custard apple, or wild banana, is a strange, rather misplaced tree quite common on the upper Potomac. It is linked, rightly and wrongly, with the tropics, and most things about it suggest equatorial connections. It is not the same as papaya (*Carica papaya*), often called "pawpaw" in the Caribbean and found as far north as southern Florida. But it is a member of that same class, Magnoliopsida, which is widespread in warmer climates. The largely tropical custard apple family (Annonaceae), to which the true pawpaw rightly belongs, has only one other North American relative, the pond apple, and it too prefers the subtropics.

So the pawpaw, single member of its family north of Tampa and with a freeze-tolerant range that extends as far as Chicago, Detroit, and Buffalo, is a bit of a freak. Its huge leaves, often a foot long and half that wide, its large-petaled flowers, colored and scented like dark wine, and its rich, outlandish fruit evoke the sultry and tropical, yet it thrives at temperate latitudes as no other of its clan.

Along the Potomac floodplain pawpaw is an understory tree, common beside the towpath for miles beneath taller sycamores and tulip trees, hickories and maples. It is rarely 30 feet tall, more often 15 or 20, its slender brown trunk blotched with gray. Alternate paddle blades of light-green leaves hang from its weak, springy branches, which sag faintly in August from both heat and the weight of new fruit.

The larvae of zebra swallowtails depend on these leaves for food, and successive broods of this butterfly—two to three per year—are nurtured from April to September. The first adults show up on cool spring days, landing on sunny wet spots to drink up both warmth and minerals, spreading their delicate striped frame quite flat for a languid half-minute, then tripping ahead in the towpath brightness. The summer-end brood is larger but still not much wider than a teabag, with ivory-edged tails half as long as one's thumb and with black outdoing white in the mackerel wing variegations. Thoroughly distinctive when perched, zebra swallowtails of summer, the riverside's loveliest insects, yet blur to dull gray when in flight, toppling and lifting like pale smoky moths, losing themselves in the understory gloom or visually decomposing in the light and shadow that sifts down through their pawpaw hosts.

About the pawpaw's fruit it is hard to make sure declarations. Many dislike it; others think it an unequaled treat. Shaped a bit like sweet potatoes, the fruits remain hard until late fall when they gradually soften and blotch to dark brown. Yet if picked while still green they will ripen fast, sometimes in as little as two days. Inside the darkly bruised rind one then finds a puddinglike flesh, tallow pale or saffron, or a deep apricot yellow. Custard is indeed what it feels like to the tongue, sweet-soft and smooth, with a flavor like bland papaya. This flavor varies with ripeness and even from tree to tree, so that novices sampling a single fruit are often disappointed, finding tasteless pulp or an unpleasant tang and never experimenting further.

If hunger makes the best sauce, we modern Americans, with our three meals daily plus snack times, are beyond loving pawpaws, whose savor may depend on being famished. Our tastebuds are jaded by plenty, our food choices ruled by affluence. How does the humble pawpaw compete with pizza or pit beef, ice cream or chocolate cheesecake? Even fruit-to-fruit it has trouble outshining oranges or bananas, which are cheap and delicious and marketed in their millions. Indeed, it was likely the banana, similar in shape and texture, which doomed pawpaws to obscurity. The former's mass cultivation and distribution near the turn of this century made the pawpaw commercially superfluous.

But its advocates carry on. In Maryland's Allegheny and Washington counties several experimental orchards now exist. The Pawpaw Foundation has been set up to promote research and development, and horticulturists at the University of Maryland are testing for commercial hybrids. They need to extend the fruit's shelf life, grow a short tree easy to harvest from, and achieve an ideal flavor.

Market success will be difficult; this remains a maverick tree. I recently picked some hard pawpaw fruits near the towpath in early September. I brought them home as odd souvenirs and gave them a squeeze two days later, though they still were mostly green. To my surprise they'd gone soft; more amazing still, when I sliced one, it was almost orange in color and as sweet and mellow as custard. My wife baked them into a cake whose moistness and flavor was the hit of a buffet supper. I went back to that spot in October, the more usual time of harvest, and picked a bunch more, though unable to find the same tree. These ripened at home to a textbook darkness, but inside were whitish yellow and utterly bland and tasteless.

I had learned the lesson of the pawpaw. It balks at attempts to tame it, to enlist it as predictable produce. The persistent freak of an old southern family, the black sheep of tropical forebears, it wants nothing of uniform culture and the monetary needs of mankind. It is fitting that it haunts the Potomac, nurturing zebra-striped butterflies and green ocarina fruits that float or fall by the towpath, unknown, unseen, or unsavored by those from a spoiled modern culture.

The people who moved through the upper Potomac valleys in the time just prior to European settlement held trees in high regard. The tree, in fact, was sacred to many, essential to their myth of creation and at the core of their spiritual thinking.

The Seneca tribe of the Iroquois nation, who frequented both the North and South Branch Valleys, believed a celestial tree gave rise to the earth and all its life. A turtle is normally perceived to be at the heart of this mythology, for, from the back of a turtle, the Iroquois believed, developed all the land on earth.

But to start with a turtle skips several steps in Seneca mythology. First there was a giant tree, not on earth but in the place where their forefathers lived, beyond the dome of the sky. The sky was a mere crust to the Seneca, and in the airy "up-above world" beyond it once dwelt the beings from which they were descended. This great tree from the up-above world was virtually the life force: from its flowers and fruit the people drew all nourishment, and from a great luminous blossom at its top their world was lighted and the air they breathed made fragrant. It was also their social hub, for around this tree the people gathered daily. Their chief partook of the sacred smoke from a plant he burned called tobacco which grew from this tree's roots, and the four directions of the world below were made up of these same roots, which reached down through the crust of sky.

The story from there is complex and has several variations, but it centers around the uprooting of this celestial tree, which creates a hole to the world below and to which a woman falls. She takes with her both tree seeds and a piece of root; the seeds become new plants on earth and the root another big tree. Beneath this tree the first earth-child is born, and from its crown springs the orb we call the sun.

A more complete arboreal pantheism could hardly be imagined. Here was a people whose reaction to the woody giants of the upper Potomac must have been reverential, indeed. We know that, in the manner of their mythic forebears, they often took counsel under large trees. The hardwoods of the primeval Potomac valley, as elsewhere in the region, were 40 percent taller than those of today, when no tree over two hundred years old can be any longer found. Historian Arthur Parker, descended from Iroquois on his father's side and an intimate of the Cattaraugus Seneca, lists chestnut, buttonball tree (sycamore), oak, beech, tulip tree, and elm in his recounting of the Seneca creation myth, so these hardwoods in particular were familiar to the tribes of old. All but the disease-vanquished chestnut are prominent beside the Potomac today. One can imagine the great age and size that many must once have attained and their spiritual impact on those moving among them.

Perhaps the most useful tree to upper Potomac nomads was the hickory. The Monongahelas of the Moore Village Site near Oldtown, Maryland, were especially fond of its fruits. Just over 12 grams of carbonized plant remains were recovered at that site, nearly 9 grams of which were from hickory nuts. These included bitternut hickory, shagbark hickory, mockernut hickory, and pignut hickory. Also found were the remnant fruits of walnut, hazelnut, plum, and oak. Peter Kalm, the Swedish disciple of Linnaeus, who traveled among the Iroquois around 1750, mentions "*kistatom,*" the Iroquois name for the several varieties of hickory, as a cherished source of food. He further relates of the Iroquois: "They make also a delicious meal of the several kinds of walnuts, chestnuts, mulberries, acimine [pawpaw], chinquapins, hazelnuts, peaches, wild prunes [plums]." All of these except peaches grow now, or once did, beside the upper river.

Indeed, to list all the practical uses that Indians once made of the Potomac's riparian tree species might very well prove impossible. Many uses were spontaneous or impromptu: bending a sapling to mark a trail, using a branch for a splint or shim, a trap, tool, or utensil. More seasoned wood was the basic material for snowshoe frames, paddles, clubs, bow, arrows, baskets, vessels, spoons, bowls, pestles, mortars, cradle boards, log water drums, and lacrosse rackets. Ash, still plentiful on the Potomac, was the best wood for baskets. Says Kalm: "The withes were thin and about a digit broad. The natives [Iroquois] make quantities of these baskets and sell them to the Europeans."

The rounded wigwams employed by most tribes in the region were made from the bark of elm, the slippery variety of which (*Ulmus rubra*) still survives here. Sheets of elm bark were stitched together with spruce roots to a tree sapling frame. And, while on quieter waters the Iroquois' fabled birchbark canoes were ideal, the Potomac's rocky rapids would have called for more durable dugouts made from pine, walnut, or tulip tree.

At least seven great nomad trails crossed the upper Potomac from today's Dickerson to Kempton and were used by the Senecas and others. Such so-called warrior paths met the river near present-day Tuscarora, Sharpsburg, Williamsport, Hancock, Oldtown, Cumberland, and Gorman and were flanked by important campsites. Long after the Monongahelas, tribes of the Algonquian language group spent time at such rendezvous and traded with peoples both upstream or down. The very name *Potomac* is said to translate from Algonquian as "where something is brought," and the tribe that John Smith called "Potowemeks," with their king Matchequeon, were established below the fall line and did business with all comers. In the last few decades archaeologists have identified an astonishing one thousand two hundred Indian sites between Harpers Ferry and the Chesapeake Bay. Dugouts of every size and shape, each of them hewn from some bankside tree, must have once plied all parts of the river carrying Nanticokes, Piscataways, Powhatans, Leni-Lenapes, Shawnees—all of Algonquian tongue—or Senecas, Tuscaroras, and Susquehannocks, speaking Iroquois dialects. Potomac trees were their transport, the pith of all things practical, their food source and counsel ground and ancient spiritual core.

The reaction of European settlers to the trees of the upper Potomac was different from that of the Indians in both kind and degree. The religion of the former was man centered, not nature centered, so they reacted to trees as mere produce glorifying their progress under God, not as ancestral links. Both groups exploited this produce, the Indians minimally, the settlers completely. Nearly 100 percent of Maryland and adjacent regions was virgin forest when the Europeans arrived, and in less than three hundred years they harvested nearly 100 percent of it.

The Potomac woodlands, for these immigrants, had dozens of intensive uses. They offered logs, boards, and shingles for every manner of building, lumber for boats, wagons, wheels, barrels, and fences, and bark for numerous tanneries. Frederick Gutheim, in his well-known book on Potomac history, underscores the waste in this latter trade: "Tanneries were everywhere, with their tanbark walks spreading in all directions, and the chestnut oak and white oak melted away, often only the bark taken, the logs left to rot in the woods." Black walnut, a precious wood today, was casually cut for the beams of mills, even bridges. And the English, starved for ship's timber, sent special representatives upriver to select the finest hickory, oak, walnut, and locust from the stands of virgin hardwood.

In the early days the greatest wood use by far was for charcoal and potash. Potash was used to make glass, a short-lived Potomac industry, while charcoal fueled the largest and most persistent old-time Potomac enterprise: iron production. For over a century iron furnaces, thick in the piedmont valleys, ate charcoal at remarkable rates. The bigger ovens in peak production took twenty hardwood acres a day, cut first by timberjacks, then reduced to slow-burning charcoal in the myriad local pits. Lime was needed in the process, too, and lime kilns required charcoal, which required still more wood. When wood-fueled steam power arrived, in the form of steamboats and railroads, the piedmont Potomac forests were so badly reduced that the ironmongers turned to coal as a last resort.

Late in the nineteenth century came the final headwaters boom, when timber was needed for railroads, mines, and urban construction, and spur lines found the last big forests. It was not just spruce and hemlock that disappeared in the high country. As Gutheim relates of that time, "It was still possible to send 'woodhicks' by the hundred into the virgin forest that framed the North Branch of the Potomac and strip it naked of hardwood for a distance of almost fifty miles."

So much for ancestral linkage. A Seneca traversing the headwaters slopes just after the turn of this century would not have felt much kinship there and might easily have found himself lost. Should he have had the price of a train ticket, though, perhaps from working in the mines or mills, he'd have found a swift track to the cities, where immigrant devotion to the god of progress was lifting new praises to the sky. The praises were wrung out not in stories, but in iron and wood, in towers rising higher than the tallest trees and proving with every foot of height that there was no dome to the sky, no celestial crust of blue, only empty, expanding space to swallow up the produce of the floodplains and hills, the fair and ancient pith of the upper Potomac forests.

A river or stream stripped of its bankside forests may have water that, in summer, is as much as 20 degrees warmer than before the trees were lost. Trout die in such bathtub flows, as do numerous other creatures dependent on cooler currents. Even if they don't die outright, their reproduction is threatened or stopped entirely. Thus the river and its floodplain forest are critically intertwined. And, while it may seem obvious that riparian trees depend on their rivers for rich silt and moisture, the ways in which rivers rely on nearby trees are less easily seen. Among all living groups on the upper Potomac there is some sort of land-water link, but trees may be the river's most important terrestrial tie.

In addition to regulating river temperature, trees provide rivers with nutrients. Indeed, most of the nutrient energy in swift rivers comes from bankside, not from the water itself. The amount of such energy derived from plants within the river—water plants, mosses, algaes—accounts for very little of the total. In one New England river study this amount was less than 1 percent, while leaves from bankside trees accounted for close to 99 percent. Since most of the major food chains in rivers begin at this nutrient level, it is safe to say that such food chains on the upper Potomac are highly dependent on tree leaves.

Critical temperature and dominant nutrient energy load—what more significant conditions for life can bankside trees affect? Consider the river's submerged snag dwellers. For this group of invertebrates the Potomac's riparian trees affect *all* the essentials of life, providing shelter and stability, an abundant supply of food, and prime reproductive conditions.

The riffle beetles of the family Elmidae inhabit flowing water throughout North America. On the upper Potomac the genus *Stenelmis* includes at least five species, all linked throughout their lives to submerged deadfall and woody bankside debris.

Riffle beetle larvae resemble those of many other aquatic insects, being slender, segmented, wriggling creatures but with retractable hooks on their abdomens for clutching objects in the current. The silvery-gray adults, less than half an inch in length, maintain this holdfast ability with specially adapted tarsal claws that penetrate twigs and branches like delicate grappling hooks. Both larvae and adults graze woody debris for algae, mosses, and root tissue. At all stages of life, and in reproduction, they depend on this debris for concealment as well. Without it small fish, amphibians, and voracious dragonfly nymphs would quickly gobble them up. Adults remain submerged in the current, often hanging from drowned branches, where, resembling silvery air bubbles, they are difficult to detect. Indeed, they carry with them, amid a layer of bristly hairs known as setae, a shiny bubble of air, and if removed to dry land they will soon seek the safety of their wet, woody lairs and resume their bubble identities. Though they do occur on rocks, it is doubtful that rocks alone would allow them to survive in the river. An abundance of submerged deadfall, from great collapsed tree boles to tangles of shoreside branches, makes possible their survival.

In this they are not alone. Water beetles of the family Dryopidae are also dependent on woody debris; the female genitalia, in fact, are adapted for inserting eggs into plant tissue, which includes fallen leaves and twigs. Many amphibians suspend their eggs in floating tree litter or attach the mass to a fallen branch, while snakes, frogs, and turtles depend for concealment on bankside mats of limbs. More than one skunk, opposum, raccoon, or fox has found shelter in a shoreside sycamore log, and birds, too, sing from the fallen giants, wedge subtle nests in their branches, or hunt from their handy perches. Fish hide in nets of submerged roots and limbs, even inside hollow tree trunks. J. A. Henshall, in his *Book of the Black Bass,* relates the following tale from an acquaintance: "A few years ago a man, Seth Whipple, living on the Hudson River, near Glens Falls, in drawing some sunken logs from the river, during the winter, for firewood, found in the hollow of one of the logs, six Black Bass [smallmouthed], weighing from a half to two pounds; they were nearly dormant." Potomac smallmouth employ this tactic in the period from December to March.

Yeasts, bacteria, fungi, algae, zooplankton, plants, insects, fish, reptiles, amphibians, birds, mammals—is there any group of organisms unaffected by the workings of the Potomac's bankside trees?

Perhaps the Senecas were not far off. Perhaps in trees there is a basic force that touches all things living. Surely they were right in viewing trees as providers. And in looking skyward, where even today great sycamores hold dominion on the upper Potomac, they were not so misguided in their reverence. Indeed, they have had much company; trees have been worshipped for centuries by peoples worldwide. In New Guinea the heart pulp of the sago palm is considered as one with man's flesh, and the sago palm is a cycad, of the same group that predated sycamores here near the close of the ancient Coal Age. The gods of the Greeks and Romans worshipped trees. And perhaps the greatest irony is that the early cultures of Europe—the ancestors of those very people who later destroyed virgin woodlands in the upper Potomac valleys—were worshippers of trees. Huge oaks were sacred to the Aryans and to all branches of their stock, as they were to the druidic Celts of Gaul, who spread their beliefs to the Britons. Lightning, it seems, often struck such trees and linked them for the old Europeans with their sky gods, who dwelt, like the ancient Seneca and their life tree, somewhere beyond the clouds.

CHAPTER FOUR

# Beside the Banks

In 1740, not far from the upper Potomac banksides, the following inventory was made of the worldly goods once possessed by Austin Choate, an unmarried male recently deceased: "one old gun, one rifle do [ramrod], one very old mair [*sic*], one dressed buck skinn [*sic*]." The total appraised value of his estate was five pounds, eight shillings. But he left no debts, so was no disgrace or burden to his heirs (in this case his brother Christopher), who might even recall him with favor. Like many young men of his time and place, Austin Choate had lived mainly by hunting and trapping. Though only twenty-four when he died, he had already exceeded the average life expectancy for a white male of his time and place.

Such was life in frontier Maryland in the mid-eighteenth century. A man was considered lucky to reach thirty, lucky to be free—for many were indentured or outright slaves—and luckier still to own fertile land, for most were tenants or worked small, poor-soil holdings. This luck was not sufficient prospect for some. Among malcontented outcasts, among opportunistic freemen and runaways alike—robust and resourceful, desperate or dangerous but determined to survive—the upper Potomac wilderness beckoned.

One such outcast was Thomas Cresap. A native of Yorkshire in England, he failed at tobacco farming, took up freelance frontier surveying, befriended land speculators like George Washington and Thomas Lee, and became a sort of real estate saboteur, deliberately wrecking the peace to scare off competition. As "point man" for politically powerful soil grabbers, he accepted their loans and land leases, then moved in to construct fortlike homesteads on desirable new tracts and make himself so dangerously vile to his neighbors that they sold out, never settled, or fled.

Along the Susquehanna River, Cresap feuded viciously with the Pennsylvanians, who called him "the Maryland Monster." He has been variously referred to as a "professional trouble-maker," "damned rascal," "rattlesnake colonel," and "murderer," and there is little to suggest these are slanders. His choicest incarnation was as a fur trader and western agent for the Ohio Company, a group of well-placed Virginians who promoted commerce, settlement, and British interests in the vast Ohio wilderness being fought over with the French.

Around 1750, at present day Oldtown, Maryland—formerly King Opessa's Town or Shawnee Old Town—Cresap dug in like an old badger and exploited the town's position as a frontier trade and travel crossroads. He cheated the fur-swapping Indians, then appeased them with free rations to earn the sobriquet "Big Spoon," meanwhile beseeching the colonial governor for hefty reimbursement. He wrongly advised visiting land speculators, helping them survey Indian-occupied tracts that could not be legally acquired. He contributed to British General Braddock's defeat in 1755 by fudging promised road improvements, supplying spoiled meat, failing to provide needed wagons, and undermining morale by gypping common soldiers. When it all blew up in his face with Braddock's stunning setback, and the French-inspired Indians wreaked frontier havoc, he retreated briefly to the piedmont. Then he returned to his fortified trading post, surrounded himself with family, and wheeled and dealed into venerable old age, a local celebrity and legend.

But Oldtown, Maryland, was an important place long before hard Tom Cresap's reign. A thousand years ago the aforementioned Moore Village Site of the Monongahela's was here, and perhaps for centuries prior to European settlement it was the foremost regional confluence of warrior paths among Shawnees, Senecas, and others. Philemon Lloyd of Wye House, Maryland, first described one branch of these warrior paths in an annotated map of 1721, indicating with dotted lines "ye Great Tract from ye Towns of ye five Nations to ye Southward" and marking where that path crossed the "Kahungaluta" (Cohongoronta, or North Branch) at "King Opessa's Town." He even showed it to certain "Sinequa [Seneca] Deputys", and "ye fellows were pleased to see their Warr Road or Great Tract to ye Southward, laid down by double Prickt Lines."

Cresap's flamboyance has overshadowed the true pioneers of Oldtown, and indeed most think he was its first white settler. In fact, long prior to Cresap's arrival an obscure Indian trader named Charles Anderson briefly farmed there, probably lived and traded there for a time with the Shawnees still in residence, and perhaps told Lloyd of the warrior path. Clearly, Anderson knew the region, for Maryland's governor, in 1722, sent him to King Opessa's Town on an unknown mission of importance. But he never owned land at Oldtown, a fact that doomed one to historical obscurity in most frontier settings.

Another forgotten figure, John Carleton, bought the first land at Oldtown, in 1739, as part of a tract called "Indian Seat," whose description makes reference to Anderson. But Carleton, like Anderson, was neither scoundrel nor monster and, thus, all but vanished from history when he sold his land to Cresap in 1746.

There were other obscure groups of settlers that toiled in the shadow of Cresap. One such was the Twigg family, whose name is common in the region to this day. Upstream from Oldtown toward Cumberland, around 1750, arrived John and Rebecca Twigg. At Sink-hill Bottom, near the town that now bears their name, a limestone sink formed a natural pond. Beside it the Twiggs built their cabin and raised two fair-skinned, blue-eyed sons, Robert and Fleetwood John. Fleetwood John habitually roamed widely in pursuit of fish and fur and returned from one of his journeys in wed to a young Indian woman. His family was furious and banished them from the household. John calmly took up residence on the far side of the pond and began raising "black-eyed Twiggs." Brother Robert soon married but remained with his parents, raising nothing but blue-eyed offspring on their side of the spring. The smoldering feud that developed held that "blue-eyed Twigg" children never played with "black-eyed" ones, and this condition lingered for generations. But there is nothing so enticing as forbidden fruit. A blue-eyed Twigg finally fell for black eyes, and the feud ended with fusion.

Ten miles below Oldtown is the village of Paw Paw, West Virginia. Near here the Potomac cuts through steep mountain ridges to form a series of hairpin bends with precipitous bankside slopes. In the 1830s the C & O Canal Company, faced with the prospect of damming the river or digging out a canal and towpath for six miles along the sheer mountain sides of these "Paw Paw Bends," was persuaded by the enthusiasm of Engineer Charles B. Fisk to bore a one-mile shortcut through the mountain itself.

As the newly appointed Fisk saw it, the tunnel would be a cinch. The ridge's natural arch of shale would protect the site from cave-ins, its relative softness would yield 7 to 8 feet per day, it would be safe from river flooding, and Fisk's able assistant Elwood Morris, working with the energetic bulldog of a contractor, Lee Montgomery—who had built a 600-foot tunnel on Pennsylvania's Union Canal and would make his own bricks for the lining with a patented machine from Baltimore—would not quit short of success. Once completed, in about two years, it would be a "wonder of the world."

The shareholders studied their options and gave in to Fisk's salesmanship. The tunnel was begun in June 1836 and completed, after appalling difficulties, in 1848, though it didn't actually function until 1850. By that time the Paw Paw Tunnel, 300 percent over budget, was the last canal section to be finished, the contractor Montgomery was bankrupt, untold suffering had befallen laborers and masons, and the canal company itself had lost its race with the railroad and was hopelessly in debt. Some still called it a wonder of the world, while to others it seemed "Fisk's folly."

The achievement was still impressive, for all its foibles and failures. Bored 3,118 feet through stratified shale with primitive black-powder charges and hand-wielded picks and sledges, with another 1,100 feet of deep rock cuts at each end, it employed a maximum of forty-four men at a time (considered a lot in its day) to remove 82,000 cubic yards of tunnel rock and another 120,000 at the north portal cut alone. It involved sinking from above four 8-foot-wide shafts, each 400 feet deep, and carving a round-arched tunnel 42 feet high and 21 feet wide for over half a mile, its ceiling and walls lined with handmade bricks four to six courses deep. Besides overcoming a grandly misplaced optimism, it survived rock slides and constant slippage of shale strata, riots, strikes, arson, firings, blackballings, slowdowns, stoppages, feuds, diseases, injuries, deaths, continual breakdown of payrolls, machinery, men and mules, and every financial crisis short of total liquidation. Amid these impediments the fact that it was even finished is a testament to old-time grit and resolve and the obsessive energy of men.

Perhaps no once-bustling place along the upper Potomac is now more shrouded in obscurity than Little Orleans, 15 miles downstream from Paw Paw. It sits at the mouth of Fifteen Mile Creek, which is named not for its distance from relatively youthful Paw Paw, West Virginia, but for its 15-mile equidistance, on the road of 1760, from both downstream Hancock, Maryland, and Town Creek, Maryland, near Oldtown. The road was new in 1760 and was built to avoid one of several troublesome river fordings that the old route, in the days of General Braddock, required. It became nothing less than the lifeline of the region, linking Forts Frederick and Cumberland and carrying to the west all manner of riders and foot travelers, oxcarts, wagons, and coaches, for over fifty years.

Though a new republic was formed about halfway through this reign, faint tinges of monarchy still colored the region. Having once hosted British militia and adventurers, this is not surprising. As late as 1795, the inn here was known as Kings Tavern; its proprietor in 1810 was one Mrs. O'Queen. But, beginning in 1811, across the ridges to the north, the new nation built its National Road, and the hamlet on the old "royal" highway was doomed.

Or so it then seemed. The canal and railroad revived it for a time, and Little Orleans became a rough camp full of disgruntled Irish laborers. The region was still too sparsely settled to insure enough full-time canal workers, so, beginning in 1828, the C & O board had begun looking for laborers abroad, securing an agent in Great Britain for the purpose. Many who responded were skilled stonecutters and masons, but most of the common laborers arrived with indenture agreements promising a specific period of work in exchange for preset wages and a fixed daily ration of meat and spirits.

The resulting ethnic mix—mostly German, English, Welsh, and Irish—was volatile; class, culture, and work skill snobberies blended badly with brutal work, inflexible pay scales, and substandard amenities. Clans and cliques competed and clashed, canal company and workers exchanged accusations of bad faith and cheating, and the "daily grog ration," deemed insufficient by the Irish but liberally augmented by local whiskey profiteers, led to more harm than good. A particularly brutal uprising started at Little Orleans in May 1838. The company had its usual problem meeting its payroll, the Irish stopped work in protest, the company replaced them with Germans, and the Irish rioted, killing two of the Germans. Matters settled down until five hundred guns from Baltimore reached the Irish, another riot flaired, and three companies of state militia moved in to confiscate guns, burn shanties, and destroy whiskey.

Surely, one feels, with the canal's completion, the hills around

Little Orleans must have gathered their ghosts and sunk peacefully into time's shade. Not quite. A final burst of activity made them twinkle once more in the light of progress. Some five miles west of the village, on a high ridge above the Potomac, over 2,000 acres of what is now deep woods was designed to be a bustling town. Near the turn of this century the Merten Orchard Company laid out two hundred 10-acre orchard plots along its prospective Main Street, which it scoured out and graded and marked with neat signs: Merten Avenue. The homes of the resident growers would face this boulevard, but the company sold plots to nonresidents as well and would clear land, plant trees, and pick fruit for them, in return for a share of the profits.

Many of the plots *did* sell. Land was cleared and apple trees planted. A trolley was planned along Merten Avenue, to serve the village residents and transport fruit to market. But the scheme finally fell apart, and both village and trolley line never appeared. Yet signs on the gravel road from Little Orleans to Paw Paw, which now cuts through the Green Ridge State Forest, still say "Merten Avenue." And the cemetery near the avenue holds some graves of those early dreamers.

The bankside hamlets downstream from there have had their high-profile history and, indeed, are lively river towns even in our modern age. Their tunes of old glory have not gone unsung; their ghosts are less obscure. Hancock was a trading post of repute in the days of General Washington, was considered as a site for the nation's capital, was a hub on the National Road, and was fought for in the Civil War. It was funnel neck for canal boats and commerce, and for farmers of a three-state region. Williamsport, likewise, was a bustling village, sat hard by the Great Valley roads, vied also for the national seat, was a quintessential canal town, and suffered through the Civil War. Tanneries, coal firms, and brickworks made it hum. And Harpers Ferry is a legend, an icon of national history which needs no further champions to delineate its stature.

But somewhat south of these places a more genteel glory blossomed, then died and was pressed on some back page of history like the keepsake of a southern garden. Just below the Potomac flourished a tidewater culture of displaced planters and old southern families steeped in traditions of gracious living. This was the Loudoun County, Virginia, enclave so dear to George Washington and his brethren—the Bullskin Creek society in which his brother Samuel lived at Harewood, a limestone mansion built by architect John Ariss, who reworked Belvoir and Mount Vernon.

Noted Tidewater families—Pages, Lees, and Stephensons—deserted their failing tobacco domains and settled thickly nearby. French royalty visited, a first lady (Dolly Madison) was married here, and the land inspired William Makepeace Thackeray and Washington Irving. Indeed, a local literati evolved around Charles Town, which Charles Washington had laid out and developed beside his own estate, Happy Retreat. In the first half of the nineteenth century the so-called Charles Town School of Walter Scott and Washington Irving imitators thrived in these valleys near the Potomac. Chief among them was John Pendleton Kennedy. A friend of Poe and Thackeray (Thackeray's novel *The Virginian* owes much to Kennedy's assistance) and editor of a Baltimore literary magazine, as well as a lawyer, businessman, and politician, Kennedy wrote descriptively of the faded Tidewater past in his novels *Swallow Barn* and *Rob of the Bowl.*

But he, like the others, seemed stuck in the long ago and could not see the life of the nearby river, canal, and railroads as a fitting literary subject. In the end the derivative focus of this school was swept away by change and progress, and especially by the Civil War, whose magnitude of horror and heroism dwarfed its effete nostalgias.

There is perhaps good reason why Kennedy and his circle eschewed the bankside existence. There was little romance and less refinement on the early upper Potomac. When life wasn't hard it was impossible, and one busted gut to make ends meet, whether man, woman, or child. Although "busted gut" is not the right phrase; it is modern slang coined by folks gone soft, by people who see some contrast between ease and fierce hard work. There wasn't much contrast in the old days: most unmonied folks worked as hard or as long as they could, almost every day of their lives. Their perspective may be lost to us now, when short hours and lighter labor let most of us savor some leisure. What short hours? you may say, and you tell me of your ten-hour days, the night you stayed late, and the now-and-then loss of a Saturday. "Wimp work," I say, and then trot out the record of those who once lived by these banksides.

Folk worked twelve-hour days, six or seven days a week, and these were the lucky tradesmen, townsfolk, or mill hands. The farmers suffered their endless toil, from childhood into old age, compounded by a lack of machinery and anything approaching convenience. And we know about common laborers, those who built roads, rails, or canals and whose misery led to violence. But, once the waterways were built, the longest hours went to the canallers—the boat captains, their families, and assorted hands and helpers. They were on duty twenty-four hours each day and actively working eighteen. It wasn't backbreaking work, just numbingly steady. Wrote one canal hand: "Generally up at daybreak and go to work. About 4 or 5 hours rest." A Department of Labor study by Ethel Springer is more detailed:

> Fifteen hours a day was the minimum reported by any of the boat families; 18 was the number of hours most frequently reported; and several families stated they worked longer. One family had operated its boat without taking any intervals for rest. One captain and his wife who reported working 15 hours a day employed no crew but depended on the assistance of two children, a girl 14 years of age and a boy of 5. The girl did almost all the driving, usually riding muleback, and the parents steered. The boat was kept moving until the girl could drive no longer, then the boat was tied up for the night. "We'd boat longer hours if the driver felt like it," said the father.

Except as a food source, wild nature wasn't much valued. But just about all else was. The cheapest discarded materials that might help one turn a buck were eyed entrepeneurially. Recycling need not be touted as goal; everyone did it from birth, leaped on the nearest resource, swept it into their humble midden to be later sifted for worth. Folks who could make ends meet in such ways were usually viewed with respect. "River rats," people of the banksides were called, and it had a certain status. From the obscure and anonymous 1859 diary of one canal worker, we learn of his scheme to collect the mule bones that littered the Potomac floodplain: "I was to get a cheap mule and take the Captain's old boat, then with another young fellow and a tow boy start from Cumberland and follow the canal down to Georgetown, gathering up all of these bones. The probabilities were that we could get a boat load which would weigh from sixty to seventy tons and that they could be sold for two or three dollars a ton which would make a very good venture."

People did not plunk down cash on a whim or buy "new" without some thought. Most goods were made by hand, from scratch, through slow and laborious labor. The items of "folk art" that we view today and add to "museum" home decors, were hard-won products of the unending harness, but viewed as nothing so special, for all were in harness together. The sparse and makeshift material conditions on canal boats, for example, were mere microcosmic emblems of the lack of comfort and plenty in the lives of most bankside natives. Canal boats were cramped river homes. The narrow bunks in the cabins were 36 inches wide, "sufficient space for one person," writes Springer, "but ordinarily occupied by two." The 4-by-4 feed box served also as a bed, when the hay was spread with a blanket. Children often slept or played on deck but were tethered in case they slipped off. Toilet facilities did not exist, nor did screens on any windows. Fuel was at a premium.

Though food was often scarce and unvaried—ham, dried bread, and molasses were the standard fare of canallers—river folk were resourceful. Water was drawn from springs and stored in wooden barrels.

Fresh pork was infrequent fare, but prepared with care and delight. Our anonymous diarist speaks of blackberry parties in summer, of "picking a two-quart pail full along the tow path," which "made a fine relish to our ham and bread." Other fruits in season—raspberries, grapes, persimmons, pawpaws—were happily gathered, as were nuts. And turtles, for both table meat and soup, says the diarist, were a staple. He devotes several pages to the art of their capture and cleaning and relates, "We parboiled the legs and then fried them making a meal that I long remembered, but whether it was my good appetite or the change from ham or the extra good flavor of the turtle I do not know but presume it was part of both."

Eels were another favorite, and the railroad town of Brunswick was once also known as "Eeltown." Indeed, American eels, with a complex and mysterious life cycle that begins and possibly ends in the Atlantic's Sargasso Sea and meanwhile brings the young females far up freshwater rivers to mature (a maturity not complete for five to twenty years, when they return downstream in autumn to the males waiting in tidewater), were long harvested on the upper Potomac by both nomads and settlers alike. Today the stony bases of disused "fish traps" or "eel pots" (weirs), whose distinctive V formations still buck the river's current, remain visible in low water at numerous locations. Highly variable in detail and quality, and constructed of rocks, brush, and wood, the traps pointed downstream, funneling fish and eels into constricting mazes or, in more recent and elaborate incarnations called "racks" that specifically targeted the seabound she-eels, up wooden ramps whose slatted openings let them drop into boxes below.

Eels were served locally in myriad ways, even used to thicken gravy. U.S. presidents were not ashamed to enjoy them. When Grover Cleveland stayed at Pennyfield Lock, during frequent fishing forays, Ma Pennyfield always asked him first if he wanted his eels "skunned or unskunned."

So in trying to fathom those days, we are all a bit out of touch. We consider good nutrition a virtual birthright. And hard work today is the badge of ambition, not the unbending rule of existence, while the standards for just what hard work *is* have been altered downward for the many. When I see canal remnants today—examine the details of construction, the fineness in the stonework or its monolithic bulk—I think of how they were wrought by hand, in the rain, cold, or heat for twelve hours a day, with a tent or shanty to retreat to, and I keenly feel my status as a weakling of the modern world.

How did folk deal with the struggle and pain? Liquor, of course, was popular but often beyond daily means. Some had religion and family. But teetotaler or tippler, devout or gone-to-the-devil, most everyone used tobacco. In the frontier days by the river, and most other places as well, tobacco was the crude drug of choice. It was frequently smoked but, in the decades before the Civil War, more often chewed. Men chewed it, boys chewed it, women chewed it. It was cheap and easy to get; it dulled assorted pains and kept one awake and semi-alert through long hours of labor. Especially by the banksides it had somewhat the status of currency. Indeed, the chomping, cheek pouching, and spitting of it throughout the young nation was a chief complaint of Charles Dickens on his first visit to America in 1842. About one railroad journey he noted: "The flashes of saliva flew so perpetually and incessantly out of the windows all the way, that it looked as though they were ripping open feather-beds inside, and letting the wind dispose of the feathers." He further observed:

> In the courts of law, the judge has his spittoon on the bench, the counsel have theirs, the witness has his, the prisoner his, and the crier his. The jury are accommodated at the rate of three men to a spittoon (or spit-box as they call it here); and the spectators in the gallery are provided for, as so many men who in the course of nature expectorate without cessation. . . . I have twice seen gentlemen at evening parties in New York, turn aside when they were not engaged in conversation, and spit upon the drawing-room carpet.

> And in every bar-room and hotel passage the stone floor looks as if it were paved with open oysters—from the quantity of this kind of deposit which tessellates it all over.

His experience on a canal boat in Pennsylvania further confirmed his revulsion: "I was obliged this morning to lay my fur-coat on the deck, and wipe the half-dried flakes of spittle from it with my handkerchief: and the only surprise seemed to be, that I should consider it necessary to do so. When I turned in last night, I put it on a stool beside me, and there it lay, under a cross fire from five men—three opposite; one above; and one below me."

Frontier life on the river and canal was hard and dirty beyond our imagining. It helped for those then living that there wasn't much else to compare it with, no image of greater comfort displayed on TV or film screen. Isolation and ignorance were an unconscious balm. Rye whiskey with breakfast (and dinner and supper, too) killed the discomfort for some, and nicotine for the many. Hard work held one's focus, as did dreams for a better future. Springwater tasted good; pork fat tasted better; pawpaws were ideal treats. There was savor amid the hardness and filth; solace in the languid river pace, in the lazy slackwater pools, in the lovely hugging hills. There were ways to dull sharp pain; there were things for which to give thanks. Turtles made good soup; eels made good gravy. Hunger made the best sauce.

Today the upper Potomac, canal, and towpath are the focus of activities and affluence that the river rats of old would have gaped at. The canallers' mule-trodden path is now a convenient highway for well-equipped hikers, bikers, campers, fishers, birders, joggers, and a dozen or so other brands of hobbyists and outdoor enthusiasts. River and banksides now run with recreation. The best park management plan could not have created a better permanent "trail" than the C & O towpath nor a finer link between history, the river, and the towns and people nearby. These links are often different than of old, but mainly different in detail. No one can deny their substance, even in this age of ephemera and haste. Perhaps this explains their persistence—as oases of opposite energy, as stable and slowed-down options in a shaky, speeding world.

Paw Paw, West Virginia, is a place where opposites attract. Once a busy railroad, tannery, and fruit orchard hub, it has fallen on hard times. Each of those industries has faded. From a peak of one thousand residents it has seen that number cut in half. The static economy gets by on movement now: on travelers visiting the Tunnel, the towpath, and the river, and on locals commuting out of town. Those in a hurry like its languid pace; those with money find its lack of wealth quaint.

Freda Kay Miller and her husband Bill run the Paw Paw Patch Bed and Breakfast. I've stayed with them before, and the first thing I mention as Kay greets me at the door is that they've lost their Seven Eleven, which I noticed was boarded up.

"Yes, yes. Well, that's not so bad because we've still got the General Store. But those were our only gas pumps!"

She soon plunks me down to some homemade peach pie, and we talk about other things. They've been running this business five years. Ninety percent of their guests, Kay says, are hikers and bikers on the towpath. They've had them from many states and several foreign countries. Kay remembers them all, and takes their pictures for posterity. The most interesting or unusual? "A playwright from Africa, whose work was being performed at the Kennedy Center in Washington. He and a friend rented bikes and biked the whole towpath." They've had a Russian expatriate, Germans who spoke little English but marveled at Bill's homemade sauerkraut (they had arrived at suppertime, and the Millers insisted they join them), and "lots of government people, from D.C. and thereabouts."

We both express amazement at the extended work commutes that people near the river often make. Many natives drive daily to Cumberland (25 miles) or Hancock (35 miles) or farther, on narrow country roads in all kinds of weather. Kay knows of one group who commute from Berkley Springs, West Virginia, to Langley, Virginia, near Washington, a daily round-trip distance of almost 200 miles. "Five of them get in this big car. Each one takes a turn driving one day of the week."

Kay's husband, Bill, has no such problem. He's retired. He is almost friendlier than Kay, if that's possible, and more voluble. We have a shared interest: river fishing. He sets out photos of his catches—big stringers of two- and three-pound smallmouth and jumbo channel catfish that look a bit like nurse sharks. His favorite water is the Cacapon, a nearby Potomac tributary that is arguably the prettiest stream along the river.

"I'm a fall fisherman, mostly," he says with some conviction. "September to December. If there's ice on the shoreline and my reel, so much the better. And the moon has to be right. I believe that, and it's true. My best catches are all by the right moon."

I can't resist picking his brain, so I ask him his *second* favorite spot.

"South Branch of the Potomac. You know Romney? First few miles down from the bridge. It's all catch-and-release there now. But three-pounders are common. I have a fly-fishing friend who won't go anywhere else. He takes three-pounders there in summer, on fly tackle."

I gaze once more at the snapshots before me, the fat dark-barred golden beauties laid out on the wet grass and leaves beside some pool on the Cacapon or South Branch. And I'm not inclined to dispute him.

Downstream from Paw Paw, beyond the Paw Paw Bends, is Little Orleans, Maryland. It's a fairly remote destination, tucked in the folds of the mountains between Town and Sideling Hills. On a spring afternoon I stroll into Bill's Orleans Grocery there. A tavern and store for a century and a half, and successor to the old Kings Tavern and the obscure Mrs. O'Queen, its ambiance has me off balance. Above the bar and on walls are mounted muskies and smallmouth bass, and creatures of the local woodlands. On the TV up in one corner the Cubs are playing the Astros, live from Chicago 600 miles away, and the shadows are slanting off the ivied walls of hallowed Wrigley Field. In my youth I sat in like taverns, but on Howard Street in Chicago, five miles from the park, and I watched these same teams after work, at just this time of day, in the P.M. Club or Chuck's Rustic Lounge, with similar fish and animals mounted above the bars. But outside, then, were the mean streets of Juneway Terrace, and the catchable fish were far to the north, at least 300 miles out of reach. Here no mean streets lurk beyond the door, and the fish are down by the landing beside Fifteen Mile Creek, in a clear-flowing river surrounded by trees, by lush floodplains and scented mountains and blue, unblocked skies. So, it takes me a moment to adjust.

It turns out that Bill Schoenadel, the owner, has relatives in Chicago. "But we don't get back much anymore." Still, it seems a very small world and very oddly connected.

Other things keep me off base. A huge wild turkey looms above the bottled liquor, as if ready to take flight. A large stock of bar mirrors flash along one wall. And there are autographed dollar bills plastered to the white drop ceiling. Thousands of them. "About six thousand dollars' worth," says Bill, "but we stopped puttin' 'em up last Labor Day. The ceiling was gettin' too dark."

What's the biggest change he's noticed in the last decade or so?

"Property values. Land that was a hundred bucks an acre when I got here in '68 is now five thousand dollars. There's an 80-by-100-ft. lot here that the owner wants eleven thousand to fifteen thousand dollars for. And most of the others refuse to sell. At any price."

Why?

"Oh, I guess they wanna keep things the way they are. Don't want it to get too crowded. That's why most live here. No crowds."

Though a few have sold. Bill's son bought seven acres from a New Yorker who owned a nice spot on a ridge above the river. "We had to track the owner down. Realtor couldn't find him. Turns out he'd moved to Costa Rica."

I ask him about business at the store. "It's seasonal mostly. But I don't push it as much as I used to. I'm retired." He is seventy and was a printer at the Times and Allegenian Company. He still runs the store and bar and the Lazy River Canoe Company with the help of his wife and sons. They drive people upriver with canoes as far as Cumberland, then let them paddle down in their own time.

"We get a lot of hikers and bikers, too." A woman in biking togs, with fanny pack and an Aussie accent, in fact, came into the bar when I did. "I thought she was your wife," Bill says to me with surprise.

The Justice William O. Douglas Anniversary Hikers just came through that morning. Douglas's highly publicized canal-length hike forty years ago, to spotlight the riverside's beauty and push for its preservation, was instrumental in its eventual acquisition by the National Park Service. Bill puts out "Welcome Douglas Hikers" signs each year. "Some of those hikers are older, ya know. A park service truck moves ahead, to prepare their campsites a bit. But I give 'em credit."

Will he ever leave this place?

"I've thought about movin'. But I don't know where I'd go that I'd like better than this."

Forty miles downstream from Little Orleans is Williamsport, Maryland. It's been called the most "typical" of the canal towns. In its heyday it probably was. Many canallers spent their winters here and made it their semipermanent home. In more modern times the Cushwa coal, fuel, and brick company and the Byron & Sons tannery have dominated its economy. It is a crossroads community, once prominent on the Great Valley wagon roads and still a ready stop-off along the modern nexus of interstates. Though close to bustling Hagerstown and Martinsburg, it harbors an intimate, small-town autonomy, a kind of wan, stubborn insistence on preserving its close-knit roots.

There is no food bargain around like that at Jeanne's Confectionery. Her tiny restaurant, a former candy and news shop, sits at the downtown hub of Potomac and Conococheague Streets. City folk may well gawk at the prices neatly posted above the counter: hot cake $.50;

hot dog \$.75; one egg and toast \$.75; bowl of soup \$.85; steamer (sloppy joe) \$1.00; steak sub \$1.35; rib-eye steak \$1.85.

Jeanne House, a tiny gray-haired dynamo who is seventy-two and has owned the place forty years, bustles from kitchen to grill to tables to register with an energy beyond that of most teenagers. She calls the regulars by name and knows what most want before they can speak. She is unphased by every mishap.

How does she keep her prices so low?

"I *have* raised them. They were lower not long ago."

"That's right," I add, "your coffee was forty-two cents just last summer."

She nods in resigned agreement. I have forced her to take a break, and we are sitting under the wall-length color mural of a mule and canal boat which was painted by a local high school girl and, other than the menu, is the café's dominant icon.

"But this is a town all unto itself," she says. "You don't make too many changes."

She contracted the restaurant out for a while, to a couple, who lasted four years. "Too much work for them," she says sympathetically. "It's very hard. You have to watch every cent. The overhead is so much higher than it used to be. The electric. The water. My insurance is out of sight."

I ask if she feels connected to the river or towpath.

"We get a lot of bikers and hikers in the warmer months. Over the years I've made quite a few friends, because they come back more than once. And we have boy scout troops that come through. They let me know in advance."

Jeanne is a modest woman and keeps referring me to other people in town—historians and folks of prominence whom she thinks I would rather speak to. I'd rather speak to her. But I can see she's busy, and I've already stolen her time.

"You should have been here earlier and talked to some of these men. I have a lot of retired men who sit back here, and they really beef up everything." She gives me a good-natured wink. "And cut everybody down."

Shepherdstown, West Virginia, about 10 miles downstream from Williamsport on the opposite bank, was another crossroads village linking north-south communities in the Great Valley. In fact, it is the oldest town in West Virginia, settled along the old Philadelphia Wagon Road by German settlers in the mid-1700s. In 1787 engineer James Rumsey demonstrated the first workable steamboat on the Potomac here, and only his untimely death foiled greater success both here and abroad. The place has always attracted skilled artisans and today has become a minor regional magnet for craftspeople with similar traditions of innovation and quality.

Not far out of town, along the Potomac tributary Opequon Creek (pronounced "O-peckin"), live Nicholas and Joanie Blanton. Nick is a renowned maker of handcrafted hammered dulcimers, and his wife is a semiprofessional folk dancer. Their house sits on 15 mostly wooded acres above the Opequon, which is visible as a broken blue-green shimmer beyond the leafing trees. Nick is busy in his shop, a two-story affair built below the house on the limestone foundations of an old chestnut-log cabin whose timbers could not be saved. He is in youthful middle age, tall and angular, with a firm gaze behind his circular wire rims but a wry and offhand sense of humor that loosely binds the ends of his seriousness and is likely to unravel at the slightest prompting. He seems almost too boyish to have long ago been a gunsmith at Colonial Williamsburg (1978–82) before his interest turned to dulcimers. His general knowledge is broad and his curiosity omnivorous; in a brief period we have discussed fishing, wildflowers, apple culture, Davy Crockett, TV journalists, pioneer economics, best-sellers, Roy Underhill, old-time electioneering, National Steel guitars, and the IWW. He is binding dulcimer hammers at his workbench while sunlight washes the floor. I ask about the woods he uses, which prompts him to show me his upstairs stock.

"The hammered dulcimer is interesting in that you can use native wood as well as tropical. My difficulty is that I need to use more tropicals because they're exotic, and the exotic is expected in the higher price instruments I make."

A modest amount of wood lies stacked around us and against one wall.

"The dark stuff is *wenge* (pronounced "wen-gay"), an African wood. The Martin guitar company got tired of wenge some years ago, and I became a willing buyer of their last stocks."

The other woods, he explains, include mahogany for dulcimer backs and something called *debingo,* "which is a *Delburgia* from Africa, often known as 'African Rosewood.' It's not a tonal wood, so it can't be used for guitars and such. But it works for dulcimers."

I'm interested in what might be local, in woods native to the upper Potomac. "Oh, I've got a jumble of walnut and cherry over there, and some faulted sweetgum against the wall."

I know sweetgum well, with its pointy, maple-like leaf lobes and prickly seed balls. But what is "faulted sweetgum"?

"When a sweetgum dies, various fungi move in and sometimes stain it in interesting ways as they spread through the wood. This usually happens before you get any weakening of the fibers. It's becoming rather trendy," he says with faint disapproval.

Nick invites me to explore the hillsides and floodplain, which I do, only to be stunned by the beauty of massed Virginia bluebells on both sides of the Opequon.

Spring wildflowers, says Nick's wife, Joanie, are a chief glory of their property. Joanie is intense and active, with dark eyes and hair and a controlled restlessness in her manner. She ticks off the names of others nearby: larkspurs, toad-shades, shooting stars, and bloodroot. She once thought of becoming a wildlife resource manager, an idea that still haunts her. Indeed, she led wilderness trips and natural science classes for years in Michigan, Ohio, Illinois, and Massachusetts. But she confesses: "After I graduated from Antioch College I fell in love with traditional American dance. So I first moved to New England where contra dancing [dancing in "long-ways sets," like the Virginia reel] is heavily centered. But I've been in this area about ten years."

She's also a Morris Dancer: "We do a type of British ritual dance that evolved in the northwest of England, done with wooden-soled shoes. There's about 12 people on my team, and about 8 or 9 of us are local."

I ask her about the changes she's seen nearby. "I feel Shepherdstown is a very nice community, but it's growing so fast that those of us who came here to get away from the big cities don't like to see it turned into a complete suburb. We don't want it to lose its character. Though it's only four square blocks. The development isn't in the town but all through the county and near the river. The town has no control over that."

What do some of the other craftspeople work at?

"There's woodworkers, blacksmiths, a number of potters, a potpourri company that make their own herbal blends, and two other musical instrument artisans besides Nick: Sam, and Larry Bowers, who builds violins. There's also a lot of building restoration and civic attempts to maintain the historic character of Shepherdstown."

This is the Blantons' seventh season of organizing the Shepherdstown Hammered Dulcimer Festival: "It takes place in all the old historic buildings, and it's a three-day weekend event in September. It draws about one hundred players, as students, who are mentored by about twelve teachers. It concludes with a concert at Shepherd College."

The Blantons' ties with Shepherdstown seem obvious. Do they both feel connected to the upper Potomac as well? "Oh yes," says Joanie. "With Jonathan [their four-year-old son] we hike and bike and fish and swim and canoe. I don't botanize as much as I used to, though.

I'm too busy." Nick invites me to fish smallmouth this season, perhaps putting in first at Opequon Creek. It goes at the top of my shortlist.

Brunswick, Maryland, is a classic Potomac railroad town. Its great brick roundhouse still stands and was once the linchpin of the B & O's eastern repair and switching center. Brunswick was the busiest town on the canal in the years before World War I. Today its downtown is faded, its economy shaky. Once there were thriving shops along East Potomac Street and various restaurants and drugstore lunch counters; today there are almost none. Of the latter group Horine's at the corner of Maple and Potomac, was best known. Doc Horine mixed his patent drug formulas in back to fill the embossed glass bottles that bore his name. The drugstore's fine walnut interior still survives, but the marble counter is gone, and the place is now an antique shop. I sit in back, where Doc used to stir his potions, and talk to Donna Huffer (née Parker), a lifelong native of the town. What does she remember of the better days?

"We teens came to Horine's for vanilla cokes and sandwiches, but there were other places, too. The cut-rate pharmacy also had a counter. Mill's, Mohler's, H & L's, and Horine's all had shelves of penny candy that we liked. We spent twenty-five cents for the Saturday movie matinee, fifteen for the movie and ten for popcorn. Then the theater burned down. A storm damaged the bowling alley, and there were other fires and closings. This was the fifties and sixties."

Are you from a railroad family?

"Yes, my grandfather Walter Crowe worked for the railroad fifty years and had a home on Tenth Avenue. My father was a conductor and my mother lived in the same house here for nearly five decades. It was fun growing up here. We girls used to wade across the 'gut' [the dry canal bed] and picnic along the river, or we biked to Harpers Ferry or Lovettsville. My husband and grandfather liked to fish and pole johnboats on the river."

How do you still feel tied to the river?

"My daughter is a cross-country runner, and her team is the three-time state champ. They train on the hills all through town and also on the towpath. I mostly walk it."

What about the town's future?

"It's what they call a 'bedroom community' now, a commuter suburb almost. They either take the train to Washington, or they drive or carpool. Most of the town does that now."

Donna commutes the few miles up to Harpers Ferry, where she works for the Printing Division of the National Park Service. Her husband commutes to Gaithersburg. "I don't think we'll ever have as large a tourist draw as Harpers Ferry. There's a lot of railroad history here, but it just isn't Harpers Ferry."

The antique shop's owner, Bonnie Keyser, isn't so sure. She belongs to several civic organizations that envision eventual renovation similar to that which put towns like Ellicott City, Maryland, on the map. "The D.C. suburbs are expanding. It's just a matter of time before we get the tax base to improve things."

Just below Mile 17, near Potomac, Maryland, is the only original lockhouse continuously inhabited since the canal was finished in 1850. This is Swain's Lock, and the Swain family has occupied the site since 1907. Fred Swain has spent all his fifty-seven years here, and operates a concession for the Park Service, renting rowboats, canoes, and bicycles and selling odds and ends. I asked him what recent changes he's seen.

"We have a lot more people moving out here. There's a two-acre zoning restriction, so they're not cluttered houses, but there's a lot more traffic. Though not much more business. Less in fact. They use us for parking, rather than pay entrance fees down at Great Falls. We run out of parking spots."

His connection to the river?

"We fish, we canoe, we walk. We enjoy the animals that come around and the beauty of the place. We hear and see wild turkeys. There's even trout in the canal. Browns and rainbows. Not many, but three or four were taken last year."

Fred is the last of a breed. His daughter and younger brother do not want to carry on here. "It's a lot of work, and real work. Not sitting behind a desk. And you can't really make a living here anymore."

Does he feel he'll be remembered?

"Probably the Swain name will be our legacy. We're proud of the area. That house up there [a fancy house on the hill], Dave Brinkley [David Brinkley, the journalist] come out and built it originally. Stayed out here, raised his kids, then went back to Chevy Chase. We watched those kids grow up. Time really flies."

Nearby a woman is walking her dog, a common activity on the towpath here. Her name is Laura Kessling and she lives in Rockville. How does she feel about the river and its towpath? "I think we take it for granted. I've lived here twenty-nine years, and it's sort of like, 'This is the Potomac River. It's always been here and always will be.' But I think it's beautiful. Everywhere you go it's special. Each lock. And I love the seasons."

Lew Barton, who I find camping and fishing down by the river, agrees. He's got big carp and channel cats on a stringer at bankside. The river is beautiful, he says, and spring is his favorite season. "I come down to get away from things."

His most memorable experience?

"My buddies slept on an island near Great Falls and it rained and the river rose. They were stuck and tried to paddle off on a log. Nearly went over the falls. One of those helicopters rescued them. It was on the news and everything."

Great Falls, Maryland, two miles downstream, is, next to Harpers Ferry, the most visited spot on the river. The Potomac drops 60 feet here in a short series of spectacular rapids. There is a boardwalk for viewing, nearby disused gold mines, rare plants and wildflowers, numerous challenging trails, and the famous Great Falls Tavern. The place was once so popular with politicos and tourists that canallers complained of their presence. It is even busier these days. The tavern is now a well-used Visitor's Center, and today Louis Wesley mans the counter. He is dressed neatly and speaks in a smooth, thoughtful voice. He has round cheeks and bright eyes and a high, receding forehead topped by billowing, shoulder-length hair. Rather conspicuously, he does not have all his teeth, which makes him look even more like a figure from the 1840s, some reincarnate canaller or railroad man whom Dickens may have met on his overseas visit. He does not, however, chew, smoke, or spit tobacco, so I'm convinced he is of the present.

"I moved here to work for the government in 1961," says Wesley. "I 'discovered' the canal in 1963. I've walked the entire length twice and biked it once. But I'm not an outdoors person and I don't camp."

How then did you walk it?

"Ten miles down and 10 miles back in a day, then drove to the nearest motel. That way, when you've walked the 185 miles once, you've actually walked it twice in a sense. One time in both directions."

What impressed you most?

"I was amazed at how different every mile is from the mile before. It all looks quite different, in different weather, and with the river at different levels. And of course in different directions. It's never the same."

I realize I've lost my hat, and I head back to Swain's Lock to look for it. There I find a shirtless man in shorts, avidly casting with a spinning rod, up and down the canal. He's throwing a big spinnerbait, working every corner, pumping the limber rod tip. His name is Alan Himes. He tells me he fishes the canal or river at least four times a week and all day Friday, his day off, from spring through fall. He takes crappie, smallmouth, and largemouth up to four pounds. "The canal is under-rated," he says. "I used to fish the river more, but it's dropped off. Used to take a hundred fish in a day, in twelve hours. Released them all. I always do."

Alan soon calls it quits and heads for his truck. There are a few more spots downstream to try. Everyone is fishing, it seems, or has fished, or wants to soon, along the upper Potomac River. It's often the first thing they mention when I ask them what they do here. Fish and fishing. They get under one's skin.

I slip down to the riverbank and watch the big dark water slide by. Too high for bass fishing. Let it come down some, let the current recede and the pools clear and then get down here on a cloudy day and . . . yes, I'm doing it too. Plotting the where and when of how I'm going to approach them. Fish and fishing beside the banks. They get under one's skin.

CHAPTER FIVE

# Of Fish and Fishing

The upper Potomac valleys are an ancient phenomenon, born of a series of collisions between Africa and North America which began some one billion years ago. The mountain peaks that resulted from these collisions are as old as any on earth and were once as high as the Himalayas. Today they are the familiar Appalachians, worn and eroded through the ages into their present softened alignments and gouged by a system of streams.

The process was extremely slow and taxes our ability to grasp it. One can glibly relate that as the peaks eroded and their vast weight diminished, their rock mass gradually rose, thus increasing the abrasion of cascading brooks, which cut down harder while the land around lifted. But one looks at the modern Potomac, snugly settled in its bed, and is vexed by this simplification. Perhaps, then, take the simple to its silly limit and imagine a vast mound of ice cream, piled on a spring-loaded platform and traversed by trickles of chocolate syrup. Warm air melts the ice cream, whose bulk falls away at the same time that freer springs raise it, and meanwhile the syrup carves more quickly and deep some pattern of streamlets down its sides.

Fish can't survive in syrup, but, ever since its streamlets came together to form a swift, clean watercourse rich in nutrients, fish have relished the upper Potomac. Presently, of the fewer than one hundred freshwater fish species found north of Virginia's Roanoke River, ninety occur in Maryland and sixty in the Potomac. The upper Potomac boasts most of these, indeed some forty-eight, about a third of which are introduced, or "alien," species.

Which, then, are the thirty-plus "native" species of the upper Potomac River? This can be hard to say and opens a fishy can of worms. The matter is complicated by many factors: the limiting barrier of the Chesapeake Bay, the phenomena of channel movement, glacial outlet, and stream capture, and the lack of historical records.

This last is perhaps the most daunting. Though frontier explorers probed some reaches of the river as early as the seventeenth century, they were hardly scientists, and the almost exclusive use of confusing common names well into the last century makes written reports unreliable. Chroniclers were more concerned with colorful descriptions, such as Captain John Smith's oft-quoted line about scooping fish out with a frying pan, than with biological accuracy. We learn of the vast numbers, especially in the lower river, of rockfish, sturgeon, and shad, but we glean little of species distribution. Frontiersman Meshach Browning, in his classic *Forty-four Years in the Life of a Hunter,* describes taking native brook trout in western Maryland up to 22 inches in length, even in the smaller streams, and in numbers curbed only by his whim. But Browning was no systematic ogler of all things finny.

Some men of his time were, yet were hardly more helpful. In 1820 the eccentric naturalist and enthusiastic classifier Constantine Rafinesque managed to garble both colloquial and Latin names in his *Ichthyologia Ohiensis,* an Ohio River fish survey and in part a failed attempt to pin down the "genus" of what he called "River Bass," comprising no less than seventeen species and listing an astonishing thirty-three common names among just six of those seventeen.

What today's scientists *do* know about the several dozen native species in the upper Potomac is that many arrived here from other regions, through assorted displacements. The Potomac River is so ancient that it probably once flowed outside its present channels. Geologic and biologic evidence suggest that both its location and volume were different long ago. More recently, increased meltwater runoff during the close of the last ice age is thought to have formed brief outlets from the Great Lakes Basin, allowing northern and western species egress to the south and east. This is the theory of glacial outlet.

But perhaps most significant of all was the well-documented occurrence of "stream capture" or "piracy," which has nothing to do with freebooters or buccaneers. This is the phenomenon by which one stream "captures" the flow, and aquatic species load, of another. In the Potomac highlands and elsewhere, streams from distinct tributary systems are often but a ridge top apart. Indeed, near present-day Davis, West Virginia, two entire drainage systems—the Atlantic drainage, represented by a trickle of the Potomac, and the Ohio River drainage, marked by a gurgling emissary of the Cheat—flow just a half-mile apart, the former east to the Atlantic, the latter finally to the Gulf. As such streams erode their banks they may cut new channels and break through to adjacent watersheds. The stream with the greatest overall downhill gradient then captures its lazier neighbor and all its biotic prizes.

Evidence suggests that the Potomac has at one time captured loops of the Cheat, the James, and the Rappahannock (while the Susquehanna has at least once ripped off the Potomac). And what was the piscatorial booty of this? For the Potomac it meant seizing the green-sided darter (*Etheostoma blennioides*) from the Cheat, the central stone roller (*Campostoma anomalum*) from the Savage (which had pilfered it from the Youghiogheny), and the silver-jawed minnow (*Ericymba buccata*), also pinched from the Yough via the Savage. Other Potomac "native" fish of western and northwestern origins which may have been gained in this way include the fan-tailed darter, least brook lamprey, American brook lamprey, spot-finned shiner, trout-perch, and mottled sculpin.

But a few of this last group may actually have arrived from the Susquehanna, and not through stream piracy. Most scientists believe that the Chesapeake Bay is less than fifteen thousand years old and was once, in fact, a river—the lower reaches of what we now call the Susquehanna—which met with the lower Potomac where the latter now enters the Bay. The seashore was some 50 miles east of its present location, and the great south-flowing river ran cool and swift, was bordered by spruce and fir, and was fed not only from the north and west but from fast streams eastward which now bleed slowly to the Bay—the Choptank and Nanticoke and others of the Delmarva plain. Indeed, the Delmarva today contains relict populations of upland fish species: the swallow-tailed shiner, the comely shiner, the black-nosed dace, the margined madtom, the shield darter, and the mottled sculpin. They are "disjunct" there now—that is, outside their normal range—but were once more widespread in the region when drainage patterns differed. Spring-fed streams in the Choptank and Nanticoke headwaters have maintained a semblance of those earlier cooler upland conditions and allowed these species to hang on.

The point is that today's brackish Chesapeake Bay is a rather new barrier to fish distribution, where it once, as a river, actually helped more than hindered the movement and migration of fishes. Who knows what species once moved back and forth from the so-called upper Potomac, to the confluence of the "old Potomac" and "old Susquehanna," and thence upstream on the latter? We suspect at least two. It seems the Potomac's stonerollers and silver-jawed minnows, predominantly western species once captured from the Ohio-feeding Yough, also occur today where they otherwise couldn't—in the lower Susquehanna—without that pre-Bay connection.

About extinctions we can only guess; there may have been Potomac species lost to pollution and habitat degradation before systematic search. Acid mine waste in the headwaters country began before this century, and, as early as 1913, biologist Arnold Ortmann noted that he couldn't survey the Yough's mollusk fauna because all were wiped out by pollution. Though not all are upper Potomac species, zoogeographer Frank J. Schwartz lists the trout-perch, Maryland darter, glassy darter, and long-nosed sucker as among Maryland fishes near extinction or extirpation. Indeed, the trout-perch (*Percopsis omiscomaycus*) is now believed to be extirpated in Maryland. According to Schwartz, the main cause of threatened extinction in the state is limited available habitat. But, as with many problems of declining fauna, this is fueled by a panoply of other ills, including outright habitat destruction or severe modification, ongoing pollution, stocking of game species, and chance introduction of alien exotics that compete with native stocks.

It is surprising to many just how widespread are introduced species on the upper river. Most people know about goldfish and carp, Asian and Old World fishes that are now prominent throughout the Potomac. But the smallmouth bass, premier gamefish of the river's swift waters, is a transplant, too, its presence here being less than a hundred and fifty years old. It is suspected that many of the smallmouth's sunfish family relatives are also introduced, including the long-ear sunfish and the pumpkinseed. Trout fishers enjoy introduced populations of rainbow and brown trout, which are restocked each year, though small non-native breeding enclaves exist in Allegheny County. The brook "trout," actually a char, is the only true Potomac native of this family, having once been the dominant upper river predator until overfishing and pollution drove it to the farthest headwaters. But even this species has been so widely planted that the best biologists around can't pinpoint native populations. Muskellunge, too, have been brought in, creating a new game fishery in certain stretches of the river. And while some contend that walleye, pickerel, and northern pike were already present, all have been stocked or restocked in assorted streams, ponds, and lakes adjacent or connected to the river.

The best-known and most popular transplant of them all is easily the smallmouth bass (*Micropterus dolomieu*). The Algonquians called this fish *achigan,* meaning ferocious. Its fighting ability when hooked has made it—next to its close relative the largemouth and the rainbow trout—the most widely introduced freshwater gamefish in North America. Its original range spanned the Hudson Bay, Great Lakes, and Mississippi River drainages, which included a region from present-day Quebec westward to North Dakota, and from there south to northern Alabama and eastern Oklahoma. Today it occurs in seven provinces of Canada and all fifty of the United States except Alaska, Louisiana, and Florida.

Smallmouth bass are of the sunfish family (Centrarchidae), a group comprising other large so-called "black bass" species (they are not black) such as the largemouth, spotted, and red-eyed bass as well as numerous smaller and well-known cousins such as the bluegill and pumpkinseed. As natives of the Ohio River drainage, smallmouth probably occurred in the upper Youghiogheny, possibly as far as certain headwaters in what is now Maryland, but did not reach the Potomac without the help of man. In 1854 Col. William Shriver of Cumberland, Maryland, accompanied by A. G. Stabler, J. P. Dukehart, and one Mr. Forsythe, suspended thirty Ohio River smallmouth fry in a locomotive water tender and moved them from Wheeling, West Virginia, to Cumberland, where they released them to the canal basin and, effectively, to the upper Potomac as well.

This was not the first transplant of the species east and south of its native range (it was initially introduced from New York to Massachusetts in 1850), but it was the most wildly successful. Within two decades *Micropterus dolomieu* was at the top of the upper Potomac food chain, which had been absent a major gamefish since brook trout were decimated over the previous one hundred years. Fishermen with hook and line began catching smallmouth in numbers, and its reputation spread. Local anglers led two hundred Potomac River smallies to the Susquehanna in 1869, and Potomac stock was soon infused into the James and Rappahannock as well. Such introductions were at times inappropriate. Edward Stabler, a Baltimore resident and father of Shriver's friend A. G. Stabler, wrote to Baltimore City Board of Water Commissioner G. T. Hopkins in October 1865: "After much delay and frequent disappointments and loss, from the lack of suitable transportation, I have succeeded in taking in the Upper Potomac, and safely transporting to Baltimore, a fine lot of 'Black Bass' [smallmouth], with which to stock 'Swan Lake,' and also those in Druid Hill Park."

The fish did not thrive and have long been absent from Baltimore's watery venues.

In order to do well smallmouth bass need clean, cold, or swift water. They are active, agile predators and demand plenty of oxygen. Fast-moving, agitated stream or river water holds dissolved oxygen in greater concentrations, as does, to a lesser extent, water that is clear and cool, such as that in northern lakes. *M. dolomieu* is very adaptable and can survive poor habitat parameters briefly but not over time. Ken Pavol, Area 1 fisheries manager for the Maryland Department of Natural Resources, affirms that, "although smallmouth will tolerate short term periods of high suspended sediments, organic pollution, and less-than-optimum dissolved oxygen, pH, and temperature, chronically poor conditions will reduce or eliminate them."

Though they are not as sensitive as certain trout species to environmental disturbances, smallmouth are a fair litmus of water quality. Says Pavol: "Lakes and rivers that possess the physical habitat requirements of smallmouth will not support them if the system is polluted. A healthy smallmouth population indicates that pollution, chemical and organic, is generally minimal."

The name *black bass* may be derived from the smallmouth's tendency, like most fish, to lose scale iridescence and change color as it dies. Dragged about comatose on stringers or held up dead for "rigor mortis" snapshots, the species has by then dulled to a monochrome darkness, as if dipped in wet soot (though the odd fish may bleach to melon-rind paleness). In addition, live fish hauled directly from their lightless midstream lairs, where some may squeeze among rocks or stumps at most times of the year, take a minute to react chromatically and, until then, are olive-black.

The smallmouth's "normal" colors vary but are notable for their beauty: persistent high tones of jade-bronze, tarnished gold, or burnt copper shade into sepias and honey browns along their slablike flanks, which are mottled deeply with vertical bars and dorsal splotches, dark broken sickles and sequential columnar cuneiforms, while a striking three-lined tattoo of inky rays emblazons each gill cover and emanates backward from the persimmon orangeness of their eyes.

Smallmouth grow slowly in northern habitats, but in fertile rivers toward the southern end of their range, like the upper Potomac, the fry may exceed 10 inches and weigh nearly a pound in only two years. In the same two years they are usually sexually mature. When the water reaches between 60 and 70 degrees Fahrenheit the male moves to a sandy or gravelly area and fans out a nest. He then herds a female (often the first of several) over this circular depression, and here she lays the hundreds or thousands of eggs that he will fertilize. Provided there is no heavy flooding, the eggs hatch two to nine days later and jet-black fry with golden irises soon swim off toward protective cover, especially that of rocks.

Rocks are key components of the smallmouth's Potomac habitat. Good rock structure means not only protection but a steady supply of food. Crayfish are a principle smallmouth meal, and crayfish, too, love rocks. The numerous crayfish-imitating baits used by successful anglers confirm this interrelationship, and it is common when cleaning a keeper Potomac smallmouth to discover some hapless crawdad half-digested in its stomach.

Rocks are difficult to avoid when fishing the upper Potomac. Considering their link with one's quarry, it is hardly desirable to do so. They hump above the river's surface, traverse its currents in oblique, broken walls, and compose much of its bed. An angler on the river, whether standing or sitting, wading or boating, is usually above some rock.

What sort of rock? It depends on where you are fishing, but it is likely one from three main groups: shales and sandstones, limestones and dolomites, or gneisses, schists, and quartzites.

The headwaters region of the North branch, below the Fairfax Stone, is a rushing series of shallow fast water bedded briefly in the sandstone, shale, siltstone, and claystone that comprise the 900-foot-deep Conemaugh Formation. Below Gormania this gives way to a shallower belt of the same materials, some 300 feet thick, called the Allegheny Formation. The water here is clear but tinted like tea by the tannins released from upland bogs; there is unseen acidity from mine waste and occasional staining of rock faces from deposits of iron sulfide.

Pure shale intrudes briefly below Westernport, is interrupted by limestone from McCoole to Pinto, and reverts to shale and sandstone again as the river flows north to Cumberland. The dominance of shale and sandstonc continues downstream from Cumberland to the town of Great Cacapon, West Virginia. Here, where the lovely blue-green Cacapon fuses with the river from the south, is the signal for a gradual change. A little ribbon of gray Tonoloway limestone flairs across the river—from southwest to northeast, like most of these formations—and parallels the Little Tonoloway into Maryland. For the next 10 miles to Hancock the river becomes bedded with limestones: Tonoloways, Cedar Creek limestones of the Bloomsburg Formation, and others of the McKenzie. Shales, siltstones, and sandstones slip in again east of Hancock, but then the Potomac enters the threshold of that long limestone corridor that is 45 river miles broad, from North Mountain to Dargan Bend, and is but briefly interrupted by a slice of graywacke and shale which encases the town of Williamsport. Gneiss, schist, and quartzite settle in from just above Harpers Ferry clear to the nation's capital, but it is limestone, and the watershed's chief limestone region, which deserves a closer look.

Called the Cumberland, or Appalachian, Valley in Pennsylvania, the Hagerstown Valley in Maryland, and the Shenandoah Valley in Virginia, the Great Valley extends north and south for hundreds of miles like a broad geologic highway. The limestones and shales that appear here were formed on the ancient sea floors some three hundred million years ago, when reptiles were just coming forth. On its east and west lie extensive deposits of Conococheague limestone, 1,600 to 1,900 feet deep, with their distinctive dark-bluish, laminate surface. These squeeze smaller veins of Stonehenge and Dolomite limestone around Hagerstown, while light blue and pale gray Elbrook and Tomstown limestone skirt the formation's far east end.

Limestones are composed mainly of calcite from compressed shell, coral, algae, protozoa, and other sea floor debris. They grade into dolomite when calcium and magnesium carbonate are present. Limestone is soluble in acid water and thus easily weathers to form pockmarked, pitted outcrops, and it tends to hold water in enlarged underground joints, or "solution channels," which may come together as big springs or "limestoner" streams, which gush forth straight from the valley floor.

Limestone's solubility is of critical importance to nearby aquatic systems. The high levels of calcium carbonate which precipitate from limestone into Great Valley streams increase alkalinity, which increases aquatic richness, what fisheries biologists call "biomass." This denser food base, from the smallest one-celled organisms on up the food chain, results in larger gamefish and is a clear boon to anglers.

Additionally, most fish species have pH tolerances of 4.5 to 5 on the acid end and 9 to 10 on the alkali end, but they do best when pH values read between 6 and 9, with 7.5 being optimum for species such as smallmouth bass. Of nine average pH measurements computed on the upper Potomac in 1991 between Kitzmiller and Shepherdstown, only three were at least 7.5, and the two highest by far were at Hancock (8.06) and Shepherdstown (7.91), both adjacent to or fully within the limestone regions of the river.

You cannot ignore limestone when, from north or south, you approach the upper Potomac through the Great Valley. It protrudes from the fields everywhere to show gray-suited elbows and knees, shoulders and arms, or a slate-toned flotsam of small and big, of bread boxes and battleships adrift on the green coves of grasses. Dry limestone walls fully four feet high line the roadways as rustic fences, barns and bridges are built on it, numerous caves are carved from it. Civil War snipers and pickets sheltered behind limestone in the pastures around Antietam; farmers ground it to enrich their crops in Shenandoah hamlets like Limeton.

In the river between Big Woods and Snyder's Landing, a virtual midpoint of this calcite bastion, one stands on Conococheague limestone or drifts above its darkness, however one is fishing, for its pocked Paleozoic reptile skin forms most of the river's bed. Faint bluish suffusions stain the flow here, pale watermarks of limestone-linked currents. A higher density of certain mineral or organic particles, often peculiar to limestone precipitations, are here held in suspension, where they diffuse blue wavelengths in the visible spectrum, much as specks of burnt tobacco shed wavelengths of blue through the particle haze called smoke, though nothing is blue in their substance. Here, of all places on the rocky road of the river, one feels there is gem-toned pureness, a cool infusion of sky shades, a flowing liquid sapphire that promises pristine glory and ideal fishing success.

But these are essentially illusions. The water here is hardly pristine and the fishing not always ideal. Pleasing though it is to the eye and mind, bluish water, blue-green water, even water that is crystal clear, is, on all reaches of the river, not without pollutants. Pollution reduces the size, number, and diversity of fish. In some degree it has always been present on the upper Potomac in the last two hundred years, was perhaps at its worst at the midpoint of the current century, and has now been much curtailed. Yet it still creates problems for fishes.

Obviously, water that shows opacity, due to visible sewage and sediments or other gross turbidities, is polluted. Concerted efforts since 1940 by the Interstate Commission on the Potomac River Basin (ICPRB) have greatly reduced such pollution in the upper Potomac basin, where once only half of some ninety municipal sewage treatment plants were judged adequate and over one hundred industrial facilities were draining untreated wastes to the river.

But modern pollutants are both powerful and subtle. When ionized in solution, certain heavy metals, like the copper in copper sulfate (used to kill algae in ponds), become toxic to aquatic organisms. Assorted pesticides used in agriculture accumulate in organisms throughout the food chain. And organic compounds absorb critical dissolved oxygen during decomposition and may combine with chlorine to produce hazardous wastes. Discarded motor oil and other petroleum products can taint fish flesh, coat gills and skin to cause suffocation, and destroy eggs and fry in shallow water. Agricultural wastes, including manure, fertilizers, silt, and silo wastes, are major degraders of aquatic habitat; a single cow or steer produces in one day as much waste as seventeen human beings, and the resultant nutrients reaching the river foster excessive vegetation. Acid mine drainage from abandoned shafts and leachates from modern strip mines are still big problems on the North Branch, and acid rain is an ongoing threat, formed when inorganic by-products from fossil fuel combustion, such as sulfur oxide and nitrogen oxide, combine with moisture in the air.

The official line among pollution monitoring agencies is that most of the upper Potomac has been cleaned up and that its fish are healthy and safe to eat. Generally this is true, but the standard often used for comparison is the deep degradation that existed up to the 1970s, against which improvements loom large.

Fisheries biologist Ken Pavol has gone so far as to say that "The river is reborn," referring especially to the North Branch. On the North Branch below Kitzmiller the Potomac's only major dam was completed in 1982 to form Jennings Randolph Reservoir. It was intended for flood control and water storage but served also as a major buffer of acid waters from upstream. Soon brown and rainbow trout were being stocked below it. Says Pavol: "A steady supply of cold, relatively high quality water from the dam's selective release tower made an immediate impact downstream. Fish, including wild brook trout, aquatic insects, and plants began to recolonize the previously 'dead' river below Jennings Randolph Dam. In 1987 Maryland DNR [Department of Natural

Resources] began stocking catchable size trout downstream of the dam, establishing an extremely popular fishery." A recent ICPRB publication pictured Pavol holding a nine-and-a-half-pound brown trout taken nearby during a DNR fish survey. Pavol adds: "We've had evidence since 1992 that both brook and brown trout are spawning in this area, and we've found yearlings, even 'adult wild' browns, which look quite different from hatchery fish."

Above Kitzmiller on the North Branch and its feeders the going is tougher. For decades the 35-mile stretch below Fairfax Stone was, despite its clear appearance, void of aquatic life, due to acid mine drainage. The Kempton Mine on Laurel Run, which shut down in 1949, still exudes a daily average of 2.25 million gallons of tainted water, and fifty-two other disused surface and deep coal mines in West Virginia and Maryland release some 118,000 pounds of acid seep to the North Branch each day. But beginning in 1992, the states of Maryland and West Virginia began to install lime-dosing machines at four locations on the North Branch and its feeders here. The machines dump up to 50 tons of acid-neutralizing crushed limestone per month directly into the waterways. The process is expensive and temporary: if the liming stops, the acidity returns. And a natural food chain of smaller organisms has yet to recolonize the main stem. Still, says Pavol, "We've now got a put-and-take fishery here for both browns and rainbows." Water that once had a vinegar-like pH of 4 or below now reads near the optimum of 6 to 6.5, and even native brook trout show up on occasion.

In the late 1980s the upper river from Luke downstream to Hancock was affected by a dioxin scare and "ban" on eating fish—what water quality experts term a "fish consumption advisory." Even tiny doses of dioxin cause cancer, reproductive dysfunction, and immune system damage in rats, and the Environmental Protection Agency (EPA) classes it a probable human carcinogen. It is an occasional by-product of pulp waste treatment formed by the interaction of chlorine with certain macromolecules. The Westvaco paper plant in Luke uses chlorine in waste treatment, and an EPA study found five suckers near the plant with 56 parts per trillion of dioxin in their tissue. The Food and Drug Administration (FDA) advises restricted consumption of fish containing 25 to 50 parts per trillion; fish flesh with more than 50 parts per trillion should not be eaten, they say.

At first the advisory was applied to all fish for 90 miles below the plant, then only to bottom feeders. Westvaco spent fifteen million dollars to improve its chlorine reprocessing equipment, and all advisories were lifted by 1993. Deirdre Murphy, head of the Maryland Department of the Environment (MDE) water quality toxic section, says: "Westvaco reduced chlorine within the plant to non-detectable levels. They basically applied a different way of bleaching that eliminated free chlorine molecules." She is not aware of any current sites that might further threaten the upper river with toxic or hazardous wastes.

The greatest pollution threat on the river from Paw Paw down to Great Falls is probably from excessive nutrients. Sediment, animal waste, and fertilizer runoff from croplands, housing developments, and domestic livestock is considerable and difficult to control. Tom Tapley of the MDE's water quality nutrient division says most sediment problems come from tillage practice and uncontrolled flow. Of the latter he says: "The actual site of a new home or housing development usually isn't the problem. It's the deforestation that goes with it. Loss of trees and woodland floor increases storm water runoff to tributaries, which increases stream flow and bank erosion and therefore sediment load."

In keeping with the next phase of the 1987 Chesapeake Bay Initiative, which calls for a 40 percent nutrient reduction by the year 2000, agencies such as MDE are trying to envision how overall hydrology is changing on the upper river, then pinpoint and address local problems. It's not easy to catalog complex and intergrading pollution factors in regions of such diverse use, let alone to solve them. Of livestock wastes, for example, Tapley says: "No discharge permit is required if the herd isn't above 1,000 animals. That's a lot of animals. Most dairy and other operations are smaller. We're trying to gradually reduce the permit minimum to 750 or 500, even 250. Support has to come from the local level, but many of these farms have marginal profits. It's hard to make demands."

Perhaps the greatest threat of all to the fish of the upper Potomac comes not from these pollutants, but from anglers. They ply the waters in ever-increasing numbers, taking brook, rainbow, and brown trout, walleye, pickerel, pike, and musky, largemouth and smallmouth bass, sunfish, crappie, catfish, and carp, and a few other species as well. While doing so they pollute and degrade banksides, disrupt shallow-water nest sites, foul the water with petroleum, accidentally kill or injure hundreds of incidental species, and introduce alien competitors in the form of "live bait" releases.

Says Ed Enamait, DNR Area 2 fisheries manager: "In my opinion the biggest potential threat to Maryland smallmouth, as well as any heavily utilized smallmouth resource, is angler overharvest." He favored the closed spring season that began in 1990 to protect the river's spawning bass. He adds: "To sustain a smallmouth bass fishery with good numbers of large fish, high minimum size limits with low creel limits or voluntary release of larger fish by anglers is essential." Too many tiny bass and not enough bigger ones of spawning size are a problem in the river and its feeders. Those blue-jeweled waters below Big Woods which flow over darkened limestone seem to suffer from just this fault. It is easy to take the nine-inch fish, hard to take three-pound lunkers.

Some of Enamait's thinking has been applied in this section of the river: keeper bass must be at least 15 inches, and but one is allowed per day (though four under 11 inches may also be taken, to encourage the culling of runts). The boundaries of this so-called Trophy Bass Fishing Area may one day need expansion. Though smallmouth bass populations on the upper river are perhaps at an all-time high, small fish (six to twelve inches) are very much the rule among those encountered by anglers.

Popular as the smallmouth is, I still see it as an underdog. Trout purists turn up their noses at its mention, and my fly-fishing friend Tommy son, who has fished the chalk streams of England with the famous Mick Lund, refers to smallies as "rough-fish." Gourmet snobs say they taste like mud; trouters dislike their big scales and dorsal spikes, distrust their warm-water tolerance, say they lack speed and stamina, say that bronzeback fishers dunk plastic, throw crankbaits, wear holey sneakers and cutoffs, and even use tobacco.

More power to us, I say. My fishing aesthetic, in their terms, is entirely déclassé. I dress down for fishing. I don't tinker mightily with tackle. I'm a lowbrow along the banksides, a river rat in a rubber raft, a madman who fishes madly but pays attention to the dream.

It is the dream that really matters. For fishing is a kind of vision, a grappling with real and unreal both, with hope and projection and half-grasped fantasy. The angler's is a threshold world, a world on the edge of the conscious. Some darkling tunnel lies below; a sun-strewn realm encases it, embowers its glassy gardens, itself reeking with mystery but suffused with light and air. The twin kingdoms are joined along a plane, an axis of glimmer and glare, a hinge forged at the waterline which lazily flaps some door back and forth between the explicit and the hidden. You come as a seeker from a plainspoken land; you leave a convert and initiate, having found untranslatable worth.

If your dream is at all close to mine, you can start at a place like Paw Paw and be unphased by predawn darkness. It is Midsummer's Night, and the darkness seems to fit. It's important to pick times and places at which humans are not much about. You inflate your craft and push off into the stream. The stars float above the mountain where the Celtic rock hogs dug their shafts to carve out the Paw Paw Tunnel. Pink soon seeps from the east. A deep slate syncline dips to the current, touches it at a bend, and here you hang your first fish. It jumps three times in the pallor and mist, you drift together with the current, you release it by a gurgling ledge. You twice pass under bridges, rusted rail crossings that hang with ivy and sprouted trees and catch the new light of day. The deep bends are played out slowly, deer pose in the shallows, freight trains rumble in the hills. Rapids burble you along, followed by slackwater doldrums. A raccoon climbs the bank; a foot-long bass grabs your crawdad mimic; the sun gets up on the ridges and turns the cedars brassy. When you haul out six miles later, blushed by sunburn and cramped like a yogi, you've done battle with two dozen smallmouth, devoured your blueberry muffins, saved your craft from disaster on the teeth of a sandstone ledge. You walk but a mile back, the shortcut that cost men their lives, past Deptford pink and bugloss alive with butterflies and skippers, past strewn purple masonry, locks leaking water and sunrays, ferns and five-lined skinks, warblers, swallows, kingbirds. In the dark dream of the tunnel your fingers touch skeletal railings, a phoebe calls through the echoed drips and cool sucking drafts, from the green far-ahead archway. You immerge in love with color and sky; you find your car, drive the gravel mountain roads that smoke in your wake like diamond-stacked B & O engines, wash down your lunch with Bushmill's at Bill's Orleans Grocery, with Harry Carey and Wrigley's Cubs lit up past the wild turkey, and how can it not be a dream?

Perhaps the dream moves to Knoxville, down in the South Mountain river gap, where the water assaults a boulder field, a broken plain of quartzite shelves cut through or drowned by rapids. It's a peak October morning and you hook up early with two big bass who jump and make their escape, while the banksides still lie in shadow and the riffles make heartbreak music. Your casts were too long and the hook wouldn't set and they each came up far away, black crescents against the glare, leaping a foot in spine-bent arcs, and your line wasn't taut but bowed through the current, greenhorn limp at the business end where the fish spat your crankbaits like plugs of black twist. You then snag three straight 10-inchers in the green hole beside a foaming chute, and they tailwalk sailfish-style, all over the pool, and you let them off on purpose to join the big slabsides you missed. The sun gets well up, and you stop to watch someone fly-fish, shooting his lemon line way out over the pools, then slipping on the rocks in his gray chest waders and slapping the surface in disgust. As anglers, we are all often partners in frustration.

You eat lunch at Cindy Dee's and make a second try, parking near

Sandy Hook and fishing under the railroad bridge that crosses from Harpers Ferry. Once in a while you must "steal" one—pluck some fishy glory from under the noses of the multitudes. The Shenandoah enters to your right, the bridge is behind and above and these days carries strolling tourists. You cast from a rock to a big deep glide where fish have been pocking the surface, and one-two-three you tie into keeper smallmouth, working them to the shoreline just out from the pylons. It's your best action of the season, you take eight fish in half an hour, the ghosts of John Brown's followers watch from the other bank, the visitors parade and look down, and when you finally make your exit and merge with the towpath, there's a yes-by-God Japanese tourist, bespectacled and with camera, who wants to take your picture. Surely it is a dream. If you told it to your wife after long hours of sleep she would say it was absurd and silly.

Or you show up one late July evening by the mouth of Catoctin Creek. Big bronzebacks are crepuscular feeders, if not, these days, quite nocturnal. You've hauled *Testubo* in the 90-plus heat, and you strip to your swim trunks by a peaceful pool and fill her full of air—her pre-float rubdown, her 500-pumpstroke massage. You sweat and catch your breath and watch the rays on the pool. Three men crash through the nettles behind—two fly-anglers and their fishing guide, dressed to the Eddie Bauer-nines—and splash in below your hole, wade single file through it as they turn to say hello, head upstream to a fish-weir ledge where they noisily flail and chatter. They have left your pool pale chestnut. To them you're a lowlife stripped to his shorts, playing with a rubber raft. You push off and float in the gloaming, past islets of gneiss and water-willow and anglers waist-deep in the current. You're walking a Rapala across the best holes, the wires are singing where the power lines cross, and a hatch is on, "white miller" mayflies a half-inch long, cottony specks being slurped by fish who also suck up your Rapala. You quit near dark after three nice fish and find a rock outcrop in the river, where you spread your foam pad and bag. Nymphal husks dot low ledges, you're surrounded by gliding water and jumping fish, green herons croak past in groups, bullfrogs bellow, and katydids feud from the bankside woods: "Katy-did; Katy-didn't; Katy-did; Katy-didn't." It's impossible to sleep so you lay awake on your back for hours, trace the Milky Way, listen to the noisy night. Staring up feels like staring down, peering out off the planet into space, into heaven's endless basin, which sometime near midnight starts spitting sparks as you've never seen sparks before. It's part of the Perseid meteor shower, and they spurt and die above you—or is it below?—and the river glides and the insects pulse from directions you are no longer sure of, and you'd cry with joy if you weren't so sleepy, so you get up and start to fish. *Testubo* drifts above the hole where you once caught a four-pound smally, and you trace vague circles in the watery black, the sky your only beacon. You are anything you imagine here: doryman off the Grand Banks, Seneca working a weir, lunatic drifting in a bathtub. Bass now and then slash your Crazy Crawler, you're too late with each blind hook set, you lose them and couldn't care less; you are happy and confused and lost in space, a husk adrift on the universe-stream, and the dawn colors in as quiet as a bruise from somewhere down the river. Its glory is no surprise at all; you've been washed in glory since yesterday. You land and release two 15-inchers on a chipped-finish Lucky 13, you haul out finally in the clean day's sun, then see your last apparition. A canoe glides above the towpath, headed upstream on the spicebush, like those visions of prairie "schooners" sailing atop the bluestem. It detours down toward the bank, and you see it is only Old Gene again, a septagenarian fisherman who walks his canoe up from Point of Rocks on a three-wheeled metal caddy to launch beside the Big Hole, where he once took a 22-incher. You don't even bother to disturb him, just watch him plow through the underbrush, his rear wheels squeaking, the twigs and verdure snapping, and the craft's red stern being closed out by green, like a snake merging into a meadow. It's early for cigars but you break one out, a slim Honduran Petite. You smoke and you watch the river and now and then you spit. You are sticky with sweat and river mud; there's pondweed in your sneakers and insects smeared on your shirt. You are dead tired and utterly alive. You are conscious but not all there, awake but somehow asleep. Such dreams are a river rat's revenge.

Fishing dreams are as many as nymphal husks. You take your pick of the best ones and store them in a private packet, in the deep pocket next to your heart. My Pennyfield dream is kept there, my vision of Ed the Fisherman who always outfished me below the lock, who patiently worked smoke grubs near shore or spun Tiny Torpedos over maple-shaded pools and would haul in two- and three-pound bass with his ultralight Mitchell outfit while I poked around at midstream. I called the spot Ed's Hole. We met often and compared notes. Then one Halloween Eve, the day before the big flood, I worked Ed's Hole for three hours straight, the water at a high gliding canter and blue like a kid's smoky marble. I hooked and lost a big fish, almost gave up in disgust, then hooked and landed another—bigger, I knew, than Ed's best. I beached *Testubo* on the bank, sat up against a sycamore, smoked my only cigar, and watched the broad hand of the river which was riffle-veined and rock-knuckled, blue with cold and pale light. I lifted the smallmouth on its stringer. Before me was a living mystery, submerged nearby since birth and revealed for the first time that day. The old-gold of the autumn floodplain shimmered from its flanks, its girth evoked every ripeness, there was persimmon in its eye. I grew light and carefree as a child, not quite grasping why.

The best dreams are interlacing, weaving fish with rocks and trees, flowers, reptiles, mammals or birds. The act of being a predator is the act of connecting with nature. You must tie threads together to make your net, or your net will not catch prey. Floating down from Big Woods one day, in the heart of limestone country, I kept watching the river's bed. The dark Conococheague limestone, darkened further by algae and age, makes the river look bottomless in places, though the pale emblems of sunken leaves, like starfish on a black sand beach, show the depth to be just a few feet. Below Taylor's Landing the limestone humps up in ridges, parallels the current or protrudes transversely, forming corridors down which one careens. Some call these the Horsebacks, but to me they look reptilian, like the dorsal ridges of dinosaurs lounging amid the flow. Both were nearly contemporaries: limestone formed as the reptiles did, toward the start of the Permian period. Two beaver that day were perched on one ridge; as I drifted near, the first beaver fled, while the second refused to budge. I suddenly hooked a smallmouth—it came up and walked on water—and with both hands full I closed on the ridge, the bass skipped toward the rock, and we all nearly came together, a waterway collision between beaver, man, and fish. But the beaver plunged off in the nick of time, slapping its tail in annoyance, and the fish worked free and bounced off the ledge, while I came up dry on the limestone. Or was it on the seafloor, with its billions of compressed shells and corals? Or on some sort of reptile whose pocked crocodilian back showed flaky dorsal plates and a dark elongate torso? Perhaps it was the latter, for I see river reptiles often, creatures from bygone epochs, ancient Permian survivors. Is any of it hard to imagine, with things all merging in the here and now, along that glistening hinge, in one's ongoing dream of the river?

CHAPTER SIX

# Reptilian Relationships

About 350 million years ago, near the midpoint of the Paleozoic era, what was once fishy began to be something else. Certain branches of a bony fish called *Eusthenopteron,* whose superficial form resembled a modern sucker, had evolved into creatures who slithered through swamps and gradually developed legs. These were the first amphibians, such as *Ichthyostega,* and they left the crowded seas and began exploiting food sources on land, where no other vertebrates yet existed. But *Ichthyostega,* like amphibians even today, had soft skin needing moisture and laid eggs in jellylike masses that would dry out on land. Thus, it was still tied to water, as were the early aquatic reptiles that appeared some 50 million years later. Yet soon after the aquatic reptiles came an animal scientists call *Seymouria.* It had hard skin and laid leathery eggs that did not dessicate in air and sun. This was the first land reptile. Amazingly, *Seymouria* represents a single order, Cotylosauria, from which evolved not only all of today's 6,000 reptile species in four orders, but all the ancient orders now extinct, including some 150 species of dinosaurs, as well as the modern birds and mammals.

Man's relationship with these ancient orders of reptiles and amphibians is relatively new, but complex and conflicted. They are often seen as both frightful and fascinating, as portentious evil or magical good. Mostly they are not seen at all. The surviving species are predominantly small, and lead secretive lives. Yet along the upper Potomac dwell certain reptiles that are both numerous and visible: those members of the 250-million-year-old Chelonia order, the turtles. They bask on logs and rocks in the river and canal, pop their heads up in the current, even hike the floodplain and towpath. But while blatant, they are bashful; while adventurous, prudent; while eminently mobile, passive. Perhaps it is this dichotomy, this yin and yang polarity, that has so long intrigued human beings.

The mythic link between man and turtle may be unmatched in the animal kingdom. At least three widespread human cultures have credited turtles with nothing less than the creation of the world. In India, Hindus believe that Vishnu, second of their three chief gods, transforms himself into a gigantic turtle who supports atop his shell the cosmic bowl in which demons and deities stir the elemental mixture that creates the world. This world dissolves every 4,320,000,000 years, when the mixing process is again renewed. A somewhat complementary myth from central Asia holds that a huge turtle in a vast ocean existed before all else, whereupon the creative power of the universe flipped it on its back and built the earth on its level plastron.

The Chinese took things further still. In one version of early Chinese cosmology a divine tortoise named Kwei spent eighteen thousand years creating not just the earth, but the location of the moon, sun, and stars, as well as supervising the formation of the universe itself. Afterward Kwei brought to life a line of superturtles designed to assist mankind, seek truth, and bear the world's problems. Chinese priests, in fact, once saw the fissures in turtle shells as coded divine edicts, and it was from reading these that some believe written symbols, and therefore writing itself, developed.

As if this were not enough, another Chinese myth insists that the divine turtle did not merely direct the creation of the universe but actually *became* the universe, its carapace forming the vast, vaulted realm of sky and spirit. In this mythos, stars speckle the carapace interior, which deflects their light to earth while the plastron, or "belly" plate, supports the seas and their great floating globe. In short, within the form of a turtle is contained all existence.

Rather more modestly, perhaps, the Japanese have long regarded turtles as supernatural symbols of peace, success, and good luck. They are emblems of happiness and longevity even in the present and are kept in ponds on temple grounds, where they reach venerable ages.

If native Americans once migrated from turtle-conscious Asia, as many scientists believe, it is probably no mere coincidence that so many creation myths in North and Central America also revolve around turtles. Here at least five tribal cultures embraced turtles in their stories of genesis, including Hurons, Leni Lenapes, Cheyenne, Mayans, and Iroquois. Indeed, Mayan beliefs were uncannily close to those of the Chinese, wherein the turtle's carapace interior formed the curved plane of the heavens. Iroquois myths, which would have included those of Seneca nomads on the upper Potomac, held that the woman who fell from the sacred up-above world landed safely atop a turtle, whose fellow watery creatures then brought up magic earth, which had dropped from the tree roots above, and piled it on the turtle's back. Here the woman planted corn, and the earth expanded, and, in some variants, a smaller turtle then climbed the sky to bring back more sun- and moonlight.

This last Iroquoian image has something of a corollary in nature, for the two commonest turtles on the upper Potomac, one small and one big, live in close proximity. These are the eastern painted turtle (*Chrysemys picta picta*) and the red-bellied turtle (*Chrysemys rubriventris*). The former is but 4 to 6 inches in length, the latter 10 to 16. Especially along placid stretches of the river and flooded canal they crowd each other for sunning room on the fallen limbs and logs, and a wee painted turtle now and then basks atop its larger red-bellied cousin, having climbed at some time prior the dark, shining firmament of the red-bellied's back.

Both turtles are often mistaken for a single species and then usually given the misleading common name *slider.* Sliders, cooters, and their taxonomic allies, the painted and red-bellied turtles, are all of the genus *Chrysemys,* and all enjoy basking in sunlight. But herpatologists make the widespread painted turtles (*Chrysemys picta*) a separate race from the coastal plain sliders (*Chrysemys floridana*) of the deeper south, the river sliders (*Chrysemys concinna*) of the south and west, and the pond sliders (*Chrysemys scripta*) of the Mississippi Valley, the latter group of which includes the red-eared turtle, whose young were so exploited in the pet trade of the 1950s and who, as a confusing consequence, have established non-indigenous breeding populations in parts of central Maryland. To muddle matters further, in the Potomac's upper reaches the range of the midland painted turtle (*Chrysemys picta marginata*) overlaps with that of the eastern painted. Meanwhile, the red-bellied turtle has the narrowest range of them all, being native mainly to the coastal plain from central New Jersey south to the Outer Banks, and inland mostly in Maryland and northern Virginia to the mountains.

A clean, healthy, adult specimen of either the eastern painted turtle or the red-bellied turtle is distinctive at close range. The eastern painted is North America's only species to exhibit its scutes (the large scale- or plate-like markings on the carapace) in nearly straight rows, side to side across its top. And, even more simply, the red-bellied is the only big (10 in. or more) basking turtle within its limited mid-Atlantic range. But, alas, confusion never really quits, for both species may be dulled with mud, algaes, or red-brown crustings, and the scarlet etchings on the red-bellied's shell are often muted by the melanism, or blackness, which comes with age, while pattern and coloration may be highly variable. Also, basking turtles are hard to approach and will slide from their perches to deep water whenever directly approached.

But, with binoculars, it is worth getting a good look at an unencrusted specimen, especially an adult red-bellied. The scarlet or red-orange vertical lines on the first three scutes of the carapace resemble molten rivulets or perhaps some vivid Chinese lettering, and this Oriental likeness in particular may be furthered by concentric meanderings adjacent to the red which form mazes of bronze-gold on ebony or curious dots and dashes, like the scriptings on enamel box work. If the turtle is not too old, its head and neck will be pinstriped longitudinally with veins of pale yellow. Should the creature come to hand, a peek underneath at the plastron reveals yellow, salmon, or pale carmen smudged with gray within a border of orange or pink. Though not quite as flamboyant, the smaller painted turtle may also be impressive, with slashes of red or yellow on head, tail, and forelegs and a carapace bordered with half-inch scales, each etched with arches of maize or crimson and appointed like the woven hem on some gaudy Peruvian garment.

Both species feed mainly on insects, crayfish, small mollusks, dead or dying fish, and aquatic vegetation, which are all so abundant in the canal and river that the turtles' leisurely lifestyle is no surprise. Unlike snapping turtles, they weren't themselves considered choice fare for humans and were not widely marketed, although as recently as the 1930s and 1940s painted turtles were sold on the Eastern Shore (perhaps as a substitute for terrapins), while red-bellieds went for seventy-five cents a piece and up in the markets of Washington, D.C. Wrote the anonymous canal diarist of 1859, somewhat misleadingly: "The snapper is the game fish of the turtle kind. The black is sometimes eaten but the spotted and painted ones never except perhaps sometimes by the blacks [African Americans]." He is here probably referring to the red-bellied turtle as the "spotted" (older ones often have reddish blotches instead of distinct lines), while his so-called "black" turtle is most likely the red-bellied in its melanistic phase.

It is easy to take painted and red-bellied turtles for granted along the river and canal. They are readily seen but rarely examined closely or rightly identified, and almost never fully appreciated. To achieve this last, one must savor the secret and subtle, must seek out a bright-shelled adult on its pedestal, half-asleep in its self-contained universe, must focus on the scarlet letters encoded on its crusted carapace, must get beneath the film of things and read the inscrutible message, some sacred sign Asian priests once studied when the world turned on a reptile's armor.

In contrast to these two veiled and wary species, the eastern box turtle (*Terrapene carolina carolina*) is the most easily studied and approachable reptile on the river. In fact it is this turtle, it sometimes seems, who does much of the approaching. Of course, box turtles want nothing to do with humans, but the way they appear in openings or cross one's heading on the towpath gives the illusion of a fellow traveler meeting you at a junction. They are irresistibly colorful and harmless, lend themselves to all sorts of anthropomorphic fantasies, and, much to the detriment of the species and the delight of children, make excellent low-maintenance pets.

But slowness is not tameness; these are utterly wild creatures that learned to survive on a very wild planet for millions of years before humans. They have adapted to a surprising variety of wild foods, can weather floods, droughts, fires, ice, attacks by assorted predators, meddlers, and machines (except direct hits by vehicles), and in some cases live a century. If dumped on their backs, they will soon right themselves by deftly tucking and twisting their head and neck to leverage themselves upright. Their flesh is thought to be poisonous (from their habit, some believe, of consuming toxic mushrooms), and this has probably saved them from wider exploitation.

Also, one must consider the role in their survival of that persistent fascination they hold for humans. It is not only children who love them, but a broad spectrum of adults. In one notable instance a pair of topnotch wildlife biologists, Charlie and Libby Schwartz, observed them for decades in their home state of Missouri and published two important studies. They learned, for example, that young box turtles may travel widely before settling down to a "home range." Among their study turtles this range averaged 12 to 13 acres, though one turtle, named Number Two, remained in a territory of just 5.6 acres. The occasional "transient" exception will continue to wander, as another turtle they named Sinbad—tracked by a radio transmitter—did for several seasons, traveling more than six miles from the spot where they first encountered him. But science is no sure armor against sentiment. Libby Schwartz, who held a doctorate in zoology and wrote with her artist/biologist husband the erudite study *The Wild Mammals of Missouri,* admitted to suffering "turtle-withdrawal symptoms" when they once moved away from their study site, and soon felt compelled to return.

I, too, have felt the pull of box turtle charms. While walking the towpath on a spring or late summer day, especially after a night of rain, which tends to spur their meanderings, I can't resist stopping to examine them, to take them in my hands and look them over closely, doting on each detail. Their carapace scutes literally radiate color, for out from the growth core of each curl assorted mosaics of orange or yellow, toffee or golden tallow, some set with coaxial hexagons, some big-blotched at first, then spotting or splashing down lacquered flanks and trimming dark edges with pale. Breeding-age males are gaudiest, sporting not just outlandish top-shells but flashy ribbons and lavalieres of red-orange or sulphur on the dull field of head and neck, and welty tesselations of similar brightness on their wrinkled legs and tail.

Box turtles aren't just gaudy, mild-mannered reptiles, but surprisingly clever predators. One in particular which I've known for years, a rather mellow-toned female, is a wonder to observe in our gardens. She can spot a wild strawberry lost in the *Vinca* from a distance of several feet and will make a beeline for it. She will track down slugs and caterpillars. And especially at dusk in late summer she is an adept at cornering millipedes of the order Polydesmidae, in particular *Pseudopolydesmus serratus,* a foul-smelling Lilliputian that barely exceeds one inch and whose miniscule movements are further veiled by stealth and evening shadow. She relishes these plentiful little "stink worms," perhaps one of the first foods to nourish her in the droughty late summers of her long-ago youth. I have sat till nearly dark and watched her pursue and gobble them in succession, lifting herself with bent-leg grace along each crack and crevice in the brickwork of the path, dropping her head low to stare or raising it to listen. At times I have thought her deluded when she lunged aside on her course to probe beneath some leaf, for I couldn't detect any prey. Yet not only one but a mating pair would often then be her prize, which she pulled out into the open with a delicate flourish of beaky snout and crunched atop her shrimp-pink tongue while sounding a satisfied "squeak"—faint and froglike in tone, and a hallmark of her gluttonies.

Box turtles touch some alter ego in humans. They are perhaps what a few of us would be if we had our choice in another life, if we could turn off our tortured, seething brains, eat and sleep and doze through existence, and now and then plod off in the wet and sun—hunting, watching, blinking, and minding our own mild business. They do all of this by the river, each a bright individual unmoved by human affairs but willing to tolerate our image when it looms up suddenly and briefly at some open alluvial crossroads. Can we say as much for ourselves?

The first thing many an upper Potomac angler will tell you along the banksides, almost as a common greeting, is "Watch out for snakes." Then often follows an anecdote about some recent encounter, straight up or wildly embellished. It's almost a kind of mythology that fishermen like to dip into when coloring their day on the river. In this mythos snakes are something to be feared, and working around or through that fear, and, by implication, some real risk, adds glory to the angler's quest. I have had fishermen tell me, on the upper Potomac and elsewhere, that the fishing looked good but "the damn snakes drove me off the river." It pleases me to hear this, and I stifle an impulse to ask where exactly they were, so I can fish there myself and be less bothered by human intrusion.

Snake fear is as old as mankind. Today the best way to see it as irrational is to compare, in any given year, the deaths from bee stings or car crashes to those from snakebite, then note how minor is man's loathing for bees and autos relative to his hatred for snakes. Man is in love with his own image, and, although he is the most fearsome thing alive, he projects his fears to the creatures most unlike him—to those legless or non-erect, to those scaly rather than smooth, to those that eat their food whole instead of mutilating it first. In some parts of the world a healthy anxiety about snakes may be justified. In Australia about 60 percent of the snakes are venomous, several extremely so. Africa, India, and Latin America harbor a good percentage of poisonous vipers, a few quite toxic, and poor human health, housing, footwear, and medical treatment accentuate the risks. But in affluent North America venomous snakes are a smaller and far less deadly faction. Out of over a dozen snake species in the upper Potomac basin, only two are venomous: the timber rattlesnake and the northern copperhead, and bites from either are very rarely fatal. More important, all snakes are secretive and relatively docile. You must provoke them to be bitten. Keep in mind, though, that stupidity and carelessness count as forms of provocation.

To understand one's risks along the upper Potomac, or one's lack of them, really, one must grasp biological reality. Two of the most commonly confused snake species here are the northern watersnake (*Natric sipedon sipedon*) and the northern copperhead (*Agkistrodon contortrix mokasen*). The watersnake is by far the most numerous, conspicuous, and aggressive of the two, and the one most bankside visitors encounter. While it has some alarming habits, it is not venomous. It is a brownish snake, two to three and a half feet long, with dark lateral blotches or bands, but its colors and markings are so highly variable as to suit broad tastes in misidentification. With its thickish dark body and bold aquatic ways, many mistake it for the venomous cottonmouth, or water moccasin (*Agkistrodon piscivorus*), which in the east, however, occurs nowhere north of southeast Virginia. Younger watersnakes and those with pale ground color and reddish blotches are the most likely to be taken for copperheads.

Different snakes have different needs, which have determined their separateness as species. The northern watersnake has evolved to feed on fish, frogs, crayfish, and salamanders, in or near the water. So its natural habitat includes such places as the Potomac banksides, where anglers stumble upon it. The northern copperhead, by contrast, is a so-called pit viper (subfamily Crotalinae, which includes cottonmouths and rattlesnakes), having between each nostril and eye a small pit housing heat-sensing organs that help it find warm-blooded prey (in Latin America the pit vipers are often called *cuatro narices,* meaning "four nostrils"). Though it may take frogs or salamanders, especially along small creeks, it has little interest in the fishy world by the riverbanks. Rather, mostly at night, it hunts small warm animals—mice, voles, shrews, birds—more numerous at other locations. Simple biological reality, then, the biology of precisely evolved species with precise food and habitat needs, make copperheads unlikely companions for riverside anglers.

This is not to say that the northern watersnakes many people think are copperheads cannot themselves be unsettling. Though most active in the evening and at night, watersnakes, when startled from a daytime doze, quickly become mobile. Herpatologist Robert McCauley Jr. relates: "Often they are so well concealed that until they begin a frantic thrashing to escape they may go unnoticed. A few specimens in my experience have fancied themselves cornered, whereupon they flattened their bodies and heads and struck viciously." Trying to catch one can be unpleasant. Writes McCauley: "When captured, adult specimens are uniformly vicious. They thrash about violently and if the head is free will bite repeatedly. A large specimen is capable of inflicting deep scratches which bleed profusely and which should be disinfected thoroughly." Watersnakes thus provoked by capture also have the habit, he notes, "of copiously voiding the contents of the anal glands," which have "a particularly vile and characteristic odor." In other words, don't mess with watersnakes, nonvenomous though they are.

Even when not harassed, watersnakes at times seem, for members of the normally wary snake family, oddly incautious. I came upon one three-footer near the bank about to devour a small sunfish. Instead of retreating, it held its ground, looked briefly in my direction, then proceeded to slowly swallow its meal, oblivious to my presence. At another bankside location well trampled by other anglers, I fished near midday in the company of two boys using bobbers, and a watersnake made repeat approaches in front of us from its post in the shoreline brush, causing the kids some concern. It's possible, I concluded, that the snake knows this spot quite well, finds dead or dying fish and bait here when anglers depart, and is not above staking its claim in this way, which more than once may have scared off competitors, events not lost to its memory.

It would be hard to find a good-sized regional snake species less conspicuous and aggressive than the northern copperhead. In this it is the northern watersnake's virtual opposite. Some field guides describe it as "lethargic" or "sluggish," even "well behaved." It reaches three and a half feet in length, occasionally longer, but most adults range only between two and three. Four other subspecies occur in the United States, including the southern, broad-banded, trans-Pecos, and Osage, but only the northern inhabits the upper Potomac drainage. A darker ground color, usually chestnut or reddish brown, distinguishes it from the paler, grayish pink of the southern copperhead, as well as the wider-waisted crossbands—the so-called hourglass blotches—along its length. Its triangular, flattish head is a coppery to golden orange or tan, and juveniles display a yellow-tipped tail that lingers till at least age two. Like most pit vipers it rapidly vibrates its tail when alarmed, and the pupil of its eye is a dark ellipse, often noted as a "vertical slit," which may aid its nocturnal hunting. Young are born alive, from August through October, after a gestation that begins in late May or June. Females bear their first young at five or six years of age and thereafter at two- to three-year intervals.

The preferred habitat of northern copperheads in this region is decidedly not riverbanks. For much of their active season, especially in the months of April, May, June, September, and October, they are commonest near their denning sites on mountain slopes strewn with rock ledges, outcrops, and talus. By July and August they may be widely scattered but still prefer stone or rock walls, crumbling man-made structures or debris piles, and field or wood edges—all places where rodents and small birds are most abundant.

Though I have seen or even captured northern copperheads in other locations, I have yet to encounter a single one during any of my outings by the river. In contrast I have come upon dozens of northern watersnakes here, of assorted ages and descriptions. Just how numerous are copperheads along the upper Potomac? To get a more informed perspective I decided to contact one of the foremost snake, and particularly pit viper, experts in the area.

William "Marty" Martin handled his first snake when he was two and a half years old. He grew up near Leesburg, Virginia, and his father sat him down one day by a creek near their house, where a queen snake liked to prowl. The boy watched and waited and snatched the small snake when it finally appeared, then brought it to his younger brother. But his six-month-old sibling was less impressed than Marty himself, who succumbed to a fascination that has lasted fifty years and seems thoroughly undiminished.

Marty has worked as a contract field biologist for the Carnegie Museum, the Pennsylvania Fish Commission, and both the Maryland and West Virginia Departments of Natural Resources. He specializes in rattlesnake surveys and may know more about regional pit vipers in the wild than anyone else living. Another respected biologist described Marty's understanding of these snakes as "incredible" and "obsessive." Like most truly knowledgeable "experts" I have known, he is modest and unassuming. We bounce along in his bespattered white truck toward an upriver location west of Hancock, and he responds with self-contained enthusiasm to a variety of questions. He's slim, with pale blue eyes and a grayish cotton porkpie hat pulled down around his ears. He agrees with my assertion that most people don't know what a copperhead looks like, and tells me a little story: "I was down in Virginia once doing some collecting, and I stopped at this farmhouse to ask about local pit vipers. The farmer tells me: 'Hell, yes, we've got copperheads all over, and a few rattlesnakes. The copperheads even come in the house. See 'em all the time.' "

Marty did an intensive search in the area and managed to find about ten copperheads, a rattlesnake, and a milk snake. He brought his collection back to the farmhouse. The farmer and his family eyed the milk snake and said they weren't surprised that Marty got this copperhead. "Finally," says Marty, "I pointed to the true copperheads. The family drew a blank. 'What in hell are they?' the farmer says. 'Never seen that kind before in my life!' "

As we move along the back roads Marty conducts an informal snake census by identifying roadkills. "Black rat," he says almost under his breath as we pass a flattened dark ribbon near the shoulder. "That's the second one." A chipmunk scurries in front of us. "Snake food," deadpans Marty.

At our first stop, a steep slope above the Potomac littered with shale and siltstone, Marty searches the rocks thoroughly, probing with his bent-tipped snake stick and illumining cracks with a hand mirror, but without success. At one rather small denning site here he has found as many as seven rattlesnakes on a single occasion. Copperheads, rattlesnakes, and black rat snakes often spend the winter together. The bigger winter colonies, he says, may house one hundred or more each of copperheads and timber rattlesnakes and ten or twelve black rats, though ten to forty of each is more usual. He reminds me that in this region copperheads, like rattlesnakes, are primarily rock crevice hibernators, and locating good rock or stone structure is essential to finding them. The largest number of copperheads Marty has found near a denning site during their mid-April time of emergence is six, though at times during summer he has found twenty or thirty in one day and as many as sixteen at a single rock. More often they are concealed under leaf litter, and so passive they can be stepped on without reacting.

"Copperheads," he says, "are fairly common in some locations near the river. But they're shy and mostly nocturnal. In the range where both rattlesnakes and copperheads occur together [mainly west of Frederick], copperheads probably outnumber rattlesnakes ten to one. But you just don't often see the copperheads. Most of those you do see will be pregnant females."

Pregnant female copperheads like to gestate on sunny rocks and ledges. Thus most copperhead bites, when a person literally steps, sits, or puts a hand down accidentally on a passive, basking snake, are from such gestating females.

In fact, gestation parameters very much determine the copperhead's range in the upper Potomac region. "In Maryland," says Marty, "copperheads are found from mountain base to top as far west as Dan's Mountain. West of there they're restricted to stream valleys. I think copperheads fall out about 500 feet lower down the mountains than rattlesnakes. Their gestation period is a few days longer than that of rattlesnakes. I suspect the season on the higher mountains is not long enough for them to bring their young to term. During some years with below-average temperatures the same thing happens with rattlesnakes on the highest mountains of the Allegheny plateau. Sometimes the pregnant females enter hibernation still carrying unborn young which they probably abort underground."

On our way to a second location along Fifteen Mile Creek we find a hapless wood turtle, a pregnant female, that has been precisely run over on the gravel road, her big white eggs cracked open around and atop her fractured shell, their yellow yolks swimming with flies. Marty cares passionately about reptiles, and this makes him furious. It's a pretty, gentle, and increasingly rare turtle, and this region is perhaps the species' last stronghold in Maryland. A driver would need to aim well to run down this obvious, slow-moving creature, and the normally mild-mannered Marty fantasizes openly about paying the perpetrator back.

We have better luck at this next spot. As we climb a steep shale hillside Marty soon calls out: "There's a rattlesnake. And a copperhead."

They are just above Marty's head, and I am below Marty. I scramble up beside him in time to see a bay-blotched copperhead slide slowly under a big slab of shale, followed by the rattlesnake. "There's another rattlesnake," says Marty, and I hear it buzz loudly and curl away to the right of the big slab. It is larger than the first one. Marty manages to head off the smaller rattler with his snake stick, then lifts the 32-incher up for my perusal. It has begun to shed, and over the next ten minutes we get a chance to witness a fairly rare event for observers in the wild. The snake moves slowly back and forth amid the warm fractured shale and sparse vegetation, gradually crawling out of its gauzy older skin. I take some photographs, keeping an eye out for the bigger snake, which has found a corner to hide in, and finally hold down the tail tip of the shedder's old skin while it emerges from the last few inches. The sloughed skin is light and spongy to the touch—a bit like those plastic bubble packing strips—and still faintly moist.

Meanwhile, the freshly unwrapped rattler is as lovely as anything living—fluid and graceful in its weightless-seeming movements, its greenish-tan ground color striped by chocolate bands, themselves edged with a broken row of buff contrasting scales. Its tricornered pendant of a head, fronted by a dark flying wedge from nostrils back through eyes, is otherwise pale and finely roughened, suggesting awl-stippled goldwork, tapering suddenly from its broad base to a wasp-waisted neck, which plays out behind like a delicate tube or cord empowered with both strength and motion. It is easy to see what might grab a man's focus, what beauty and grace and mystery might take hold of his youthful fancy and haunt him throughout his life. The day has gotten warm. We leave the pit vipers on their dry, shaly hillside, surrounded by a midday buzzing of both insects and birds which suggests obliquely, atmospherically, the serpents' famous rattle.

After lunch we try one more location nearer the river, just upstream from Hancock along a railroad embankment, and though Marty turns over rocks, checks out a rotting signalman's shed, enters small caves and scales sheer walls of limestone and shale to explore the ledges above, we find no other vipers. Fench lizards scuttle about; American toads abound; a young black rat snake stretches out along a weedy edge in the shade. But, true to type, copperheads are elusive. We had picked early June, within the season of female gestation, and had lucked into the cloudy skies that Marty said would be best. We had searched in some prime locations, amid denning sites and varied structure, both away from and near the Potomac. And with a half-century of know-how in the lead we had glimpsed but a single copperhead at a place rather far from the river. Step lightly, ye anglers, along the Potomac banks. But fear not the secretive copperhead. Fear instead your hysteria, your ignorance and cruelty. You are more of a threat to yourself and others than this coppery ghost is to you.

Fifty million years is a fair chunk of time. Yet that is the headstart amphibians had over their younger relations, the reptiles. The tactics that succeeded back then, which were tried and tested by eons, have held the group in good stead. Success does not want change. The surviving orders of amphibians have retained their smooth, porous skins, their need to lay eggs in jellied globs, their critical links to water. But the larger ancestral amphibians, such as *Lysorophus* and *Diplocaulus,* proved ill equipped for recent epochs and long ago died out. Two other traits, not limited to amphibians, had turned out to be crucial in the line that carried on: small size and secretive ways. If an animal is tiny and knows how to hide, it can outlast great calamities. But it won't get much respect from that upstart *Homo sapiens.* Man values many things, but shyness and frail stature tend not to be among them. Such creatures must rely on the mavericks among men, on those with peculiar perspectives, to pay them proper homage.

The first fans of amphibians were mavericks indeed, at odds with their own fellow citizens. They were known as witches. Witches used amphibians—frogs, toads, even salamanders—to concoct their infamous brews. The choice was not merely random. Many amphibians ooze viscous fluids, or "slimes," through their porous skins, and these slimes are often toxic. Evolved to discourage predators, amphibian slimes may be much more than poisons, for today medical science is exploring their other properties—as potential antibiotics, antivirals, even anticarcinogenics. Their alleged miraculous attributes are gaining unlikely attention.

Ed Thompson is neither witch nor warlock, doctor nor pharmacologist. But he is something of a maverick. He was passionately focused on nature long before it had special meaning for the many. Amphibians have intrigued Ed since childhood. Today he is regional ecologist for the Maryland DNR's Natural Heritage Program, which attempts to pinpoint and inventory the state's rare and endangered wildlife and work for its preservation. In this capacity his focus is not just "herps" (biologist slang for the herpetological animals, reptiles and amphibians) but all the threatened species in other groups as well: plants, insects, fishes, birds, and mammals. This suits him fine. "I've always had a need to know what natural things are and how they fit in with everything. I want to know what exists around me," he tells me during a late spring excursion near the North Branch.

It's a need he has largely fulfilled. Perhaps no one is more familiar with the flora and fauna of western Maryland than Ed Thompson. In the past fifteen years he's gained a reputation not only for knowing what's around him, but for finding and knowing the previously unfindable and unknowable. He does not like to toot his own horn, but I manage to draw out some details.

It began in the late 1970s with the Jefferson salamander (*Ambystoma jeffersonianum*), a long-toed, blue-specked member of the "mole salamander" family (Ambystomatidae). Prior to 1977 only seven breeding sites for the species were known to exist in Maryland. Ed applied his passionate focus in the field and ultimately documented some fifty-five Jefferson salamander breeding locations in the state. This raised some eyebrows in a day when the breeding ranges of most regional fauna have been well defined for decades.

He was next put on the trail of *Aneides aeneus:* the green salamander. This rare, jewel-like creature, with its greenish gem flecks strewn on a blackish field, had not been found in Maryland since sometime in the 1960s. It was reported to inhabit damp cracks in rocks in the region's remotest uplands. For over a year Ed searched in vain around numerous caves and ledges in every prime location and was beginning to give up hope. Finally, on a haunting occasion forever etched in his memory, he shined his flashlight in a crevice and gazed not merely on his first green salamander, but on a female guarding eggs. It was, he says, one of his most satisfying finds. Yet, not content with this, he went on to discover the species at forty more locations in Maryland, and his reputation grew.

Ed's quest for the northern water shrew (*Sorex palustris*) was perhaps more memorable still. He relates:

> In 1982 a number of people wanted to list the water shrew as an endangered species in Maryland, but there was some debate as to whether it even existed here. The single record suggested it was only in a border swamp that was actually in West Virginia. So the first place I went was Hammel Glade swamp in the middle of Garrett County. If I could find it there, there'd be no doubt. I was new at it. I set hundreds of traps for almost a week and hiked back and forth through the middle of the swamp in my hip boots. One day I went down in quicksand, the real stuff, not this sticky oatmeal you see in the movies. I guess there were springs underneath, but the top looked solid as hell, like firm sand, and I stepped in and immediately went down over my hip boots, which filled up. It was as if I'd walked off the edge of a table. Fortunately the stream wasn't that wide and I just used all my adrenaline. I finally got out and it was like, "Holy mackerel, this water shrew stuff . . . !"

He managed to capture a single water shrew after over four hundred "trap nights" (four nights setting 100-plus traps), which established the first reliable record. Then he examined old data in West Virginia, visited sites there to better learn the habitat type, and returned to search similar places near Deep Creek Lake. After exhaustive fieldwork he ended up with seven confirmed sites in Maryland, where none had existed before.

Among other finds, Ed Thompson has established the first Maryland record for the ebony sedge (*Carex eburnea*), an evergreen shrub called Canby's mountain-lover (*Pachistima canbyi*), and the rock, or yellownose, vole (*Microtus chrotorrhinus*) as well as the first nest record for the winter wren (*Troglodytes troglodytes*). Also, by identifying additional rare state populations, he has significantly added to the knowledge base of at least twelve uncommon species of plants, eight species of butterflies, one species of fish, six species of reptiles and amphibians, five species of birds, and six species of mammals. And all this by the age of forty-one.

So I'm feeling more than humble as we rattle along in a state-owned truck toward the mouth of Lost Land Run. It doesn't keep me from talking, though, or peppering Ed with questions. Just upstream from the North Branch confluence we pass the big lime-doser that DNR Fisheries has installed on Lost Land's banks. What does he think about lime-dosing here? "I have mixed feelings," he says with deliberation, but the expression beneath his beard and wire-rim glasses looks pained, and I take this comment for diplomacy. After we've stopped to check it over and watch its loud step-lever tip pounds of raw lime into the sparkling creek at roughly half-minute intervals, turning the water milky for hundreds of feet downstream, he questions its effect on brook trout and wonders aloud if the thing is not misplaced.

But today we are focused on salamanders. Not the elusive green, which is not a North Branch habitué, but more bread-and-butter species linked closely with Potomac valleys. These include two important genera: *Plethodon,* the woodland salamanders, and *Desmognathus,* the dusky salamanders. All are part of a huge family called Plethodontidae, whose members breathe through their skin and mouth lining rather than with lungs.

The woodland salamanders are some of the most widespread and common, especially the red-backed (*Plethodon cinereus cinereus*), which is found throughout Maryland and the Mid-Atlantic, the Northeast, and the upper Midwest. It is no less striking for its abundance, being a sleek little amphibian (usually less than four inches long) with a skin like oiled vinyl and bedazzling pigment variations grounded mostly in dark slate or oxblood but often with broad mid-dorsal lines of garnet, orange, or copper, golddust stippling near its flanks, and a salt-and-pepper belly. It does not require much wetness, lays its eggs away from water and has no aquatic stage, and hides beneath varied objects. By far the commonest *Plethodon* east of the mountains, where I often find it under rocks beside the towpath, it competes along the North Branch with such relatives as the slimy (*Plethodon glutinosus glutinosus*) and the Wehrle's (*Plethodon wehrlei*) salamanders.

Among the *Desmognathus,* a more stream- and spring-linked genus, the northern dusky salamander (*Desmognathus fuscus fuscus*) is most widespread, found throughout the state but crossing the range, in the west, of both the mountain dusky (*Desmognathus ochrophaeus*) and the Appalachian seal (*Desmognathus monticola monticola*). This is a baffling group in the region where these species overlap. Color and pattern vary widely with age and size; individual differences are pronounced and local populations distinct. It takes someone with Ed Thompson's acumen to sort such critters out.

We start out looking in crevices. The sandstone shelves on wooded hills above the North Branch, their tawny, wet fissures mortared with moss and dappled with sun ray and shadow, come under the beam of Ed's flashlight. Before long we find a mountain dusky salamander peering out from a cavity. It's a squat-looking three-incher, freckled and root beer brown. The standard way to tell a mountain dusky from a northern dusky is to look for the former's cylindrical, rather than flat, or "keel-edged," tail. But Ed finds heads diagnostic as well:

> More often than not they're facing outward in these cracks, for whatever reason. . . . And when you see enough of these sal-

> amanders you notice that the head shape is different in all of them. You can even tell them by the shape of their nose. Mountain duskies have a bulbous nose. Compared to other species, I call it a "Jimmy Durante" nose. In contrast, green salamanders, which I also look for in crevices, have a very flat profile. Mostly you'll just see a glimpse of a salamander in a crack, so you have to pick up on all these little differences.

Color is an unreliable guide:

> Especially with mountain duskies the color varies incredibly. Sometimes they look yellow or coppery like red-backed salamanders. The *Desmognathus* also have a whitish line that goes from the eye to the corner of the jaw, but they can lose that when they get older. Their back legs, though, are much larger than those of the *Plethodons.* In fact with those big back legs duskies can jump almost like a frog. Of course there are other more technical differences that have to do with the shape of the nares [nostrils] and the teeth and so forth. But I don't use that in the field.

Next we turn over rocks in a clear seep below some ledges and find a nice Appalachian seal. It's a bit bigger and darker than the mountain dusky but just as stocky, with that glassy, false transluscence that I've always liked about salamanders. "Along cool, shady streams," says Ed, "you can sometimes see these seal salamanders sitting up on rocks, with their front legs propped somewhat like a sea lion. That's partly where they get their name." The seep here is afloat with a variety of drowned or struggling insects, and I speculate that at night it comes alive with prowling salamanders.

Now Ed leads me on a climb up the wooded mountainside. He takes time to study other things—insects and herbaceous plants, snails, fungi, birds—but especially the broad-leaved trees that have here reached considerable size: black locusts, sugar maples, red oaks, and cucumbertrees. The slope, he says, has an "old growth" aspect—

nothing like what he has seen in the Great Smokies but still nice to see. Almost no alien species have moved in under this canopy. We wander, instead, amid pleasing natives: pipe-vine and trillium, ginseng and yellow lady's-slipper, jewelweed and slender nettle.

Beneath some decay in a cascading seep Ed locates a slimy salamander. The big, black *Plethodon* struggles to escape but finally quiets down in Ed's palm, where I gaze on its oddball physique—limp, big headed, pop-eyed, with an outsized, licorice-whip tail and legs all akimbo—and its uniform peppering of platinum flakes. In the look-alike Wehrle's salamander these flakes and spots are supposed to be absent dorsally. "That works fine," says Ed, "except some slimys also don't have dorsal spots. But, then, the Wehrle is more slender, and when you get them in your hand you can tell." As its name suggests, the slimy exudes sticky secretions, though in this case they seem mitigated by a crumbly sprinkling of wood rot and loam. It turns out to be our last herp of the hike, and our focus shifts more to the landscape as a whole, to the fragile, threatened beauty that abounds on this North Branch hillside so close to expanding humanity. While descending to the truck we solve the world's problems, verbally at least. Talk then turns back to amphibians and I comment on their strangeness, on what some describe as their exotic or "alien" beauty.

Ed doesn't buy this. "To me the beauty is that they're *earthly,* not something alien. They're natives, right here around us, which is all the more amazing. It leads me to question our need to do things like exploring outer space, because it's often a throwaway mentality, a 'disposable earth' way of thinking. There are fantastic things in our own woods that people know nothing about. Let's first appreciate *them.*"

This strikes me as some sort of bottom line. We are connoisseurs of the obvious, lovers of glitz and spectacle, of flashy adventure and heroic exploration. Thus things quiet or subtle, secretive or strange, which also wield bold charms, often seem to us either boring or out of place, though present in our own backyards. We set our sights on distant stars while grace and glory of the highest order are all but ignored at our feet.

Perhaps, in the long run, it is just as well. Let the upper Potomac valleys shelter their secretive worlds. Let reptiles and amphibians hold, as they have throughout the ages, to their crevices and cracks, and let man work out his destiny and ignore these creatures where they hunt or sleep. Perhaps the last race, after all, won't go to the strong and swift but to those whose secrets keep.

CHAPTER SEVEN

# Mammals Three

Far ahead, as you round a bend in the river, a creature stands still on a gravel bar. The dawn light is dim, the ground fog lingers, and your sense that it is living fades, for a great brownish snag absorbs the immobile outline. It now seems all of a piece and the "creature" but a wooden illusion. But your boat drifts nearer, and the simultaneous cocking of a slender head and rotation of an upright, mitten-size ear, together as distinctive as a dog's wagging tail, confirm your first impression. The chestnut doe then stiffens and completes her stare, faintly lifts her tail, and merges with casual grace, a few mincing steps at a time, back into the bankside forest. The little pang comes afterward, in the moment just past parting, when you recall the doe's frugal movements and dignified silence and you savor that sense of fleeting beauty which is the true taste of wildness.

Encounters with the white-tailed deer (*Odocoileus virginianus*), along the upper Potomac and elsewhere, were rather rare forty years ago. Now they are common. From a stable population that, prior to European settlement, was kept in check by limited grazing and abundant natural enemies such as wolves, cougars, and bobcats, deer numbers rose in response to fur trapping, forest cutting, and farming, which decreased predators and increased prime habitat and food supply. But then they began to plummet from ongoing woodland depletion and persistent overhunting. By the start of this century white-tailed deer populations had reached an all-time low and were not soon to rebound. The country was hard used by a resourceful citizenry that was still essentially rural and knew how to live off the land. Meat-starved Depression-era hunters and farmers kept deer numbers down through the 1930s, and, even as late as the 1940s, seeing a wild deer was an exotic event for most.

But post-World-War II America changed the equation forever. Suburbia boomed, and suburbanites don't hunt fields and woodlots with high-powered rifles. Instead they plant gardens, fruit trees, and succulent shrubs, and take to watching, not eating, these large and graceful herbivores. Then, too, farming changed. What was left of it became production intensive, and the once-common practice of burning off fields and pastures to clear them for eventual new growth gave way, through increased use of fertilizers, to the concept of perpetual harvest. Fields were rarely barren, and when cut, by sloppy jumbo combines, left ample waste grain behind. In addition, woodlands began to return as total farm acreage shrank, and deer do best in a habitat of forests mixed with food-rich openings. The adaptable white-tailed deer had found a growing exploitable niche.

Concurrent with these developments was a sense that deer were in trouble (*Bambi* was a film of the deer-scarce, pre-boom 1940s), and game managers wished to increase their numbers. From Maryland's Aberdeen Proving Grounds just after the war, a few dozen whitetails, which themselves had grown from but five animals received from a Pennsylvania game farm, were transplanted throughout the state. Hunting laws protected the does, and the does fed and bred. They fed and bred so well that their offspring pushed out into neighboring states—Virginia, Delaware, Pennsylvania—and mingled with other stock. The resulting "hybrid vigor" made the genetic base stronger, and by 1992, some forty-five years later, the whitetail herd in Maryland was close to 200,000. South of the Potomac, in neighboring Virginia, the estimated population is now 1 million, believed to be five times higher than it was in 1600.

The white-tailed deer is a highly efficient ruminant. Big males can weigh 400 pounds (the record is 425) and females 250. They crave 10 to 12 pounds of food per day and can get it in one or two hours. They will eat almost anything succulent or green (and, like goats, many things that are not), and they have four separate stomachs. This is a crucial advantage, as it means they are cud chewers and can eat now and chew later. Their main storage stomach, or rumen, holds 8 to 10 quarts of food, so by rapidly tearing and gulping in the open spots where they graze, they can wrap up this vulnerable business fast, then retreat into cover for the rest of the day, to swallow and bring up their cud in a lazy digestive process that may take thirty-six hours to complete. Originally a tactic for reducing exposure to their natural predators, this eat-and-hide plan for survival can be just as effective today.

Further aiding their proliferation has been the fact that nutrition and birthrate are directly linked. A female whitetail getting just enough food will breed in a year and a half and produce a single offspring. A well-fed female may breed at six months, when she is really just a fawn (most birthing occurs in late spring and mating in late fall), and these days twins are the rule, with a good share of triplets and the odd quadruplets or quintuplets. So ample food both hurries ovulation and increases the crop of newborns.

Meanwhile, helped by modern game laws that, until recently, have forbidden the taking of "antlerless deer," these super-fertile females now outnumber bucks by three, four, sometimes five to one. Even conservatively assuming a three-to-one ratio of females to males, when the roughly 150,000 Maryland does give birth in spring (also conservatively estimating an average fawn crop, per female, of 2.35), they briefly *double* the whitetail population of some 200,000 which existed in late winter. And, with few natural predators and a doting majority of human neighbors, whitetails—lovely whitetails—are now virtually out of control.

Maryland's 120,000 licensed deer hunters—a figure that seems like a lot to some but is actually just 2.85 percent of the state's 4,217,000 people (1980 census)—are today outnumbered by their white-tailed quarry by some 40,000 to 80,000. Of this small fraction who hunt deer, only a third or so are successful, taking 45,000 to 60,000 deer annually during all three legal seasons (bow, muzzle-loader, and firearms). The vast majority of hunters dress and eat what they kill or give their kill to others for the purpose. This is in contrast to the many deer killed by vehicles or starvation, whose meat is usually wasted. Yet for those who still cry bloody murder to all this, it helps to remember that the four million-plus other Marylanders who don't hunt get all their meat—including that of infant sheep and cattle (lamb and veal)—from food stores, neatly wrapped in plastic, the living critters having earlier been clubbed and hacked to pieces at production line abattoirs remote from consumer view.

I am a nonhunter myself and a great lover of graceful animals such as white-tailed deer. But I also love biodiversity and the full range of flora and fauna that compete with deer to survive. Sadly, the deer's more balanced competitors, both near the river and elsewhere, are badly losing out. Many regions now hold forty-five to fifty deer per square mile, when fifteen to thirty is the most such habitat sectors can easily support. Besides enjoying grains and grasses, leaves, fruits, and nuts, deer are fond of woodland wildflowers and tender herbaceous plants, many species of which are endangered throughout the Potomac valleys.

In 1990 William McShea, a wildlife biologist with the National Zoo, began a ten-year study of whitetail forest feeding habits in Shenandoah National Park. He hoped not only to understand better the degree of damage deer do to native flora, but also to see if there was a link between the dwindling forest floor plants deer often feed on and the shrinking numbers of small mammals and birds that breed in such habitats. At a dozen ten-acre wooded plots, some protected by fencing and some not, thousands of assorted seeds have been planted. Wire baskets on poles catch falling acorns to gauge good and bad food years, and mounted cameras shoot passing critters to sample their number and species. The litter sizes of mice and squirrels, which fluctuate with food supply, are counted in man-made nests conveniently hung from trees.

Within the fenced plots preliminary results have shown far more surviving seedlings, both of trees and herbaceous plants, and much higher plant species diversity. And, says McShea, "Already there seems to be a significant correlation between the density of the forest understory and the diversity of near-ground-nesting birds, both in terms of species and numbers of individuals." This is a long-range study, and McShea stresses that his data is far from complete. But, he adds: "The absence of deer had a significant impact after just one year. Overall, after four years, the difference in the protected areas is obvious. Everything's bigger, greener. Forest-floor vegetation is easily a foot higher."

Regardless of McShea's conclusions, severe problems are already perceived by expert observers elsewhere. The redoubtable Ed Thompson of Maryland's Natural Heritage Program, who regularly scrutinizes the North Branch watershed, believes that extinction of some forest species because of too many deer is well under way and perhaps, in certain cases, already complete. Furthermore, vehicle collisions with deer are on the rise and are potentially fatal to the drivers. Ed Golden, forest wildlife supervisor for Maryland DNR, confirms this: "Collisions have been increasing. In the last few years we've averaged 1,600 to 2,000. Ten or fifteen years ago the numbers were 800 to 1,000. It peaks in October during the rut. Nationwide, in 1993, over 130 people were killed in such accidents." Meanwhile, Lyme disease, a severe bacterial infection transmitted by deer to humans through its carrier, the deer tick, has also been increasing. In 1987 Maryland had 27 confirmed cases of Lyme; in 1991 there were 283. The case count dropped to 185 in 1992, but Meheret Woubeshet, a researcher in epidemiology at the

University of Maryland, where a long-range study is being conducted in conjunction with the Maryland Department of Health, says "that is the year when stricter reporting and confirmation criteria were applied." Despite the stricter criteria, confirmed cases rose to 206 in 1993.

Solutions to the deer imbalance are often suggested, including intensive hunting, relocation, contraception, and food source manipulation. All are unproven, complicated, and expensive. Some have suggested that humans caused the imbalance to begin with and should finally stop interfering. This is a bit like suggesting that, because we have dirtied our bedroom with assorted vigorous activities, we should leave the bedroom dirty, as cleaning it up would be an added vigorous behavior.

Fortunately, the white-tailed deer is a much-studied mammal, and from such close scrutiny an answer may arise. We've come a long way from the days of English settler John Lawson, who wrote in 1709 that the whitetails (which he called fallow-deer) of North Carolina "had abundance of Bots [maggots] in their Throat, which keep them very poor. As the Summer approaches, these Bots come out, and turn into the finest Butterfly imaginable, being very large, and having black, white, and yellow Stripes." Like many of Lawson's observations, this is a quaint mix of partial fact and wild fantasy. Though the butterfly description fits that of the eastern tiger swallowtail (except for the white stripes), its larvae, like those of all butterflies, feed on plants, not deer tissue (nose botfly larvae may feed in whitetail nasal cavities, but they become flies, not swallowtails).

Yet perhaps what we now know about whitetails is as intriguing as Lawson's archaic fiction. We know, for instance, that deer can jump an 8-foot fence from a standing position, run 40 miles per hour and swim nearly a third that speed, broad jump 30 feet, grow antlers a yard wide, and live seventeen years in the wild. We know they grind each piece of cud with an average of forty chews and that spaghettilike papillae (protrusions) in their first stomach's lining, which aid digestion, number one thousand six hundred to the square inch. We know that does stay clear of their newborn fawns but return to nurse them some ten times a day, that doe's milk has three times the butterfat and protein as that of domestic cows, and that fawns shadow their mothers for a year, at which time they are rudely sent packing. We know that testosterone regulates antler growth, that it also occurs in does and that too much makes does sprout horns, and that a buck's rack may have 76 points (though 6 to 8 is more normal) and is a function of nutrition, not age. We know that the bone marrow of well-fed deer is 90 percent fat, that it turns white, then yellow, then pink, then red if the deer cannot find food, and that bright red marrow has been drained of fat to a level below 2 percent (at which time the animal is doomed).

But for all we know about details, dangers, and depredations, for all we know of grim statistics, we know the deer's beauty best. When prowling the upper Potomac we leave our data behind and are touched more by grace than gravity. Along roadway, towpath, river, or trail, to see the white cotton dust mops of the does go up as signals to their fawns—who gambol at some pace behind, turning to stare and listen, twitching ears and tails, then suddenly, at the tardy perception of peril, bounding left or right, all legs and lovely innocence—is to feel the zest of living. Or, more rarely, to watch some buck with an eight-point spread who is busy watching *you,* and then to start thinking like the predator you are—What direction is the wind? How long has he been watching? Are there other deer nearby?—is to watch yourself through the glass of time: you the upright biped, the dweller on savannahs with binocular vision and deft, opposable thumbs, who needs to assist your struggling tribe, to convey what you have seen, to form a word for this moment, this wonder, this chill along your spine.

Today the moment seems less crucial. But is it? Your lips come together, roundness seems right, you form them in a trembling circle and consciously exhale an *O* sound. "Who," you say to the staring buck, not caring if he flees. "Who," like the voice of the night. Is it a question, this primordial human sound? Does the question have an answer? Or does it just pose another and another after that? Who will at last solve the riddle? Will we ever really know the deer, grasp our proper stance toward it in a world beset by imbalance? Or will we only be able to wonder and watch and echo the hoot of the owl?

Near dawn at a certain boat landing along the river, the sound that often accompanies my 500-stroke inflation of *Testubo* is a loud *ka-blat!* or *ka-thwack!* From my station above and away from the bank it resembles the sound of a big flat rock being dropped into the water. But it recurs three or four times, and no other humans are about. If I stop my labors and creep to bankside, I can make out a prow-shaped wake cutting back and forth in the water, silvered faintly by emergent daylight and centered by a darkish blob. It is only *Castor canadensis,* the beaver, objecting to my presence by slapping its tail on the surface.

Casual human visitors to the river are often surprised to be told that beaver not only live there but, in places, are fairly common. To confirm this for themselves they would have to walk the banks, ride in a boat, or approach a landing like this one before dawn when no one else was about. On the banks they might find tree stumps, chiseled to a point like stockade posts and littered round with chips, or perhaps see or hear the chiseler as it boldly patroled the shoreline. From a boat, if they knew what to look for, they could spot beaver den holes in the steep banks or observe the odd stockpile of branches.

The beaver is a mammal more studied even than the white-tailed deer, and its fall and rise, along the Potomac and elsewhere, is in some ways more amazing. Some have estimated the population of beavers, in the region of the present continental United States before 1600, at no less than 60 million. Around 1620 the French explorer Samuel de Champlain noted that every lake, pond, river, brook, and rill in the mountainous Adirondacks was "thickly peopled" with beaver, and, after fifty years of trapping, that area alone was judged to still hold some 62 beaver per square mile. Since the beaver's range blankets North America, and Canada—unaccounted for in the above estimates—was a major stronghold, one can make one's own guesses about the staggering total size of its original population (though one informed source has suggested 400 million).

In the Europe of that day, beaver fever ran high. The story of the fashionable craze for beaver hats is well-known (it raged for over three hundred years, beginning in the 1500s), and because of it beaver pelts often had the status of currency. But castoreum, a musky secretion of the anal glands that was thought to be a cure-all, was an equally valued by-product. The French and Dutch cornered the beaver market first with the help of Indian allies, who were not new to the business of beaver barter. By the time Chief Samoset first greeted the Pilgrims near Plymouth Rock adorned in pelts of beaver—and was instantly propositioned about supplying them—the trade already existed.

Before long numerous European companies trapped and swapped beaver products without restraint or conscience. In one early instance three-quarters of the pelts brought to auction were burned to manipulate prices. By 1800 the one million Adirondack beaver had been reduced to 5,000, and, meanwhile, the whole continent north of Mexico was being scoured. When the steel trap was invented in 1823 the slaughter intensified. An Arizona trapper took 250 beaver in two weeks, and the next year a party of twenty trappers in Montana killed 95 beaver in a morning, 155 in one day, and 5,000 for the season. Later in the nineteenth century the Hudson's Bay Company alone traded 3 million beaver pelts in a two-decade span.

The results were predictable. By 1820 Adirondack beaver numbers fell to 1,000, and by 1895 just 5 beaver were known to exist in all of New York state. New Jersey lost its last beaver in 1820, New Hampshire around 1865, and Pennsylvania by 1890. Eleven other Eastern states were also devoid of beaver before the turn of the century. At that point most knowledgeable people considered the beaver to be near extinction. In the span of three hundred years one of the most numerous fur-bearing mammals to exist anywhere had been all but completely destroyed.

Many states finally closed their beaver trapping seasons altogether and gave beavers complete protection. Then wildlife managers in such states as Wyoming, Minnesota, Wisconsin, and Michigan, where beaver still existed, began sharing their meager stocks with others. New York imported six beaver in 1904. In 1917 Pennsylvania introduced beavers from Wisconsin, and others were stocked in Virginia in 1915 and West Virginia in 1922. In the space of a few decades the species had recovered so well that nuisance reports poured in. Beavers can flood and kill valued timber, stop up ditches and drainage channels, destroy irrigation systems, or inundate roadways. After much research and data collection, trapping seasons with precise limitations were established by many states. Studies had shown that beaver populations can remain viable even when reduced each year by 30 to 35 percent, as long as sound habitat remains.

According to Peter Jayne of Maryland DNR's furbearer program, beaver along the upper Potomac may never have completely disappeared. In any case, the possible survivors were augmented in the 1950s and 1960s by transplants from such places as the Aberdeen Proving Grounds in Harford County. The population has increased dramatically ever since. While no complete census figures exist, trapping statistics offer clues. A record high of 693 beavers was harvested statewide in the 1986–87 season. But such figures fluctuate with fur market price levels, since some trappers back off when pelt prices fall; the 1993 harvest was just 298. A better gauge is the number of nuisance complaints registered, which has continued to rise. Have beaver, like white-tailed deer, reached troublesome levels? "Certainly," says Jayne, "there are nuisance sites. But we consider beaver a positive resource at this time. We're right on the edge of having to do something about them."

In any case, it's a phenomenal comeback and proof, if anyone needed it, that the beaver is a highly successful and adaptable animal. Just what sort of stuff is this shy but resilient mammal made of? A few have commented that the beaver is like something from a fable, put together from weird spare parts: a duck's webbed feet, a carpenter's chisel for teeth, a fat man's heavy body, and a tail out of Lewis Carroll.

But the reality, like many things in nature, is even more striking than the whimsy.

Only the beaver's naked hind feet are webbed, and the toenail of the fifth inside toe on each back foot is split to function as a comb, essential in the beaver's constant grooming, which removes lice and fleas, smooths and streamlines its fur, applies castoreum for waterproofing, even draws splinters from its teeth. The equally hairless and leathery front feet, or forepaws, also have five toes with long nails and, closely examined, resemble a monkey's paw or, some say, a human hand. Indeed, though lacking an opposable thumb, a beaver's forepaws are nearly as dexterous as hands and can grip a variety of objects.

The beaver's four chisel front teeth, actually incisors, never stop growing. If somehow misaligned and not constantly worn and sharpened by gnawing, they may circle back in an arc and prevent the beaver from eating, even ultimately pierce its skull. The enamel of these teeth is naturally bright orange, not simply colored by tannin or poor dental hygiene. In fact, this outer layer of enamel makes them self-sharpening, for it is much harder than the rearward section of dentine, and, as lower teeth grind against upper, the dentine wears away behind to form a front-to-back beveled edge.

The beaver's seemingly outsized body is in fact Lilliputian compared to that of its ancestors, some species of which weighed 800 pounds. The 40- to 60-pound average adult of today needs this bulk to keep warm in its cold, wet habitat, and the rotund shape is no accident. Such roundness presents a small surface area relative to its mass, an important thermodynamic efficiency.

A beaver's tail is multifunctional, being oar, rudder, paddle, and diving plane in one. It is also a tool for communicating, may do duty as a weapon or distraction device, is used as a rear prop, or "stool," while the animal is stationary on land, and, with its finlike flatness and tough scaly surface (which caused the first explorers to classify the beaver as a fish) requires a minimum of body heat.

But the beaver's physiology is more interesting still. Its ears and nose are valvular and thus automatically seal when it dives beneath the surface. Transparent eyelids serve as natural "diving goggles," and folds of skin on either side of the mouth prevent the inadvertent leak when, as often happens, it chews wood under water. Its fur is double layered, having soft, slender guard hairs outside and a dense wooly lining beneath. For complete insulation it regularly smears this dual coat with the oily castoreum obtained from two glands (the castors) on either side of its cloaca, an efficient anal cavity that simultaneously houses its excretory, reproductive, and scent organs. Castoreum, the alleged panacea of European traders and medicos, has subtle properties of fragrance retention and release, holding any odor that caresses it and surrendering it slowly to the direct influence of body heat. It is still used as a perfume base, a trapping scent seductive to all furbearers, and, of course, by the beavers themselves as a form of communication.

A beaver can submerge for fifteen minutes and swim below the surface for half a mile. Its relatively large lungs and liver store much air and oxygen-rich blood, its heartbeat slows as it dives, and its respiratory system tolerates high levels of carbon dioxide. Blood vessels to its extremities constrict, while blood flow to the brain remains normal. When it surfaces to breathe it exchanges some 75 percent of its lung contents (while humans exchange just 15), and is thus well supplied with oxygen for any further dives.

Perhaps its greatest asset is an ability to eat most things vegetable, especially woody plants. This has allowed it to survive in cold climates and adapt to the flora of varied regions. A large gland in its stomach secretes enzymes that reduce bark and cellulose. Additionally, by a process known as *coecotrophy,* it passes its once-digested glutinous food mass from its anus, then eats and digests it a second time to glean every morsel of nutrition. The twice-digested true feces that it finally excretes are so devoid of food content that they resemble pure sawdust. On its strict vegetarian menu are such myriad staples as grasses, rushes, sedges, burweeds, duckweeds, water lilies, cattails, irises, spatterdocks, roses, berries, mushrooms, many types of farm crops, and numerous species of trees and shrubs, including their bark, twigs, leaves, roots, flowers, and fruits.

On top of all this the beaver is smart. Swiss biologist Georg Pilleri determined from much analysis that its cortex is far more developed than that of any other rodent. Indeed, in 1982 another biologist, the Frenchman P. Bernard Richard, reported that beavers solved daunting problems. A willow protected by wire mesh at its base was sized up by a beaver, who piled litter beside it to a height above the mesh, then climbed the handy platform and gnawed away above it. In another test a beaver out-thought a Norway rat, considered by many to be highly clever. A chunk of bread suspended on a string was jumped at by the rat, as well as by a muskrat, who both attempted to tear and shred it with each crude upward leap. The beaver found a way to get above it and simply cut the string.

Beaver along most of the upper riverbanks lead a life rather different from that of their northern relatives. The classic beaver "lodge," that conical or rounded stick-and-mud mound that serves as winter quarters and is often depicted in nature books, is missing from all but the colder Potomac headwaters. So also is the beaver dam. Since these two features are the most well-known and conspicuous artifacts of beaver presence (and, indeed, in the North make possible rapid aerial population surveys), their absence makes many believe there are no beaver here.

Yet beaver sign, of a subtler sort, is evident the length of the river. As mentioned, they still gnaw down trees and leave "stockade post" stumps, but they generally focus on small trees and saplings and use the wood not for lodges and dams but, rather, to build food caches and stockpiles. At this latitude mild winters, mostly ice-free water, and long growing seasons make dams (used to create deep water and facilitate lodges) largely superfluous. Plant food is available year-round, or nearly so, caches can be built above waterlines, and far fewer trees, or none at all, need be felled.

Without the need for elaborate stick lodges, most upper Potomac beaver simply tunnel into the muddy banks and widen out a "den" at the far end. Den entrances, where visible, appear as circular, oval, or squarish holes, one to two feet wide, at varying heights in eroded banks, sometimes concealed by tree roots and often along islands, where dogs and human intruders are less frequent. Sometimes there is a "high den" and a "low den" to allow for easy entrance with the river at varying levels, and some are interconnected, but a single den will do. A food cache of neatly gnawed branches and twigs may be visible nearby, just out from shore, but is often entirely absent. In the face of frequent flooding, planning for permanent amenities may seem futile even to a beaver.

Beaver families are close-knit and matriarchal, the dominant female bearing two to seven kits (though four is average) in spring and, with her monogamous mate, closely looking after them for their first two years of life. The so-called beaver colony consists, in any given summer, of the two parents, their kits of that spring, and their young of the previous year (yearlings). Second-yearlings (young who have overwintered twice with their parents) are abruptly kicked out when they reach age two, but, if they fail to find their own living space upriver or down, are sometimes allowed to return.

These two-year-old "nest flee-ers" form, at strategic points as they wander, neat piles of mud soaked liberally with castoreum. All beavers do this to mark family territory (and trespassers are rudely treated), but it is the young adults in search of homes and mates who most often pile such fragrant mounds at conspicuous spots near bankside. As in the Seneca creation myth, where a beaver (among others) submerges to bring up earth from below, beavers in fact do just that, diving to the bottom to scoop up small loads of mud. Then they surface and transport it to the chosen site, to be coned up and perfumed distinctively.

Along the upper river these days it is not so rare to view beaver in brightest daylight. Matters have come full circle, for beaver were originally diurnal. Early trappers and explorers wrote of seeing them perched on their lodges, peacefully soaking up sun. The extreme persecution that followed made them creatures of the night. Recently, I've seen them off islands, on rocks at midstream, or swimming back and forth near shore, even on the sunniest days, and, in one case, while I ate my lunch at noon.

Yet, regardless of the time of day, it is hard not to find them attractive. They are animals possessed of traits even humans can admire: industry and intelligence, patience and gentility, family values and faithfulness, toughness and adaptability. On the river they do not stand out, and, for anyone concerned with their nuisance potential, this is one more reason for tolerance. They build beside the banks without destroying, work and play and raise young without creating a fuss, without spreading noise or pollution, without sowing hatred or violence. If any creatures have a right to remain, it is surely these sturdy, oddball survivors, which came so close to extinction.

Unlike the white-tailed deer and the beaver, the river otter (*Lutra canadensis*) is one of the scarcest mammals on the upper river. At the turn of the century none existed in the western counties of Maryland, the result not just of over-trapping but of hideous water quality. Sediment and chemical pollution from the badly regulated timber and mining industries had wiped out the fish and other aquatic animals it thrives on. The few surviving otters had little or nothing to eat. Such severe degradation of habitat is not easily reversed. Until 1989 there were still no otter in Maryland's three most western counties: Washington, Allegheny, and Garrett.

By that time, however, better logging practices and mine reclamation had so improved the water on such rivers as Garrett County's Youghiogheny that a transplant program was begun by Maryland's Department of Natural Resources. Each spring for five years a half-dozen or so otters were captured on the Eastern Shore, where their numbers are stable, and introduced to the Yough. In some years the high cost of flying the otters westward (the safest and best way) was beyond the department's budget but was picked up by the Pennsylvania

Game Commission, who, being co-steward of that north-flowing river, were partners in the restocking effort. In all, Maryland moved some thirty otters to the upper Youghiogheny (and Pennsylvania an equal number to its sectors) before the program was completed in 1993.

Members of Maryland DNR's furbearer program then turned their attention to the upper Potomac and neighboring Allegheny County. In the spring of 1994 they began live-trapping river otter in the Eastern Shore counties of Dorchester and Caroline, then flying them west for release near the Potomac tributary of Town Creek, a few miles below Oldtown. Additionally, a man-made den site was implanted along Town Creek, with the hope that this year's immigrants (eight for starters, of a projected thirty in all) would adopt it.

Because Maryland DNR's budget has been badly reduced, it took some creative management to achieve this Potomac introduction. Furbearer program leader Peter Jayne relates:

> We had to get funding where we could, outside our own agency. The State Highway Commission operates under a "mitigation" regulation whereby they've got to create a wetland if they destroy one. I guess they've destroyed a couple, because we worked out a deal with them over otters. They found some specs on den construction and built this artificial site near Town Creek. The site is basically a pond. A big pipe goes into the pond bank on some private land. But the part we really can't afford is the expensive airfare. So they made available about four thousand dollars for otter transport.

A ban on all trapping of river otter in Garrett and Allegheny Counties is currently in place, but, eventually, if the otter take hold, Jayne envisions reopening the season "once we determine their occupied range and get evidence of their sufficient presence, from accidental trapping or other deaths."

Curiously, although no otter are presently known to exist in downriver Washington County, the state still maintains a one-per-season bag limit there. Doesn't Jayne see a contradiction in having an open season on otter in a place where they probably don't exist, especially in view of the trouble and expense his own agency is incurring to restock the animals nearby?

"That's a good point," he says. "I suppose it does seem a bit contradictory. But we don't think anyone is deliberately trapping for otter there right now. It wouldn't be worth their while. And if anyone happens to accidentally take an otter while setting for other animals, we want them to feel free to bring it in for proper tagging under the regulations. We don't want them to feel they poached it and not report it. Then we lose that data."

All otters legally taken must be presented to the DNR for tagging. The tagging data thus collected is basic but, according to Jayne, ultimately useful: date of capture, county of capture, length, weight, trap type used, watershed collected in. From length and weight such factors as age can be estimated. Over time tagging data have shown, for instance, that trappers take more males than females and that most females are taken in the month of March. Data also delineate the annual statewide otter "harvest" (seeing the whole trapping process as a kind of natural resource "farming" is key to understanding the perspective of both trappers and state wildlife managers). Dorchester County, on the Eastern Shore, traditionally yields Maryland's greatest harvest, averaging, in the last five years, 51.4 otters per season, with a high of 77 in 1992–93 and a low of 32 in 1989–90.

The other two upper Potomac counties in Maryland not yet mentioned, Montgomery and Frederick, maintain the only nonintroduced otter populations above tidewater, though at very low densities. Once again these are gauged largely by extrapolating DNR tagging statistics. The Montgomery County section of the upriver watershed, though hard by the nation's capital, seems to contain the most otter: 16 were trapped or accidentally killed in the five years from 1989 to 1994, with a high of 6 in 1990–91 and a low of 1 in 1991–92. Though admittedly just some fraction of the total population, this is not a lot of otter. The number is even less upstream in Frederick County, where the five-year total was only 6, with none at all in both 1989–90 and 1993–94.

River otter are secretive and nocturnal, and their general whereabouts in these stretches of the river are known mostly by the people who trap them. To get a better sense of their presence I put myself in touch with Ron Leggett and his father, Pete, each a past president of the Maryland Trappers Association. Both have trapped on land and water most of their lives and steadily as a team for the last twenty-two years. They are dairy farmers by profession. Like many others who work the land, trapping is for them a second job, not essential to their survival but an important added income. Being commercial harvesters of wild furs has embroiled them in what has been called the most persistent and virulent debate in the history of wildlife management. They have been cursed and vilified by those who oppose trapping, and have even received death threats. So they greet my suggestion of a trip on the river with a good deal of suspicion. Yet both are conscientious and likable, and they go out of their way to cooperate.

The Leggetts manage to find a lull in their grinding farmwork and meet me with their boat in western Montgomery County. Ron is mid-forty-ish, with short dark hair and a sturdy medium build. Pete is an older, grayer, and stouter version of Ron, a bit more talkative and extroverted. Earlier I had asked what appealed to them about trapping on the Potomac. "Basically just bein' out on the water," said Pete, "and bein' able to see wildlife and do the things we've always done." Said Ron: "The solitude. It's so peaceful. You're on the water, it's just quiet. You get to see everything without interference."

It is a warm morning in early summer. They have warned me beforehand that otter sign may be hard to find in this season, what with rank vegetation and the adults lying low with their new spring pups (the one to five otter pups are born blind in April or May after a ten-month gestation). And they know from what I've said that, while not opposed to trapping per se, I would like the sight of river otter here to be more than a very rare event. This, I feel, would require some sort of moratorium on otter trapping wherever their numbers are low. I'm not exactly the enemy to Ron and Pete, but I sense that I'm close to the line.

On the other hand, when I said I'd like to see more otter around, Pete chimed in, "I would too!" and his enthusiasm wasn't just economic or professional. He thinks the big weasels are beautiful. Indeed, both have made plain their love of animals, have said they wouldn't be dairy farming if it were otherwise, and, when you think even briefly about that line of work, it's hard to doubt their sincerity. On the upper Potomac, in fact, they have taken just five otter in their lives, none in the last six years, and they don't target the species without a specific client request.

"If we're settin' for beaver or 'rats [muskrats] in an area and we see otter sign, we give the place a pretty wide berth," says Ron. Even without such precautions, they insist, accidental trapping of otter (with beaver or muskrat sets in water and raccoon sets on land) is very rare and their taking of nontargeted species in general extremely low.

I ask what kinds of sign tell them that otter are around. "One thing we look for is slides," says Pete. "The otter make a path down the bank that's slick and narrow. A lot of times where they cross the end of the island, up from that point, they go up one side and down the other. And then there's tracks. Look kinda like a big dog's tracks. You can look where they been walkin' up these slides. Also, they'll eat whole fish, and they can't digest the scales. So they'll regurgitate all the fish scales in a pile—we call it a 'slime pile'—and you find that too."

We cross the river in their metal johnboat and head up the mouth of a creek. The water is shallow and rocky, and the sun glints down through the sycamores and maples and dapples the surface with gold. These are careful, experienced men. Ron works the throttle deftly, picking his way upstream. When it gets too shallow he grabs a pole and stands, levering us smoothly up through narrow riffles and runs like an artful, rustic gondolier. We find one spot at the outlet of a stream where a slide has been neatly fashioned across a high point of land, and indistinct tracks scar the mud. But beaver make slides as well, so the evidence is inconclusive.

We drop back to the river's main stem and head downstream, exploring a long channel behind a series of lush green islands. For Ron and Pete it is a trip down memory lane. They haven't been back here since the winter trapping season (which runs roughly from December to mid-March), and each hole in the bank, each system of undercut tree roots or disturbed shore mud reminds them of a muskrat or beaver they've stalked or taken in the past. Indeed, looking for sign, they stare intently at the exposed line of bankside mud as if perusing old snapshots in a family album, commenting to each other in low, intimate voices as we work down with the current.

When we reach some deep water near the end of one island, beaver sign become common. Their high-water den holes are prominent in the steep banks and their tracks visible at bankside. Otter, too, make den holes, but conceal them with greater care. Now Ron and Pete point often to places where they've seen otter slides or tracks before, though none are apparent today. It was near here, says Ron, that they had their only close encounter with a living otter. "One thing otter do," says Ron, "they hang out by these undercut banks with hangin' roots. They'll get under there and lay for the day. And we pulled in here to make a muskrat set, I think. The roots came clear down over the bank into the water, and as the boat came up and touched those roots that otter came right down past the corner of the boat—a beautiful thing. I'll never forget that."

Pete adds: "You just don't run into 'em everyday on the river. You'll see a lot more sign than you do see the otter. You could probably come down here, even at night with a spotlight, and run this river for a week and not even see one."

To me this says a lot about the animals' extreme scarcity, not just their secrecy.

In the next half-mile of river we find two good otter signs. One is a doglike paw print, in the mud beneath some sycamore roots on a little slice of island where no dog would likely visit (all four otter feet are webbed, but the webbing rarely shows in prints; the impression of the five claws is prominent and, in an adult, some four inches wide). The other is a patch of dug-up sand on the point of another island, imbued with a musky fish odor so distinctive that Ron's experienced nose tells him an otter dawdled at the spot. This is, in fact, the place where Ron and Pete have in the past found slime piles, the little heaps of fish scales contained in a viscous, yellowish ooze, vomited up by otter sometime after dining.

The contention that otter eat lots of gamefish such as trout and bass has been largely put to rest (biologists in the upper Midwest gathered hundreds of dead otters from trappers and analyzed stomach contents; crayfish topped the food list, followed by rough foragers like carp and sucker), but was the source of a persecution many centuries old. Ostensibly to protect trout and salmon the English gentry employed mixed dog packs—foxhounds for trailing otter, poodles for routing them out, and a half-dozen shaggy "otterhounds" for tackling them in the water. Today British otters are protected.

Finally, after a long downriver search that has revealed much evidence of muskrat and beaver but very little of otter, Ron and Pete take me back to the landing and we say a brief good-bye. They are friendly enough, but their suspicion has never quite vanished. I've got too many points against me: I don't trap, I don't hunt, I don't work the land, and indeed I'm one of those "city people," out of touch with their reality, whom they've more than once referred to with barely concealed contempt. On top of all this I've got a soft spot for river otter.

Still, on a certain level I sense we're not far off in our love of wildness and the natural world. But we've grown up in different places, nurtured different habits and ways of subtly connecting, each of which we're fond of and which helps to make us tick and, as hard and short as life is, we've no intention of discarding. And yet, who knows, just a little twist of fate can spin love of wildness around. Back in the 1920s, on another great river, the Mississippi, a professional fur trapper named Emil Liers acquired a pair of young otters. Before long he fell in love with these playful and fun-loving mammals, gave up trapping, built a life around raising and breeding them, and took them with him while he traveled and lectured to school groups. Though he stopped trapping, "The Otter Man", as Liers came to be known, never swore off hunting. His otters, in fact, became top-notch waterfowl retrievers, doing their work with more skill and panache than any dogs he had owned.

The love of wildness is in all of us. We often wish to caress it, to possess it, however briefly or vaguely. And to do so, though the attempt is always futile, we take different paths. Wild paths on the upper Potomac are complex and many and are not just followed by men. The river otter has its path, too, a path it follows in secrecy in order to survive. For that we must surely respect it, and protect it where it falters.

CHAPTER EIGHT

# Grace Notes in the Green

Beside the river it is hard not to notice, for all one may chase after fleeting or secretive wild things, the least mobile but gaudiest natives of all, those pastel-petaled grace notes, the wildflowers, tucked about in the warm-weather green. Upper Potomac wildflowers herald each season of growth yet are most plentiful and striking at two times of the year: during the cool and fickle spring of mid-April through May and in the lush, sultry days of late summer which stretch into early fall.

Springtime may be botanically splendid here but not always for the obvious reasons—those of vernal moisture and rich valley loam. For in the Ridge and Valley section of the upper Potomac highlands, just east of the Alleghenies, eccentric conditions of geology and weather have combined to produce a flora like no other in the region, a flora that thrives on adversity. Here Devonian shales have been fractured by time and stresses to cascade slowly off ancient slopes and form anchors for arid gardens. These beds of broken gray bits are as porous and quick draining as a pebble beach, often more sunstruck and heat-retentive than desert sands, and lie in the lee, or "rain shadow," of mountains, where water is squeezed from laden clouds just prior to their arrival, leaving little for the shaly hillsides.

The result is a rocky landscape, dry and hot, which often has annual rainfall of less than 30 inches and daily temperatures reaching 145 degrees Fahrenheit. These are the so-called shale barrens, a term first coined by botanist Edward Steele in 1911. For any living thing that can adapt to this stressful environment there is one important payoff: most other species cannot, and thus competitors (the chief drawback in more pleasant habitats) are few. The ecosystem thus forged over time today harbors at least thirteen species of "endemics" (plants that are confined to, and in most cases have evolved in, a single geographic region) as well as a long list of non-endemics that are nevertheless scarce or unusual.

One of the more dedicated shale barrens observers in the upper Potomac watershed is Dr. Melvin L. Brown. Coauthor, with Russell G. Brown (no relation), of the voluminous *Herbaceous Plants of Maryland,* Melvin Brown grew up in the Potomac highlands of Mineral County, West Virginia, taught at the University of Maryland, and now resides with his wife near Cumberland, Maryland, in, fittingly enough, the dry rain shadow of Dan's Mountain. On a sunny May morning I've made a date to revisit with him a favorite shale barrens habitat, one we scoured together the first time we met and toward which he is something of a steward.

Melvin Brown is a rather bulky man in his seventies, with lush eyebrows and a soft, leisurely voice. He came up the hard way as a sturdy hill country farmboy in the days of the Great Depression. As I lean my car into the sweeping curves of the North Branch Valley below Cresaptown, I press him for some of the details. "It's the old country boy story," he says. "We were poor but didn't know it. We did for ourselves, and I didn't know till much later how thin the margin for error was. Butchered three or four hogs in the fall and made sausage that lasted all year, made tubs of apple butter and filled the cellar with potatoes. Lots of potatoes. My first cash-money job was fifteen cents an hour, making hay. We baled 60 bales a day by hand, that was the standard. For fifteen cents an hour." He stares out onto the green slopes of Dan's Mountain as if struggling to believe his own past.

Eventually, Melvin got a good education and became a teacher. He taught physical education and a subject that, in those days, was simply called "science": physics, chemistry, and biology all in one. How, I ask, did his interest turn to botany? "What adds more beauty to the landscape than flowers?" he sums up simply in his offhand boyish drawl.

We cross the river at Keyser and drift eastward toward Patterson Creek, a north-flowing Potomac tributary that splits and meanders around Headsville, West Virginia. I park in the shade of a large red cedar; Melvin dons his white plastic pith helmet and, bearlike, rouses his big frame into the sunlight and squints at the shaly slopes beyond the creek. This is a place called "Larenim," a shale barrens preserve set aside by Mineral County in 1992 and watched over in part by both the county and volunteer caretakers like Brown (the name resulted from a contest among local school kids; the winner simply spelled the word *mineral* backwards). Shale barrens are fragile, and even careful hiking among them can degrade their delicate features, so we mostly stick to the gravel road above the creek which follows the winding hills.

Already it is hot, a function as much of the heat-convecting shale as the steadily warming day. Prominent on the baking talus are clumps of pink-flowered beardstongue, named for the hairy stamens within their trumpetlike flowers, and thick colonies of prickly pear cacti, the East's only cactus species. Neither is limited to shale barrens but both enjoy dry conditions, what botanists call *xeric* (a plant adapted to such terrain is technically termed a *xerophyte*).

The rarest flora of the barrens favor south-facing slopes, where, due to the steadier sunlight, the competitor-limiting dryness and heat is most pronounced. Beneath a scattering of scrub and post oak, and a growing contingent of invasive Virginia pines and eastern red cedars that threaten to shade out the sun-loving oddities, live unusual woody plants. We first notice a dwarf hawthorn (*Crataegus uniflora*), with its spiked twigs and serrated leaves, which, barely four feet tall, clings to a scorched shale shoulder just above the road. Dwarfism is a common plant adaptation to poor, dry soils. In some cases individuals of a normally tall species are simply stunted by local conditions; in other cases a completely separate species has evolved to handle the stress. Of the latter, dwarf hawthorn and dwarf hackberry are notable among woody plants here, while dwarf dandelion and dwarf skullcap, of the herbaceous plants, show this species adaptation.

In fact, nearly all plants are somewhat smaller on shale barrens. Flora of reduced stature require less food and water, expose less surface area to the scorching sun, and are less prone to dehydration. Scorching and evaporation are also countered by pubescence (hairiness), sclerosity (stem tissue toughness), and both linear (needlelike) and deeply cut leaves, one or more traits of which mark most plants growing on the shale.

Melvin Brown doesn't talk much while afield in his favorite barrens. Perhaps he, too, has learned to conserve vital energies here. He once more looks bearlike in his movements and stature, shuffling up heavily and bending to his charges, staring, gently touching, seeming almost to sniff with his nose. Then, satisfied that this or that species—Oswego tea or shale barren pussytoes, birdfoot violet or moss phlox, rock twist or lespedeza—is in order, he snuffles to himself, backs off slowly, and resumes his loose-footed gait down the trail.

Most shale barrens species bloom in spring. In such roasting habitats as these you had best bring your sexual essence early to the fore or else run the risk of it cooking to a crisp. These are not big sexual plumes, these careful blossoms of the barrens, these bindweeds, skullcaps, primroses, ragworts, pimpernels, clovers, and cresses. But they are of varied and subtle hues and of especially delicate structure. In many the little perfumed lip, the turned-down petal or corolla, however small, is a wildly miniature landing strip for each welcome prospective pollinator, each minute aviator bee or wasp, each airborne sexual go-between.

They are brought forth, these xeric flowers and fruits, with nothing at all to spare, without the least waste or extravagance, but only with the sheerest economy of every cell in their being, with a precision of resource application that less harried living things cannot match.

Many are under siege from more than just heat and dryness. Hoary puccoon, a lovely orange-flowered member of the forget-me-not family which favors arid soils, is becoming scarcer at Larenim. We found none in the expected places last spring, and this time we come upon a single lonely specimen drooping beside a cedar. "Deer," says Melvin quietly. "Deer are changing the whole flora in some of these areas." And they are not alone. Additional threats to shale barrens habitats come from introduced alien species, reduced light from invading trees and shrubs, use of herbicides and fertilizers, excavations for fill dirt, overgrazing by livestock, too much human traffic (both foot and off-road vehicle), and overcollecting by botanists.

Not so long ago shale barrens botany was largely a mystery. Traveling European scientists were the first to notice the odd species we now know as shale barrens endemics, beginning in 1805 when German botanist Frederick Pursh collected shale, or velvet, bindweed (*Convolvulus purshianus*), an erect, white-flowered member of a normally creeping group which resembles the dooryard morning glory. In 1877, along the South Fork, Gustav Guttenberg discovered a similar vinelike plant, shale leatherflower (*Clematis albicoma*), and in the same decade Timothy Allen found yellow buckwheat (*Eriogonum alleni*) on the slopes of Kate's Mountain near White Sulphur Springs, West Virginia. This last turned out to be a disjunct species from the Far West, where related forms dwell in the Rocky Mountains, and the theory suggested by Edgar Wherry, a noted shale barrens expert, is that yellow buckwheat once ranged the continent but was wiped out eastward by climate change in all but these shaly hideaways.

At last Melvin and I come upon the most famous of these nineteenth-century shale barrens finds: Kate's Mountain clover (*Trifolium virginicum*). One plant protrudes from an embankment, and a few others are scattered above it on a particularly bleak hillside. Superficially, it is not unlike others of the clover clan but is prostrate and solitary, the whitish flowers drooping, the trident of leaves on each stem long and bladed like spearheads, with pale, V-shaped variegations that vein the inside surface. It has recently finished blooming, and Melvin stoops to twist off the dried brown flower heads, then ambles around the slopes like a New Age Johnny Appleseed, scattering the hope of the future.

A man named John K. Small takes the main credit for finding this plant on Kate's Mountain in 1892. For a number of years that was the only known site for its occurrence anywhere in the world, and it was studied and collected there by avid visiting botanists. Then others began to find it elsewhere, in Virginia, Maryland, even Pennsylvania. Of course, it had always existed at these places, but suddenly people knew what to look for, and where, and the plant became much less "rare."

This change in its status was partly the result of applying what some call the "search image." In fact, Ed Thompson told me a story about the search image directly related to this species:

"The existence of a 'search image' is a known phenomenon in predatory animals," Thompson explained.

> This includes people. A good example is when I was looking for Kate's Mountain clover, a real cryptic plant that, if you have never seen it, you can go to an area where there's a bunch of them spread on a slope and not see one. But as soon as you find one, you look around and start seeing all of them.
>
> I had a botanist who was working with me in shale barrens. I sent him to this one little area and told him: "There's clover there, just go up there and it's all through the opening, you look around, you'll see it." He called me up the next day and said he tried but couldn't find it. So I met with him there the next week and I showed it to him and, well, he felt like a fool. It was all over, but it's so cryptic you may not see it. Once you do, and you go to another area, you've got that search image in your brain. It's sort of a

composite image of the species' little details and how they look overall against the landscape. It works for almost everybody. Mushroom hunters use it too. It's not magic, you can cultivate it.

It may not be magic, but some folks apply it with greater skill and persistence than others. When Thompson started with Maryland Heritage, Kate's Mountain clover was known at just five or six sites in the state. He went on to discover no less than eighty sites, of five to twenty plants each. (Incidentally, Ed complains, his success at locating new colonies of rare species has a catch-22 drawback: the more sites he identifies in the interests of preservation, the more anti-environmentalist factions use his findings as evidence that the species are too numerous to need protection.)

In any case, at Larenim I apply my own search image tactics on the walk back to the car and notice Kate's Mountain clover at one additional spot. But I soon get a better chance to prove myself. Melvin wants to check up on one of his favorite threatened shale-related species, twisted milk-vetch (*Astragalus distortus*). Most shale habitats in the region are unprotected and often merely comprise some farmer's back-forty grazing land. This is the case at our next stop. It's just a dry hilly pasture above the road, littered with scrub pines and cedars. But the beautiful birdfoot violet grows here, its pale or dark purple petals suspended above an emerald clump of deeply cut "bird-footed" leaves (most other violets have heart-shaped leaves), along with pussytoes and moss phlox and waddings of prickly pear cactus. And, somewhere, the elusive twisted milk vetch.

Indeed, the milk-vetch has become so elusive that we simply cannot find it. We found it here last year, talked briefly with the smiling farmer who was tickled by our focused interest, even took a few color slides. Yet today Melvin is baffled. He leads us back and forth in the place he knows it should be, but without success. Did the cattle finally destroy it, we wonder? I fumble in my mind for a better image of the plant. Leguminous, and therefore compound leaved, like locust or acacia. Stunted and sparsely scattered. A little low clump with oppósite, mouse-ear leaves and purplish flowers, all of it compact, dwarfish, contained, in greenish relief against gray shards of shale and reddish pine needles, like a miniature bouquet of beach-peas. And I find it. Melvin comes over to confirm things and locates others nearby. *Astragalus distortus* is still hanging on where it should be here, but for how long is anyone's guess. Still, our morning ends on a high note. It's a tiny triumph in the ongoing wars—the threatened species wars, you might call them—wherein many more battles are lost. Today's search celebrates our hopefulness; tomorrow it may signal our despair.

Yet shale holds but a fraction of the river's flowery wonders. Best known are the upper Potomac's rich floodplains, where spring can be a feast of discovery and even the casual towpath tramp may sate a hunger for sly color and showy, emergent life. From Cumberland down to Carderock the fat alluvial soils, drenched with vernal sunlight still unchecked by canopies of leaves, bring forth their fragile gardens. The pageant is perhaps sweetest in the limestone swath of the Great Valley, between Williamsport and Dargan Bend where, at intervals, sheer cliffs of limestone crowd the canal bed, dangle wetly with columbine and creeper, spleenwort and saxifrage, hepatica and rock cress.

Feeder valleys indent these bluffs, small green harbors off the brown straits of the towpath and swollen river. And here, amid deep silt and crumbling boles of long-dead trees, bloom fantastic colonies of Dutchman's breeches, their winged ivory flowers suggesting just-pulled teeth, but delicate and neatly massed, a-dangle in clumps above reddish stems gone translucent in the showering light. Fairy shrimp (Anostraca) swim inverted in temporary channels, schools of foot-long carp spawn in the flooded canal bed, doing oval or figure-eight dances, and all along this forgotten ditch burst forth bluebells and red trillium, squirrel corn and trout lily, wild ginger and cut-leaved toothwort, anemone and bellwort.

Here, too, small caves pock the hillsides and bluffs, their entrances sentried by brown bats and pipestrelles, suspended as serenely as spruce cones from the beveled lips of the archways. Inside, death-pale amphipods, like tiny platinum shrimp, lurk in hidden pools beneath faintly dripping stalactites. Cave spiders feed on salamanders, flies and beetles devour dung and detritus, while pickerel frogs and cave moths—some gaudy, some merely handsome—collect near the wettest openings. Nearby, stems stretch above mud or moss, sweat-bees stick to stamens, butterflies lift from brown muck. All around is a backwater. No great triumphs or disasters swept these limestone citadels, only the slow pace of time, growth, and death, the pulse of petal against leaf in the shattered understory dimness, the ghostly drip in an alkaline dark, repeated ten trillion timcs.

A kind of botanical fantasy erupts here in spring. An earth force has been loosed, concrete and tenuous both; its firmest manifestations reflect each basic geometry, embrace every structural design: disks, keels, rays, wings, bracts, spurs, crests, corollas, styles, cymes, umbels, spikes, racemes, panicles, corymbs. Its balance blocks and ladders are lobed and toothed, whorled and entire, clasping and perfoliate, opposite and dissected, compound and alternate, heart-shaped, ovate, palmate, lanceolate, and linear. Yet all is frail ephemera, a six- or eight-week stock show, a carnival raised for rapid disengagement, its balloons all broken by the first of June, its main-frames torn down by the solstice.

It is *Brigadoon* on the Potomac, where a trefoil banner like red trillium, known also as wake-robin, may be hoisted for a matter of days, and one finds it waving by a limestone rill, back in some mossy alcove full of tree roots and rotted windfalls. And without moving from the spot one suddenly spies two more, to the left or right, which did not seem to be there before. Of course this is mere illusion, but wonderful to bask in. One feels a brief sense of homage and awe, retreats a few feet to regroup on a rock, and almost tramples the mother lode: a foot-tall concert of half a dozen more, trembling in the breeze together, flashing their little three-part code—three triangular blood-red petals, on three triangular bracts, above three triangular leaves—which seems to communicate some meaning. One rests for a spell, the light beams down through a fractured cloud, the air is full of fust. Fantasy, illusion, ephemera—the lurking upland numina seem near, disguised as simple flowers and tweaking, in all their seasonal haunts, the persistence of one's reason.

There is nothing very illusory about the massive rock palisades just above the Potomac's fall line, 12 miles upstream from the nation's capital. The so-called Great Falls of the Potomac that looms over steep-sided Mather Gorge is an impressive dose of reality, abruptly dropping 60 feet in a spectacular series of foaming cascades, then descending another 85 feet to tidewater at Washington. Yet in its own gradual way Great Falls, too, is ephemeral. Indeed, the transitory nature of its rocky habitats—the persistent change in them wrought by time and periodic flooding—is crucial to the survival of its astonishing number of floral oddities, many of which bloom in late summer and early autumn.

In contrast to the hugely slow pace of change in the headwaters shale barrens, where plants have had undisturbed eons to evolve into species with inflexible needs, the plants of the Great Falls floodplains depend on dynamism and motion, on the occasional release of furious force, without which they would neither arrive nor survive. The whole stretch of the upper Potomac riverside can be seen as a vast floral migration and emigration corridor, wherein seeds and rootstocks from afar have had a chance to flee their native turf, while Great Falls often becomes their final home, a melting pot of botanical foreigners from west, east, north, and south.

Great Falls is no sleepy backwater, then, but a busy and crowded crossroads in energetic flux. The narrow confines of the C & O Canal National Historical Park, from Cumberland to Georgetown, harbor some 170 rare, threatened, or endangered plant species, but fully 130 of those are crammed into the roughly 10-mile stretch of the Great Falls gorge. And this total does not include all the "disjunct" species, that is, species that may be common elsewhere—on the southern coastal plain, the Appalachian plateau, even the Midwest prairies—but that curiously occur here well beyond their normal range. Nor does it account for the many Maryland "Watchlist" species that survive here—increasingly rare flora for which state biologists have registered formal concern.

Besides being stressed and altered by constant floods, this mob of displaced floral vagabonds is pressed continually on all sides by masses of kinetic human visitors who come to view the falls and tavern, to boat the canal and river, to picnic, hike, and bike, to sunbathe on the outcrops and cliff sides, to play chicken with the roaring chutes that parallel the main stem in ancient fissures of metamorphic bedrock. The C & O Canal is the eighth most visited national park in the country, competing not so unfavorably with the likes of Yosemite and Yellowstone, and Great Falls, Maryland, is the busy knot in its ribbonlike length. Annual guests in the hundreds of thousands tred the boardwalk on Olmstead Island to the Great Falls overlook or slog the precipitous Billy Goat Trail on adjacent Bear Island. And some three or four drown each year from being a little too kinetic in just the wrong ways.

A place of such diverse tumult and dynamism requires high-energy overseers, active of mind and body, versed in both social skills and stewardship, in both the ways of human recreation and of subtle natural phenomena. Such an overseer is Chris Lea, resource manager at Great Falls since 1989 and a fifteen-year Park Service veteran. Though only in his thirties, Chris has worked for the Service as ranger and rescue officer, trail guide in the mountains and canyons of the Far West, even guardian of Independence Hall and the Liberty Bell in downtown Philadelphia. But his special interests are geology and botany, and, in attempting to integrate both, he is also pursuing a master's degree in geologic plant ecology.

On a rather autumnal day we take a late-summer stroll together through some of Great Falls' best floral habitats. The temperature climbs from the middle fifties, the sun sparkles on the rapids, and a dry cold-front breeze pushes the clouds around, a breeze that has been transported, like a number of the plant species near us, from somewhere in the nation's heartland.

Along the Olmstead Island boardwalk we come upon a showy grouping of downy false-foxglove (*Gerardia virginica*), a tall spire of a plant with toothed leaves and big, bell-shaped yellow flowers. Three species of false-foxglove exist here, all striking but none very unusual. What is unusual is the tendency of this genera to parasitize the root systems of other plants, especially those of oak trees and grasses. In the dry, poor-soil habitats in which they exist, this insures them a secondary source of moisture and nutrients during times of particular stress.

Closer to the overlook we find more yellow blooms: the starry sulphur array adorning dense-flowered Saint-John's-wort. There is also a bright pink blossom of halberd-leaved rose mallow, and, near a bulge of tan rock, the big white flowers of the poisonous thorn-apple, or jimsonweed. In a wet swale below us we notice bottlebrush, gamagrass, and a scattering of wild oats.

"These swales often have standing water until sometime in May," comments Chris in his quiet voice, "and are a sort of microhabitat in themselves."

> You've got pin oak growing in here, red maple, and sometimes willow oak. Any little high point will be a non-wetland again, so just a few feet of elevation makes a big difference.
>
> What we're actually walking above here is the Pleistocene floodplain of the Potomac. The ice ages arrived and sea level was lowered as much as 300 feet when water got tied up in the polar ice caps. In the coastal plain, where you have softer deposits, the Potomac cut down rapidly, whereas here in the piedmont, where you have hard crystalline rock close to the surface, it carved very slowly. This differential is what created the sudden drop, the so-called fall line near D.C., which extends all up and down the east coast. But even though this rock is resistant, the steep gradient that

> was formed here meant faster-flowing river water, which down-cut quickly relative to the areas on either side, and formed this gorge. This two-mile stretch of it has long parallel fractures and joint lines, and when the river finds these joints in various stages of flood, it cuts down that much more quickly.
>
> Eventually, with the river down-cutting relatively fast, annual floods just didn't get up this high, making it fairly dry. On the other hand, every twenty to one hundred years, depending on the exact elevation, you do get a flood coming through, and it's a very dynamic thing, very violent, scouring and cleansing much of the botanic community. It's these rare flood events that are the controlling and shaping factor for what lives and what doesn't in this whole series of bedrock terrace communities. They take out trees before they get very big, making it more sunny and open, and prevent a lot of rich soil from building up. There's less competition from the commoner piedmont plants, so rarities or disjuncts can compete more favorably.

So, in other words, it's not enough that floods may carry seeds here from more western or northern habitats, or that others may arrive with birds, mammals, or hurricane winds from the east or south, or even have been here all along. What's important, in conjunction with this, is that periodic flooding and the relative dryness, openness, and lack of loamy soil between floods limits competition. In this competitor-limiting sense, I ask, isn't it a bit like shale barrens?

> Maybe in that sense, but otherwise not. We don't get many endemics here. In fact we have none that I know of. Nothing really evolved here. Most of the plants we have are common in some other part of the country. It's not so much the species that are unique here, it's the communities. There's just a lot more diversity, more strange combinations of things. Much of it is dictated by the varying elevations as well. At every few feet of elevation you have a totally different flooding regime. You've got all these little micro-

> habitats. And yet this two-mile stretch of old floodplains is still of relatively constant elevation. Now when you get about two miles further downstream, those older gorges have widened out and slope more gradually, so at best the bedrock terrace habitat is a narrow strip.

We soon descend from the boardwalk and find a rocky, sedgy wet spot where a little colony of erect water-hyssop (*Mercadonia acumentata*) is just beginning to put forth its tiny white flowers. It represents nearly the entire Maryland population of this southern wetland species, which occurs here at the far northern limit of its range.

When we reach the falls overlook we look down to observe in the cracks of the cliff face that slender, yellow-rayed dwarf, riverbank goldenrod (*Solidago spathulata*), a state-threatened species which here exploits the lack of competition in an arid location that has almost no soil.

Numerous members of the legume family occur around Great Falls: wild peas, bush clovers, tick-trefoils, vetches. Many species of this large group are able to make their own nutrients thanks to a symbiotic relationship with specialized bacteria living in the nodules of their root systems. These bacteria can actually "fix" nitrogren from the atmosphere and make it available to the plant's vascular system, an obvious advantage in regions of poor and thin soil in which nutrients are scarce.

Several wet terraces below the boardwalk, cut by small channels, are strewn with the tiny shells of the Asiatic clam (*Corpicula flumina*), in some places to a depth of many inches. Chris shakes his head.

> This species was brought here from Asia and first found in the Potomac in 1979, and now, as you can see, it's by far the most abundant mollusk. It's a real threat to the native mollusks, of which there are maybe twelve or fifteen species, most either rare or in decline right now. The Heritage Program is currently doing a mollusk survey from Washington County on down to the D.C. line. They're finding many relic shells of the native species, but not as many live animals as they'd like to. You can almost stick a shovel

> blade into some of these Asiatic clamshell drifts and not find the bottom. It's been speculated that in areas like this you get such huge deposits of shell that there may even be a calcerous [calcium and, thus, alkaline] influence on the native flora.

Yet, he points out, this is not the first time an alien mollusk has reached the upper Potomac. "Actually, a mollusk native to the Ohio River drainage was introduced to the Potomac in 1854 when smallmouth bass were brought from the Ohio to Cumberland, Maryland. A lot of mollusk larvae parasitize fish gills, which makes their populations more mobile. This species had apparently done just that with those first introduced smallmouth."

Chris next leads me down to Bear Island, which has the greatest number of rare or threatened species—some eighty amid its paltry 140 acres—and the most floral communities. As we leave the towpath on the lower end of the Billy Goat Trail and enter a thin and rocky mixed hardwood forest, we find a blooming clump of rock skullcap (*Scutellaria saxatilis*), a candidate for federal protection. Its blue-violet flower has a delicate hooded canopy and flared, finely cleft lower lip. "It starts blooming in May," Chris says, "but stays in bloom a long time."

> It's more of a mid-Appalachian plateau species from Kentucky, western Virginia, that area, but 95 percent of the rock skullcap in Maryland is in these rocky woods on Bear Island. Maybe its seeds floated down with floods over time, or it may be a relict from cooler times, when it was widespread throughout this region. Or maybe some other factor.
>
> Some geologists would say that there's basically one terrace that forms most of this habitat on Bear Island. Others would say there are many. As you go upstream toward Great Falls and Olmstead, that area gets flooded more often because it's narrower. There are some lower rocky barrens near the river that get flooded annually or maybe every other year. They pretty much get blasted by floods. And then within those areas there are little sheltered subcom-

> munities where you get dense thickets of things like deciduous holly, American hornbeam, and other small trees and shrubs. Then there are scour bars in the river that are another kind of habitat.

So people disagree as to just how many terrace habitats exist around Great Falls?

"Yes. To some extent I'll be investigating that in the next couple of years. Part of my thesis will attempt to correlate vegetation with specific geologic terraces. Already about half a dozen different alluvial soil types have been mapped around here by geomorphologists."

In the same thin forest we soon come to another distinct habitat, a vernal pool, which is now quite dry and almost indistinguishable from the surrounding woodland. "These slight depressions hold a fair amount of water in spring and are mostly dominated by red maple. We recently found more erect water-hyssop in a similar pool, and in another I found *Proserpinaca,* or mermaid weed, which is not rare on the coastal plain but is here on the piedmont. There's only one location in the park for it."

The Billy Goat Trail takes us down near the rocks by the river, and here a little mix of pools, barrens, and semi-open prairies creates a small confluence of communities that alone shelter ten state-rare species. Little bluestem mixes with water cordgrass along a sandy wash, and a high, vibrant stand of sunflowers nods faintly in the breeze. "This is another more western species," says Chris, as he reaches out to touch it. "These barrens are good for a lot of Midwest prairie species. The hairy wild petunia is an odd one around here, too, and it's more western."

Before long we come upon another sunflowerlike Composite, *Coreopsis tripterus,* a normally southern plant, and wild false indigo, a state-endangered spring bloomer well known in the Midwest. "We use the term *disjunct* a lot, but it's really imprecise. We don't know if they're part of a relict population, or arrived in some other way. It's still a pretty big mystery."

In a particularly bare and sunstruck rocky alcove near the river

Chris points out low clumps of *Paronychia virginica* var. *virginica,* the yellow nailwort. If it weren't currently in bloom, with a little blush of saffron fluff to enliven its elfin crown, one might take it for something quite common. "This variety," Chris casually imparts, "is one of the rarest plants in the country. The second or third largest population in the world is here at Great Falls. Most of its population is in the Appalachian region of the Potomac watershed and then in the Arkansas Ozarks, where it's a bit more secure. It's rare but it's not that picky about the substrate it grows on. It's found on limestone, shale barrens, and on metamorphic rocks, like those of these scoured river barrens. Its one imperative is full sunlight."

The litany of oddities continues: climbing dogbane, tall tickseed sunflower, fetterbush, live-forever, prickly pear, passion-flower, butterfly-pea, more wild false indigo and riverbank goldenrod and, in an area of low ponds bordering an open woods, where beaver sign is evident, another rare *Scutellaria,* the veined skullcap. In a stony little savannah-like stream valley that holds a dozen other state-listed plants, we look for, but can't locate, Canada milk-vetch (*Astragalus canadensis*). Three of its four known populations in Maryland survive here. In such small valleys as this, relatively frequent cycles of floral community extinction may occur, both from furious floodwater scourings and from the interim shade thrown by fast-growing hardwoods whose canopies wither the most rigidly sun-needy species. But it is all only temporary, until the next big flood or hurricane deposits the proper seeds and a new community takes hold.

Flux. In a world ruled by flux the Great Falls gorge is flux times ten, flux to the max, its sense and symbol and stronghold, the system that sums it up best. Even the falls themselves are in flux, steadily wearing down as the crashing waters abrade them. And, yes, the terrace floral habitats are in flux as well, not just rising or sinking with the riverbed, but moving further west. Observes Chris, as we wrap up our morning walk: "When you think about what's going on over the very long haul, the river is probably creating more of this habitat upstream toward the falls itself. It's moist and frequently flooded up there now, which will eventually erode the area and leave the terraces higher and drier. Meanwhile, secondary erosion is widening out and breaking down the dry terrace both here and downstream. So in a very slow sense this whole group of terrace communities is actually moving upstream."

Thus it continues—the huge ephemeral pageant of the upper Potomac floodplain. It is played out not just week to week and month to month in the blooming schedule of its plants, but decade to decade, century to century, millennium to millennium, on the very ephemera that the plants call home—their seemingly static and immutable beds, their firm plateau moorings of chlorite and schist, quartzite and graywacke, all of them changing, becoming something else, moving this way and that, waxing and waning down the long beach of time like so many tides of stone.

Nothing stands still by the Potomac. Nothing ever will. Its varied beauty mirrors movement, hinges on the fleeting and flowing, scintillates over time like sunlight on rapids, is a kind of trembling and lifting off the dark stream of the ages, and in passing is a kind of flight.

CHAPTER NINE

# Lullaby of Birdways

If I've launched *Testubo* above Point of Rocks on a brisk April day, with the current tawny under bankside maples whose leaves are still gnarled buds, and drift down between the cold blue-brown hills, I've done so for more than just fishing. I've done so because, like all living things at this season, I am restless and wish to be about. The sky is still winter clean, the air is a medley of old and new dampness, my casts are wayward and distracted. I am not much of an angler now but more a gatherer of news, a looker after the landscape, an old bear alert for fresh signs.

Other creatures in motion seem few. The movement instead is of light and clouds, tree branches and current, snags a-bob in the eddies. Except far ahead, where tracks of frothy water somehow rise off the surface in parallel lines and direct themselves downstream. This is not hallucination or miraculous levitation but the natural surface turmoil brought by birds taking wing, by, in this case, a brace of common mergansers walking water to get airborne. Their dark forms all but invisible from afar, they leave only this wake of whitened spray to signal their passage into flight.

And *passage* is the word of the hour. Throughout the region the water birds of winter, having sat out storms and snow squalls on a thousand inland waterways, have for weeks been making sorties, heading west and north incrementally toward their breeding grounds of summer. Most cling to the coastlines in winter, spending, as seasonal visitors, what for them is a southern vacation off Atlantic and Gulf Coast shores. These are the so-called bay ducks, which raft beyond the beaches or in brackish tidewater estuaries, often by the hundreds.

But bad storms, pecking order squabbles, hunger, ill health, or inexperience break up their numbers and lure them to anomalous hideouts on the piedmont or coastal plain—to lakes, ponds, marshes, reservoirs, or rivers—where ambitious birders spy them out: the grebes and goldeneyes, buffleheads and ring-necked ducks, greater and lesser scaup, oldsquaws and scoters, redheads and canvasbacks, loons and mergansers. The untutored layman sees Canada geese and mallards and a host of bobbing gulls. The birder may find a falcated teal, Eurasian widgeon, or white-fronted goose and share the pleasurable secret with only a knowledgeable few. On the upper Potomac such birders and their cohorts can be found around Swain's Lock or Seneca, Pennyfield or Blockhouse Point, Hughes Hollow and Sycamore Landing, White's or Edward's Ferry, from October, when the first migrant waterfowl arrive, to the time of their pullout from March into May. Along open waters above rapids or off big islands, theirs is a game of searching for stragglers or strays, in which a flock of one hundred goldeneyes, sixty buffleheads, or a dozen red-throated loons turns heads, while singles, twos, and threes of a species are the usual modest reward.

All these birds are travelers. The mergansers that kick up their ghostly wakes on my float of early April are headed for the forested North—to Michigan, Ontario, New York, Vermont, Quebec—but their species' range, like that of the other birds mentioned, reaches northwest to Alaska and the Aleutians, to Alberta or the Yukon. In the north they share quarters on blood-dusk lakes with ululating loons, nest in tree holes or rocky niches, dive after perch and sauger, and drag their trains of manic chicks across spruce-shadowed bays and inlets. A few may linger near Great Falls or Seneca—the old or immature who have trouble managing the flight. But nearly all are gone by May Day and most by April Fool's. A single such wintering species, the hooded merganser, has been known to remain into June at locations around Hughes Hollow, where some suspect it may breed.

But from fall to early spring there are local peregrinations of the birds that merely overwinter, and one never quite knows what mavericks may call the river home while conditions remain right—the water not high or frozen, the fish or mollusks abundant, the weather not too severe. Birders are driven by mystery and surprise. Yesterday's barren channel or point may be tomorrow's birdy bonanza, and the chance of a strange encounter is what gets most birders out of bed. It is not just a checking off of species on life lists, state lists, year lists. The dry actuality of data is balanced by its polar opposite, a thing rarely spoken of but often keenly felt. In the sudden glimpse of a wandering duck whose presence seems improbable there is something not merely thrilling but even a bit unreal.

On some bitingly cold winter trek, when a single striking bird shows up off the banks, or in a flooded stretch of berm or canal, there is the sense of a visitation. Perhaps an oldsquaw, a species as peculiar as its name, has somehow materialized in four feet of water and triggers a fit of wonder. Why, one ponders, is this sole sea-going oddity here? Why this gregarious creature so at home in great flocks on the Arctic or Atlantic coasts, whose haunting *ow-owdle* melody carries more than a mile and suggests the baying of hounds, thus leading to its many monikers, among them *scolder* and *scoldernore*; *squeaking duck* and *hound*; *calloo, coween, quandy*; *old wife* or *old injun*; even *uncle Huldy* or *John Connolly?* Why this Indian file highflier, this tundra breeder that dives so deep it is caught in trawl nets at 200 feet? Why this most curiously patterned of waterfowl, alone of all duck species to have two distinct male plumages, each the other's obverse: in winter, pale, dark-blotched head and ivory torso inlaid with brown; in summer, dark, pale-blotched head and brown upper torso on ivory. Yet here, to one's amazement, is that ivoried male from the ice floes—swimming where in summer prowl egrets and tropical warblers—turning placid circles on the water's dark mirror, casually out of place as if just dropped off by a zookeeper.

And thus for a fleeting moment—often not fully savored until later beside a fire or warm glass of whiskey—the humdrum and objective short-circuits, and the sight of such lightness and vibrancy, such cleanness of pattern and detail, such offhand embodiment of strangeness and grace, makes you muse on what forces are in motion, what confluence of weathers and urges has brought you both together; you, who should not sensibly have pursued such a frigid foray, and the bird, who should not—or could not, from the convincing impression of its frailty—have flown to or flourished in this spot. It all seems the fragment of a dream or some brief sunlit chimera. Yet it is real-life juxtaposition as well: the alert, agile, and intact bird, afloat in a wilderness of hardship.

Such are the visions of winter. But drifting down now with the April current there is a sense of that hardship having passed, of winter's wilderness vanquished. Indeed its crucible of frost, wherein miraculous creatures perish or prevail, was perhaps just a fortunate prelude, a curing rack for the staples of the earth, the harshest elements having set now, and mingled, and bonded with diverse fertility to pour out the rich broth of spring. Besides a few more mergansers, I see wood ducks jump up in a channel and *woo-eek* out of sight. Permanent Potomac residents—the males as gaudy as a Chinese New Year—they will haunt the river on my every visit, seeming almost to enjoy being startled, bursting forth from brush piles and logjams and squealing till above the trees. Far downstream another call, this one a quick-whistled *chewk-chewk-chewk,* rings out over an island, and I spot my old friend the osprey, back from its winter in Peru or Brazil, Florida or the Bahamas. It hovers for an instant, cocks its black-wristed wings, and plunges precipitously fishward, its river entry a boil of white, its exit a thick desperate flapping, like some moth's from a wet pool of candlewax.

A great blue heron is about. I appear to drive it ahead of me where it takes up perches on sycamore snags, dares me to drift ever closer, then spreads its pterodactyl wings, croaks with equivalent antiquity, and beats its way downstream. Many great blues stay all winter, but even now others of its wading clan are returning from further south: small green-backed herons, the commonest herons of summer, and, much rarer, both least and American bitterns. By summer the mélange of waders will grow. Surprised anglers will wonder to see white-plumaged stalkers in the shallows: great and even snowy egrets, and sometimes immature little blue herons that are neither blue nor little, but white and three feet tall. These days such species disperse up rivers after nesting concludes on the coastal plain, their numbers finally growing after decades of market plume-hunting all but doomed them near the start of this century. One decidedly unwhite species, the curve-billed, bronze-toned glossy ibis—appearing black from a distance—may also work the summer pools upriver, having pushed its range from Florida clear to Maine and Quebec.

The sycamores now, leafless and suffused with strong sun, are perhaps at their height of distinction, stretching nearby like great dappled masts or gargantuan, boa-skinned serpents. Those far downriver suggest some post-industrial dockside long overgrown, a montage of lost shipping wharves, of eccentric tilting spars and derricks, corroded pearly gantries and buffy, nickel-pitted cranes. Above them hawks and buzzards blemish the blue and white bowl of sky: an even-winged red-tailed hawk turning perfect circles, a red-shouldered just at the treetops, screeching *kee-ah!* even as it sinks out of sight, and two black vultures, with their stub tails and whitened wing tips, flapping beneath the rocking glide of a thermal-linked turkey vulture.

Three dark cormorants charge upstream past my boat. These with the ripple necks are double-crested cormorants, breeders of the southern coasts who are also expanding their range. All year small bands wander inland to exploit the abundant fish crop on rivers like the Potomac. Grebes, too, hunt fish here, and one swirls and dives in the eddy off a point. This is the little pied-billed, with its beak set off by a vertical band, its head too big and its tail too short, and its habit of swimming half-submerged. Other less common grebes, much prized by birders, may dawdle this time of year: horned, red-necked, even eared grebes, the latter a western species that has shown up at nearby Lilypons.

Lilypons, in fact, is noted among birders for its rarities. Not far from where I'm floating, just east of Noland's Ferry, this man-made treasury of fish ponds and water plants has been the scene of close encounters between humans and avian oddities: unusual shrikes, bitterns, ibises, swans, grebes, sandpipers—all have been found near the water and fields or winging high overhead. The fishy lagoons lure some species, but success also turns on access and focused attention. Easily reached by legions of D.C.-area birders, Lilypons sits near New Design Road, whose farm fields in winter attract snow buntings, pipits, horned larks, and larkspurs, and thus lead to the road being scoped its full length from Buckeystown to the river.

Indeed, coverage has all to do with impressions of birdy abundance. The sport of watching birds grows apace even as numbers of migrants decline. The Potomac is no particular mecca for exotic wintering water birds. While its upper reaches remain relatively clean and food filled, the tidewater sections and the Chesapeake Bay are plagued by ongoing problems that affect the vitality of birds, especially waterfowl, as do problems in the places where they nest. More eyes seek avian prizes and thus lists continue to grow, but the lenses that find the rare grebe or goose are no substitute for breeding success or healthy wetland habitats. It is intact systems that count most, not anomalous individuals. I would gladly give up my fragmentary dream birds—my ghostly, white-waked mergansers and chimeral, isolated oldsquaws—

for the great primeval spectacles that once crowded water and sky here, which drew their beauty not from scarceness but from awesome fullness and fecundity.

*Testubo* has had a fair run. There is no big smallmouth on my stringer, but I've managed something more. I've broken out of my winter husk; I've charted things afloat and aloft, watched water and sky stir with movement, tasted briefly of the vernal broth. I beach *Testubo* by a sycamore knee, haul her out and pack her down. I gulp some warming coffee, smoke a brown-leaved cheroot, stay alert to the seasonal signs. It's too early for the choicest songbirds, but rappings and tappings abound. The floodplain is full of staccato voice, the rhythm and pulse of a secretive tribe who make themselves known through their woodwork. I stand now at bankside, brush the humus from my trousers, sling *Testubo* to my shoulders, hike out to admire old crafts.

The upper Potomac floodplain has become a haven for woodpeckers. When canalling and tree cutting stopped, the timber slowly came back to some semblance of its early prominence. Today, cycles of forest succession and disease, plus periodic flooding, kill or weaken many trees which in turn harbor ample insects and their larvae, chief foods for these chisel-beaked birds. Fully seven species of woodpeckers can be found here during much of the year: the downy, hairy, red-bellied, redheaded, and pileated, plus the northern flicker and yellow-bellied sapsucker. Each species fills a niche, has a separate voice or behavior, even special ways of beating on wood or chopping out edible morsels. And each hammers not just to find food and fashion a home, but to lure or signal mates and to mark its breeding boundaries.

Balancing elusiveness with flamboyance is basic to woodpecker survival. But elusiveness comes first. Woodlands are patrolled by accipiters, a group of swift and agile hawks that feed on other birds. Silent and highly maneuverable in trees, with short wings and rudderlike tails, they are the bane of unwary passerines, or "perching birds," whom they close in on from the rear and silently snag with their talons. Thus, constantly foraging in forests, woodpeckers rarely perch as such but, rather, present a restless, erratic target, camouflaged by zebra stripes and herringbone dorsal plumage, flattened close to bole or branch, jerkily moving upward or down, sideways or in spirals, flying at intervals with dips and bobs, and not crooning from a central stage but tapping or drumming as they edge along, or emitting sharp notes and rattles, each of them echoed by hollowed wood, deflected and misleadingly refracted through the tuning forks of the trees.

Further specializations aid woodpeckers: opposing toes with sharp claws for clutching bark; stiff tail feathers, called rectrices, which maintain vertical balance as they climb or descend on trees; a thick-walled skull and membrane-cushioned brain to absorb the shock of their hammering; extra-strong muscles in skull, bill, and neck for maintaining that hammering at length; and a wildly extensible tongue, barbed and bristled at its tip and as long behind its base near the throat as it is out to the front, thanks to two cartilaginous "hyoid horns" that curve back cordlike, from a tongue bone in the mouth, then up and over the skull to the forehead, where they fasten inside the nostrils.

Such adaptions evolved early on, for this is an ancient family, the Picidae, one of the first to exploit the forests, related to the primitive Old World "wrynecks," which contort their necks when feeding in the manner of many serpents. At feeding, in fact, modern "pecks" are eerily adept, frequently boring directly to the burrows of parasites beyond view. The precise method by which they locate this unseen prey is mysterious, though hearing is believed to be foremost, followed by the trick of inserting their bill in the wood and "feeling" briefly for vibrations.

Elusive and self-sufficient as they are, these birds still need to communicate. Thus, the fanfare of red crests and head marks, bold dark-and-light wings, penetrating calls and rappings. The little downy woodpecker, most abundant of the bunch, is also the most vociferous, frequently issuing its sharp *peek!* or *pik!* plus a series of *tsik-tsik-tsiks* ripped off in horse whinny fashion. And from late winter into spring it pounds on posts and tree trunks in drawn-out *trrrrrrrr* drummings that are preludes to sex and nesting and fill the woods with rhythm. The hairy woodpecker, a shade larger and louder than the downy, is something of its musical twin, but its tappings are slightly shorter and it throws in, too, a prolonged grating rattle. Both probe bark and wood for their meals and make stiff little hops as they hunt, ascending tree bole or branch or working down in hitches.

The red-bellied woodpecker is also common, a good deal larger than the downy or hairy, and rather badly named. The abdomen under its rump is rusty red but rarely seen; instead, its red nape is showiest, extending to the forehead on males, so that some call it redheaded woodpecker, though that is a separate species, one scarce by the river and elsewhere in the East—a declining bird of clean tricolors, fond of parklike openings, and which sometimes can be found near Seneca. The red-bellied, by contrast, has expanded its range, especially to the north, and throughout the Potomac watershed its distinctive series of nattering calls, from flickerlike *wick-wicks* to softer *churr-churrs,* are well-known floodplain cadences. Its rapping is a drumroll, spirited and loud, and heard, too, are its workmanlike taps as it digs after grubs in deadwood.

The flicker is an eater primarily of ants, a ground driller and manic snickerer, *wicka-wicka-wick*ing and *kik-kik-kikk*ing as it glides below logs and circles anthills, jumping and jabbing and thrusting its outsized tongue. It migrates in groups and is the least "woodsy" woodpecker; thus noisy "flickering" confabs grace parks, lawns, and gardens in both spring and early fall. It is handsome, its head, neck, and throat neatly set with mustaches, black cravats, gray hoods, scarlet tattoos.

Especially among fruit trees and salubrious maples, the sapsucker lingers, calmly drilling through bark till the juice flows and gathers, then licking the ooze right away or returning later to do so. Meanwhile it utters a welter of sounds: *cherrs, yewicks,* and *tucks,* soft *hoih-hoihs* and *kee-yews* and catlike *mews* and *meows.* Otherwise it beats poles and rooftops, taps faintly on Potomac sassafras, raps loudly on fat black cherries, occasionally gets drunk and falls to the ground, having sipped too much of the pooled and fermented nectars. Its belly is faintly yellow, but more striking is a crimson forehead and throat, a deep ebony bib, and contrasting dorsal patchworks and veins, worked out in pitch and pale cream.

The big noise of the woods is the pileated woodpecker, a chicken-size bird that loves carpenter ants and leaves middens of chips a foot deep. Pileateds sport red crests and great two-toned wings that flash in flight or fold into grave black capes as they land to hack out domino-sized hunks from the riverside hardwoods and conifers. Their voice is the cackle of a madman or witch, a wild, resounding *kuk-kuk-kuk* that gives their presence away, as do the battle tattoos that define their domain, and, in the dampening riverine dusk, their solemn pre-roost drummings.

In spring all these woodpeckers are present, and the result is a sensory paradox, with birds intent on both shyness and show erratically flitting through the forest, low and high, loud and silent, light and dark, scattering their forms like shadows. As I dawdle back on my April trek I hear the downy's thin staccatos, the hairy's louder embellishments, the red-bellied's vibrant clucks and rolls, the sapsucker's squeal and the flicker's wicker, the pileated's jackhammer drumbeat. A shard of speckled movement on the trunk of a scaly river birch gives away a downy, a flash of white rump and golden wings reveals a fleeing flicker, and an undulate, crow-sized silhouette against the sky-gap over the towpath marks the passage of a pileated, as brief and elusive as a pleasant sensation.

This last bird is the glory of the floodplain. Often during my wayward floats it crosses the river, cackling, dipping deeply in the glide between wing beats, lifting me with its grandeur and, in this age of extinguished wonders, its against-the-odds survival. The rational in me resists it, yet I see it as an augury of promise and at such times feel touched by grace. If I hear one along the towpath and lower my pack to stand or sit quietly nearby, I may pick it out through the branches, clinging to a snag in the sunlight, or glimpse it in flight as it finally swaps trees or sails out over the water. Sometimes by stealth and patience I can approach it and gaze on its haunting presence and proportions at impressively close range. It is not all that shy of humans, as the ornithologist T. Gilbert Pearson reported early in this century: "Pileated woodpeckers frequently show an absence of fear of man which one would not expect in a bird that is so distinctly a forest dweller. While camping in the hammocks of central Florida, I have now and then walked up to within thirty yards of a Pileated Woodpecker busy at work on some rotting log, without the bird paying the slightest attention to my presence."

Indeed, one once swooped down where I sat, breaking its dive with a big thrust of white and black and coming erect on a stump. Then I examined the vermilion crest, the alert and listening pump of its head, the pigsticker beak and balance-wedge tail, the circling, dancelike direction of its step—pivoting to peer in here, back-stepping there, quarter-turning left or right to detect the proximity of prey. The pileated woodpecker's appearance near the ground is often startling or abrupt. At one memorable location I thought I was facing a raccoon, for I arrived to a glimpse of movement, to the stirring of something rather large behind a log, and to a scratching and play of shadow. Finally a head popped above the bole, rapier-billed and red-crowned, and we briefly stared each other down before the big bird fled.

Thus a kind of dramatic tension marks woodpecker presence by the river. They speak but are not often seen, signal with rhythmic clues, show up with arresting suddenness. They deal in the coded message, these birds—a cadenced language of implicitness and caution which whets the psychic appetite, which hints at denouement or reward, but whose final value is a sidestep and a hedge, whose charm is the tease of mystery. In mystery lies all myth, and myth's absence today is the certain proof that our vision of legends has failed. But perhaps it still falls weakly on the world of Potomac woodpeckers. For here we see creatures who climb trees like men, ladder-stepping skyward with stiff upright postures; who ring out rhythms and sharp cries, who strut handsome colors and body tattoos—mustachioed creatures who hop and dance and get drunk on their own concoctions yet remain essentially enigmas, visiting man bravely but in snitches and, much like the demigods of old, acting out dramas in dim woods, inventing their own songs and praises, chasing their own airy dreams, and appearing, unannounced, at odd or portentious moments. The biggest of their numbers are oracular birds, birds of fate and foreboding who inferred the sacred not only among nomads but also among Europeans, who called them "Great God Woodpecker," "Good God Woodpecker," "Lord God Woodpecker," reinforcing their deistic aura.

Above all they are deft specialists and survivors. What startles some about wild lands is the fact that they, too, house competents. We so often see man as master that we give little weight to nonhumans, smugly assuming that they muddle through with some hodgepodge of crude ways and habits. Yet, in fact, within their own niches, they are awesomely accomplished. No one does it better than the whale, or the wolf, the woodchuck, the woodpecker. They simply do it without fanfare and fuss, without self-congratulation, without analysis and accrued reward, without much more than efficiency. And, oh yes, with beauty and grace, which we undervalue as well. This suddenly slaps us in the face when afield, when we finally get a good look: an expert shares our space, is of finest hue and detail, strong in proportion to its weight, graceful to the point of astonishment, efficient beyond our grasp. In an instant, up truly close, we see and know this; in an instant we are put to shame; in an instant our egos take over; in an instant it is once more just a bird.

Perhaps there is greater eloquence in shadows than there is in explicit forms. If so, these birds speak volumes, for they dwell in dappled shade and themselves are a sprinkling of shadows. My April trek is suffused with light, but around me move dark flickerings, counterpoints of murk; agile, feathered umbras of shyness and evasion; code senders, myth hoarders, mysteries unread—the rhythmic equivalent of the signal-smoke that made frontiersmen wonder. Yet their senders are not tribes of red men, but an age-old guild of timber tinkers, rhythm merchants and drum dancers, keepers of the forest shadow-song, a society as ancient as a bristled tongue, a sharp-clawed foot, a language proclaimed in wood.

Beginning in late April, when Orion is completing his winter trek to the west with the twinned feet of Gemini close behind, the black sky is haunted as well by other, less colossal migrants. The tiny "wood warblers" of the family Parulidae head north to their breeding grounds, sweep against thc constellations in nightly waves, crash by their thousands into skyscrapers and transmitters, and stop off in greater thousands among mid-Atlantic woodlands. Of fifty-six exclusively North American species, some thirty-five employ the eastern flyways and reach the upper Potomac from the southern states, Central and South America, Mexico and the Caribbean, many soon moving as far north as Canada; others, about twenty-seven species in all, remaining to nest in the region.

These are light, mothlike birds, nervous flitters and flutterers, birds of thin bill and stuttering wing, intent on their soft-bodied prey. Their hottest colors—mostly yellows, oranges, and whites—are fused with arresting contrast to grays, blacks, and olives. They are restless, furtive, preoccupied birds, clean and minutely compact like bright mice with wings, and above all they are songsters—sweet trillers and subtle note-smiths, buzzers and lispers and weavers of pennywhistle pitches, masters of the slurred or tumbling refrain.

But before the great nightly flocks come a spattering of early arrivals. One of the first is the yellow-throated warbler, sometimes showing up in late March from wintering grounds in Georgia, Florida, or the West Indies. Indeed, in the Deep South many reside year round—creatures of moss-hung live oaks and cypress swamps, of pine forests and ruined plantations, where the handsome males whistle clear, down-drifting phrases from exposed or lofty verdure. But, more often, the great river floodplains further north comprise their summer homes, from the Missouri to the Wabash and Ohio in the West to the sycamore bottoms of the steep Atlantic drainage. They are still, in fact, called "sycamore warbler" by some, often choosing to nest and forage among the pale leaning giants, probing for insects beneath loosely curled bark, circling dappled limbs on serpentine courses, cocking their torsos to and fro, flitting out and back in quest of mid-air morsels.

If you move up a feeder creek when the river is April high and the brown water glints with muted arboreal reflections, you may glimpse a marauding male, gold bibbed and black cheeked, braiding downward on a great bare trunk to where the roots hang twisted above the bank like precarious nests of snakes, and observe the bird stunting and feinting on the leather-dry bark, tilting its head, twitching to a stop, pinching its beak into seams. Then, with apparent whimsy, he may fly up in stages to the highest branch, backlighted black against blue, and deliver his claim to this plane-tree kingdom: "Teee-yoo, too, too, too, too, *wee!*"

Back down in the streambed a related early migrant, the waterthrush, will likely be about. The boldest of its clan arrive with the late March winds, seek out the sheltered creeksides, teeter up and down as they hunt among rocks and tangled deadfalls, along gravel banks and sandbars. The song of both species, Louisiana and northern, is a shrill declaration, seeming quickly to lose heart and ending in decrescendo, a strangled down-slur of broken notes whose echoes die in the shadows.

The pine, prairie, and parula warblers are early birds, too (some will nest on the shale barrens slopes of the far Potomac headwaters), as are the tail-twitching palm warblers headed further north and the zebra-striped black-and-white warblers that may stake out their nest sites locally. Yellow-rumped warblers, a few having overwintered here, also drift northward after an April peak abundance, while ovenbirds, yellowthroats, and yellow warblers—all local breeders—trickle in throughout the month.

But the big neotropical push builds up near the first of May, when piping orioles fill bankside maples, black and crimson tanagers ascend from South America to forge summer homes in the hardwoods, and wood thrushes *eee-o-lay* in every understory alcove. A savvy birder, in a single day, can log over one hundred species by the second week in May, and the floodplain bulges with color and song, with strange or brilliant avian forms that will stay just a matter of hours or remain to raise their offspring. For those seeking warbler species it's a time for scanning treetops, for picking out flashes of rump or tail, wing bar, breast streak, throat patch, or eye ring. It's a time to be teased and tantalized, foiled by fleeting glimpses, thwarted by thickening leaves. It's a time when songs not heard in a year must swiftly be recalled, when tapes reviewed during winter become suddenly insubstantial, when field marks so obvious in books seem now mere half-grasped mirages.

Some of the best warblers hug the canopy: ceruleans and blackburians, Cape Mays and bay-breasteds, emitting jumbled slurs and twitters, rasps or faded ditties. Blackpolls squeak like tricycle wheels, perhaps clouding, as you strain your ears, the first rapid riffs of a Wilson's. Nashville and Tennessee warblers skulk or chant two- and three-part melodies. There are black-throated blues and black-throated greens, chestnut-sideds and magnolias, golden-wingeds and blue-wingeds—the hope of a mourning or Connecticut, the longshot of an orange-crowned or Swainson's. In the lower growth flit redstarts and transient Canadas or a sprinkle of shy local breeders: hooded and Kentucky warblers, worm-eating and prothonotary.

None are sweeter or more striking than this last, a warbler whose voice and habits are synonymous with rivers. It is a bird dipped entirely in golden maize, then fitted below the nape with a shawl, of satiny bluish gray, which falls over wings and tail. Its song is a piping strand of *zweet-zweet-zweets,* projected from thickets above the banks or, obliquely, from the dimness of bermside swales, caught and carried on the vernal gusts, wafted from deep shade to sunlight for the pleasure of the nearest ear. Named for the papal notaries who sported yellow hoods, the prothonotary warbler suggests anything but ecclesiastical duty, being a wild and uncommissioned beauty, a wearer of nature's robes unfettered by clerical function, stitched instead to the wind and sun, to the fluvial reek of the springtime freshets, to the high, open ceiling of the sky.

At times even the best birders find birdsong confusing. Most of the tunes—pre-breeding vocalizations—come but once a year, are heard under changing conditions, are at least as varied as the range of species, and often seem to the human ear to be more alike than different. As if this weren't enough, recent scientific research is confirming what experienced birders have long suspected: that individual birds of identical species have distinct and personal songs, and that each singing male has a private repertoire, a spate of variations on the same basic theme. So much for "reliable" bird tapes and written descriptions in field guides.

Yet the evidence seems irrefutable. Steve Nowicki, a Duke University associate professor of zoology and an award-winning teacher, has long studied neuroscience and animal communication, with a special focus on birdsong. He actually raises young songbirds in the field, physically manipulates their vocal apparatus, and captures and examines their singing with soundproof chambers, audiotape players, videotape recorders, and sophisticated computers.

As Nowicki and others have observed, the typical bird "song" lasts about two seconds and is a tommy gun blur of some fifty separate notes, each as brief as ten thousandths of a second and delivered five times faster than humans can reel off syllables. While the songs of the males are best known, both male and female may have five to twenty call notes, phrases, alarms, or soft verses and, by virtue of a vocal organ called the syrinx, which has two vibrating membranes that can modulate separate tones simultaneously, can actually sing duets with themselves.

Yet Nowicki has discovered far more. The syrinx, located just under the bird's breastbone, was previously thought to be its only song-making instrument. In fact, Nowicki has learned, birds also use their beak and throat to modify vocal resonance, altering the length of their full vocal tract and thus changing its natural frequency. He has also found that breeding males improvise, or "jazz" in effect, singing eight to twelve basic song types but varying some many times. Indeed, young birds learn to sing better, he found, when played tape recordings of adult male songs that contain a rich variety. At the risk of tampering with nature's jukebox, he is even trying to train baby birds to sing numerous song variations, to see just how vocally versatile they are capable of becoming.

Such delvings pique my interest but also make me wary. For all that science aids our grasp of the ongoing riddle that is birdsong, there are ways in which it detracts. Analysis is reduction, and reduction is a form of diminishment, however pleasing to a human brain that wishes to cradle and caress—smoothly and concisely, as if in the palms of both hands—the assorted globes of mystery. But springtime, birdsong, and indeed a kind of wildness in the human spirit itself, resists the twin-palmed caress of excessive rational scrutiny.

On some fundamental level I see the songbird cacophony of April and May as a clamor of unreason, out of sync with analysis and the world of measurable events. It is an undertone of confusion, a nonsense tune on the rim of sleep, a layered lullaby of birdways, of life just beyond full focus. No one can fathom its profligate discharge, its ephemeral tease of opulence, and perhaps no one should try. Its tremors concuss some placid film, disturb some fluid cushion around the soft gray matter of reality, and induce hallucination. The Potomac sprites we call warblers are goads to the verifiable, abraders of smooth-edged reason, tormentors of the knowing and known, gremlins defying the clerics of science and the hoarders of concrete data.

Often, when I was young, warblers appeared in my dreams and were things beyond attainment. This hints perhaps at their essence, at their role in relation to our spirit. They are not a clutchable race, and, so being, they continue to inspire and instruct. We vainly chase them with lenses and tapes, but how sad if the task became easy! Today, mostly through loss of habitat, songbird numbers dwindle on the upper Potomac and elsewhere, and a scientist may someday corral their remains and bring their enigmas to "solution." Then the two manias will have smoothly converged: man's compulsion to destroy and his matching compulsion to examine. The last chapter of the songbird tome will be both neat and fitting, yet still be a single chapter, as the last breath of a dying man is some fraction of his full existence. But the life of these birds is ages old, the preceding chapters were many, and it is those that command closest reading. Warblers were teases of color and note long before they were lifelist jots, microphone medleys, or studies in migrant declination.

First there were profligate discharges in the spring of man's existence, fluxing constellations against a darkened sky, things he could not name or know or plausibly absorb, ripples on the film that cushioned his reality, subliminal, abrasive dream tones beyond the range of reason.

CHAPTER TEN

# Natural Signs

Gold was discovered near Great Falls, Maryland, in 1861. In a creek on the Collins Farm, near the junction of Great Falls and Old Conduit Roads, one Pvt. John Cleary of the Union Army's California Volunteers found bits of pure gold flecking the stream gravel and in the nearby hunks of rose quartz, sugar quartz, and honeycomb quartz that littered the banks and pastures. A veteran forty-niner of the Sacramento gold fields, Cleary eventually sunk test pits, had the ore assayed, found backers, bought the Collins farm and others, and was one of several entrepreneurs who began mining in the Great Falls and Cropley regions after the Civil War. On and off for the next sixty years there were outbreaks of "gold fever" near the Potomac here, and schemers, promoters, and engineers made the old National Hotel, at Sixth and Pennsylvania in downtown Washington, their favorite place to gather. About thirty gold mines came and went, with a few 1870s veins yielding $150 of gold per ton (a handsome return in its day) and with some stream nuggets weighing three or four ounces each. The largest operation was the Maryland Mine, active periodically from 1900 to 1939 and eventually producing five thousand ounces of gold.

It is the Maryland Mine I'm approaching on this cool spring day, dressed in my favorite old sweater and taking my time in the woods. I have no great love for mining. In fact, I can't help but dislike an activity that degrades the land so badly. The gold mining process was (and is) especially noxious: shafts 150-feet deep were dug here, with numerous lateral tunnels, some disgorging five hundred tons of ore in a single peak month (modest by modern standards yet destructive nevertheless) and forming lofty above-ground mine dumps from the hundreds of tons of "waste" rock. Generally, a ton of hard quartz was crushed to get each half-ounce of gold. Toxic mercury was then often used to draw gold dust from pulverized quartz in another messy process, and throughout the surrounding woods remain the shallow trenches, pits, cuts, shafts, tunnels, spoil piles, and rusted boilers and engines from this and other operations.

But I am focused on other things: the stately, straight-boled tulip trees that have replaced the great chestnuts of old. Through their branches sunlight sinks shafts to the toothwort and wild geraniums, bluets, spring-beauties, and Dutchman's breeches. Somewhere nearby grows a rare species of coral-root, awaiting patient search, and black birch shows up in these forests at the southern limit of its range. Huge oaks and beeches exploit the steady wet at streamside, while clumps of waxy mountain laurel glisten on the hills near ruined Civil War entrenchments. Vireos call—red-eyed, white-eyed, yellow-throated—and visiting rose-breasted grosbeaks whistle in the canopy. It is almost two miles to the Maryland Mine, but protection has made the land rich again, and the trek is full of interest. I stop to watch a warbler, glimpse the white flags of retreating deer, or tip over rocks and fallen limbs to gaze on red-backed salamanders.

At the top of a steady rise the mine's water tower comes into view, crowded by box elder, dogwood, and tulip tree and by fences and multiflora rose. The main shafts interest me little, but, near a peripheral maze of old boards and stumps, I'm drawn to a circular pit, shallow-sloped like a bomb crater and entwined with verdure—with violet, geranium, honeysuckle, and deep green clumps of Christmas fern. It's an ugly area, really, except for this sunken digging rank with growth, where a tiger-beetle seems to lead me on, to flash its metallic signal ahead and tempt me into the crater. The ironic potential tempts me, too: What might a modern searcher "mine" in this disused, overgrown pit? At the bottom, in deepest shade, I lift a hunk of milky quartz, hoping for a further sign. What I find startles and delights me both: a delicate northern ringnecked snake, curled like a lovely necklace. It's a young ringneck, maybe eight inches long, with a satiny, slate-gray back and darker, big-scaled head. But most striking of all, as I roll it gently with my finger, is a deep yellow belly like a beaten gold strand and a complementary ring at its neck, unblemished and entire and as gold as the finest jewelry. It's a treasure greater than I'd hoped for; I feel once more the childlike lightness, the sense of wonder and amazement, the conviction of a priceless find.

But it's not until after I've held it in my palm, examined its intricate details and returned it to the rock, then retreated to the rim of the crater, that the full irony strikes me. Here, where men stripped the fields and forests, gouged out craters and gutted hills in pursuit of a few pounds of gold, their effort is largely forgotten and brings no one much delight. But one thing does bring delight. It's a creature weighing less than a nugget and appointed with the nugget's hues—and with those hues, in fact, worked like gold itself into mocking mimics of jewelry—which has reclaimed the very center of a pit that was once scoured for lifeless minerals. It's a subtly uncanny business, a page for my book of small wonders, my Potomac journal of the strange. It is one more natural connection, too, a further frail strand in my fabric of riverside discovery—muted, beautifully woven and essentially ignored, like the frayed old sweater I'm wrapped in.

A month later, in mid-May, I am far upriver, on the South Branch of the Potomac, close to its mainstem rendezvous. On the surface, once more, there is little going on: I'm trying to catch some smallmouth bass at a locally popular fishing hole. It is warm mid-afternoon; the river is bright and bluish green. Parents and children are down on the rocks, eating, shouting, and splashing, fishing and skipping stones—which they mix as if one activity—and enjoying a festive Sunday. In a yard above the road someone is endlessly mowing a lawn, and, without *Testubo,* I'm trying to find some quiet stretch that can also be reached on foot. When this fails I fish among the ruckus in the gaps that evolve as folks leave or move, and the surprise is that I begin to catch fish, not big ones, but 9- and 10-inch smallies that are fond of my crawdad imitation. Indeed I'm rather surprised, under these conditions, that I've taken any fish at all. When the last big party leaves, the final skipped stone sinks, and the lawnmower runs out of gas, I reclaim the shoreline near the deepest holes, where the locals had been most active.

Again, to my surprise, I hook four small bass on four straight casts, the sun beats into the jade-tinted water, and I start to wonder if skipping stones has potential as a new way of chumming. Then, as I unhook another young smallmouth and release it in the shallows, my peripheral vision picks up a shadow—of a two- or three-pound bass finning slowly just a few feet from shore. I cast to the fish repeatedly, merely flicking the bait in front of it and working it slowly past. The smallmouth swims back and forth but is otherwise apathetic. I try out every bait I have and still it shows no interest. I grow bored and move down the bank, only to spot another big bass—this one three pounds or better—likewise cruising the shallows. And, it turns out, likewise unmoved by my lures. I pull these so close to its passive maw that it literally has to turn away to avoid colliding with the bait.

Then I begin to focus on the bottom, on the little gravelly openings between the confusion of rocks. There are paler patches of pebbles here comprising ragged ovals, and I realize all at once that I've been watching spawning bass. These are the big breeding females, driven to these "nests" by the males and preparing to release their eggs. At such times they are unmoved by thoughts of food and will resist most presentations unless they feel the nest is threatened. Young males, meanwhile, the so-called bull bass of springtime, can become highly aggressive, especially if left with no nests to build or females to find and escort, and will attack baits with abandon. Thus, the ease with which I hooked smaller fish is explained by these age-old events.

But what makes this episode intriguing was the reaction of the human visitors before they pulled up stakes. Though I'd watched them fairly closely, I never detected their interest in these fish, which I'm sure, had the bass been noticed, would have brought some pointing and shouting and a concerted deployment of fishing lines directly above the females. To a child, indeed to most adults, a three-pound bass in a magnifying pool is a monster worthy of attention. The water was tinted but essentially clear, and once one picked out the shadowy forms they were easy to keep track of.

But, of course, they were no more plain to the visitors than the ringnecked snake in the mine pit. We moderns lack subtle focus in the wild and are blind to many phenomena. We are losing our "peripheral vision"—not just our literal sidelong sight, but a kind of attunement to marginal clues which our predatory forebears once nurtured. We have lost sensitivity to shadows, to stipples, glimmers and glows, to the loose, hanging edges of the naturally woven world. Cued to slick events, to loud noise and flashing lights, to blatant electronic impulse, we retain the senses of the hunter but only with vestigial keenness. Our "search image" aptitude atrophies and our full perception narrows.

"So what?" says the average citizen. We are no longer hunters and gatherers. We get what we need with less bother. True enough for the present. But the balance may one day swing back, may be doing so already, and the trade-off is perhaps a poor one. With a dimmed awareness of loose threads in nature, of the oddly raveled detail, we also lose sight of its linkage, of the pattern it is connected to, of the whole cloth that binds our spirit and the fabric that cloaks our soul. Perhaps we should relearn the weaver's touch, the mender's gift for connections. When one picks out dangling edges, is forced to see selvage and hem, one fashions a broader responsiveness to the complex garment of life.

We need now and then to find strands under rocks, to detect the frayed lines of a fish, to once more make nimble our ancient "gatherer" skills. By the river one constantly gathers, for the river gathers itself. It collects bits and pieces under rocks; it draws up the yarn of shadows; it entwines each stipple and glow—that long-handed upper Potomac, riffle-veined and rock-knuckled, that old darner, that weaver.

Yet some of the river's threads are so thin they are barely visible, even to those with keen sight. Three hundred years of scrutiny have still not revealed them all. On yet another fine spring day my wife, Donna, and I meet Warren and Jil Steiner in the Red Byrd Restaurant near Keedysville. Warren is an entomologist with the Smithsonian Institution in Washington and Jil an ecologist for the Maryland National Capital Parks and Planning Commission. While both know their way around wildlife, Warren is an expert on beetles, particularly the Tenebrionid family, whose minute, shiny members live beneath bark and are sometimes called "darkling beetles." Because most species are secretive and small, bark beetles frustrate discovery. Yet Warren hopes to uncover a few on the nearby limestone ridges.

After an ample breakfast we drive to Snyder's Landing and hike the downstream towpath. We all take pleasure in the wildflowers: green and white filagrees of Dutchman's breeches on the margins of the path, vibrant Virginia bluebells in the wetter and sunnier openings, and pockets of blood-red wake-robin on the slopes of the dry canal bed. While the rest of us hunt for harbinger-of-spring, an inconspicuous tuber that sprouts tiny parsley-like leaves and even tinier whitish flowers, Warren pokes about among tree trunks and logs, prying and peering under bark. He becomes so intent on his search, in fact, that he often leaves us behind, and when we finally reach Killiansburg Cave, a vertical limestone concavity above the canal which sheltered frightened Sharpsburgers during the battle of Antietam, he completely disappears. Nick Blanton, taking a break from his Opequon Creek dulcimer shop, soon shows up on his bicycle and we all have a fine time botanizing—ogling and photographing bellwort and anemone, broadleaf sedge and liverleaf hepatica, trout lily and ginger, even the northern white cedars that, outside their normal range here, persist, scaly and twisted, on the highest limestone ridge tops.

But Warren sticks mostly to his private quest, probing, like some bipedal woodpecker, the treebark cracks and fissures. When Nick departs after noon and we've had our fill of combing the hills, we head back along the towpath. Though it's a chilly April day, Warren has removed his trademark sandals and, Huck Finn style, is walking barefoot on the rough, damp path. He stops at most of the shaggier trees, and I can't help asking if he's looking for something special. "You never know what you'll find in these underscrutinized areas," he replies, eyeing a weathered old locust. "There are still lots of species to discover."

Even in this long-settled region?

"Oh yes. In the eastern United States alone there are something like twelve thousand known beetle species, but it's estimated that an additional 3 to 4 percent of that number are still unknown or unclassified."

You mean, in this day and age, there are three hundred to five hundred animal species, of a single group and in a heavily scoured region, which remain taxonomic mysteries?

"About that many. Yep. And even the ones that are known are greatly understudied. We know little about how they live, their habits, food, reproduction. Most are just specimens in jars. Some may go extinct before they even have names."

He detours to examine the locust, patiently peeling back bark strips, gently parting wood rot, deftly snatching some scurrying adult, cupping it gently to confirm what it is, then releasing it back to its niche. Warren is no mere eccentric obsessed with finding bugs. He cares deeply for the world of insects and nature, cherishes living systems, and, in a time of vanishing species, is committed to finding what's left before it's gone for good.

Biologists estimate that, worldwide, at least forty-five plants and animals become extinct each day. Insects are no exception, and we wonder aloud, as we dawdle back to the landing, just how many species were lost near this river before people even started looking. And how many now, in the face of swift growth and change, will die out before they are discovered.

When we stop for coffee in Shepherdstown, Warren finds one more chance to keep searching. We visit the old town waterfront, where the Swearingen Ferry once crossed and James Rumsey plied his steamboat. An old mill stands deserted; waste treatment tanks line the roadway. Two men are fishing for catfish at the creek mouth and we stop to exchange some small talk. Except for Warren, of course, who is busy nearby probing bark. He's put his sandals back on, though, for the place is a boat ramp and parking lot, too, full of broken glass and metal. Then, with offhand elation, he declares he's found something good on the trunk of an old box elder.

"*Prateus fusculus.* It's from a primitive group of the Tenebrionid family that likes hollow, decaying trees," he calls, coaxing it into a specimen bottle as the fishermen trade bemused stares. "It's known from Long Island to the Gulf States, but it's so small and cryptic that it's rarely been collected anywhere. I'll have to check, but I'm fairly certain it's a first record for West Virginia." Donna, Jil, and myself show as much excitement as seems fitting for a creature at the bottom of a two-inch jar that is roughly the size of a poppyseed.

Yet it's one more tiny triumph. Draw up another loose thread. Where an engineer knew victory of old, beside this very bank, a biologist knows it anew, however small and unsung. In the place where Shepherdstown began, on the frayed margins of its past, there is still a fresh glimmer in the fabric, some natural sign that discovery persists despite violent change and crisis. So it goes by the river. Pull a few strands from one spot, weave another back. Keep an eye on the ragged hem, hope it does not unravel, darn loose edges where you can.

Summer on the upper Potomac is a time of morning mists. The days are sultry and dreamlike; damp heat collects in the valleys and is cooled into fog overnight. It is a rank, lulling, torpid time, a time when wildlife stays hidden, when birds stop singing, when the air induces sleep and blurs clear distinctions.

I may bathe at midday in some cooling creek, having spent the morning getting sweaty in pursuit of smallmouth bass, but dawn is the time when I'm first about, when I walk the crack between worlds, a time as different from the coming noon as darkness is from light. The identical spot on the river, at daybreak, is unrecognizable at ten, as if, in the interim, someone changed the scenery, pulled the *Brigadoon* backdrop and replaced each veiled detail with ones so sharp and glaring that their very essence seems other, seems a separate molecular construction.

I am thinking especially of a certain stream that, while winding back from the river, supports beech trees beside a bend. By July most warblers have stopped singing, and the only persistent medley is that of the warbling vireo, a drab little bird with a spritely voice—of melodious, burbling undertones well suited to the dreamy mornings. If one drifts an extended riffle or wades to the purl of the current, the bird's bubbling blends with the water song, and both tunes become indistinguishable. The high banks, in fact, and the density of foliage and dampness, seem to hold these sounds and distort them, to refract each ever so slightly with a spooky sort of ventriloquism.

There is also a special odor here, for summer is the prime time for fungi. Enhancing the usual leaf rot smell is a certain fungal reek—like the one described by Nabokov near Vyra, the Russian estate of that author's childhood and which he dubbed the "boletic reek," for the Bolete family of mushrooms so prominent in the neighborhood. Indeed, the fleshy and colorful boletes are well represented near my stream: after rain in July or August there are showy Frost's boletes and chestnut-capped bay boletes, yellowish ornate-stalked boletes and my favorite local edible, *Boletus bicolor,* a garrish, maroon-topped, salmon-stemmed fungi that is good in stews or stir-fry.

Thus the overall dawn atmospherics by my tributary bend—mists and murmurs and effusions, blended with the sight of beech boles stretched like torsos in the wispy gloaming—are, even to the dullest mind, charged with mysterious suggestion, even mystical potential. It is the sort of time and place in which people begin to see things, create forms out of the fog curl, toy with other-worldly visions.

But fantasy can take one too far; sentiment and escapism are easy traps to get caught in. I do not see gnomes under toadstools, glimpse fairies in the gathering light, or search the sandbanks for Bigfoot's track (though there's a local guy who does this). Being once more attuned to detail and design, I take solace from the sense of them. I like the firm tarmac of evidence, enjoy taking off from its runways on speculative flights of fancy, but reserve a place to re-land my craft and do not jam the radar of science. And I apply the anthropomorphic—the projection of human traits—mainly in descriptive metaphor, as arresting analogue, as a way of drawing attention to nature's vivid dramas and of goosing poetic impact with the language of familiar reference. But there are lines I will not cross. I see fairies suggested in the hummingbird's flight but do not believe in fairies.

An essential pleasure in the natural world is this grounding in design and detail. It doesn't do to invent too much, for nature has invented it for you, in far more interesting ways. Scrutinize the structure of a beaver or bass and you need not fool with fiction. I will always recall my disappointment on reading *Lord of the Rings,* Tolkien's elaborate fantasy of life in a mythic realm. At one point he describes forest trees that reach out and touch his travelers. An unmatchable anthropomorphism, this idea, to me, of touchy-feely humanoid plants was the farthest thing from delightful, and crossed my line of tolerance. There is the very strongest evidence that trees, unlike humans, don't step or shuffle, reach out or caress. And the fact that trees are not human is to me the core of their solace. It is their irrefutable *otherness,* their immunity from being mere men, which constitutes much of their charm. If you want science fiction and are looking for inhuman aliens, you need no bizarre invention. Merely gaze at your neighbor, the tree. So it is in all of nature. Its reality *exceeds* simple fantasy, is better in the finest ways. Its complex, creative designs, if the human mind could but grasp them, would stagger that mind senseless.

So I take no interest in the sentiment that says, when one reaches a place like my tributary dell—with its lulling boletic reek, bubbling bird and brook song, and reverberant beech-haunted streamsides—that pleased or fretful trees are watching nearby or, to take a more Disney-esque fantasy, that gnomes are processing mushroom stalks—in some workshop beneath the tree roots—into gay picnic umbrellas, while the fumes of their ardent industry thus scent the magic air.

The reality, once again, is so much more intriguing, even on the simplest levels. If one stays to see the sunrise, one can watch the mist fall away, see the beeches change their color and tone, being one moment lavender blue in the shade and then turning silvery pewter. If one bothers to walk the banksides, one learns that the stream needs compression to speak, for otherwise, free to expand its waist where the banks have broadened with erosion, it reclines in lazy pools and utters not a sound. If one makes a brief study of the boletes, one sees their inertness as a virtue, their pigments as useful clues, and their down-to-earth fragrance and fleshiness as the essence of their edibility. One further notes how they spring up after rain, not prodded by elves but by weather, by vagaries of moisture and light, by the welcome laws, however inscrutible, of our planet's precise limitations, by tropospheric alignments that converge to bring sunshine or storms. And if one takes in these things altogether, one can mark how the brain wields our senses, processes multiple inputs with an intricacy past all fiction, so that strewn atmospheric amalgams—brought together at the bend of a stream to trap rank boletic effluvia, birdsong and brooksound and beechtone—can soak us in the magic of the real and invite our legitimate wonder.

Yet for all my faith in a "real" world, I remain something of a mystic, which is also what makes me a madman. I am split like a dual personality. For all my belief in Darwin and my conviction that dog will eat dog, that frog will eat snake, or vice versa, depending on which is bigger; for all my belief that Bigfoot is a myth, not because he could not sustain himself or that nature could not invent him but because we are hopeless dreamers and see too much in the mists; for all my awareness of limits and my grasp of imminent extinctions, I believe in a natural magic. And my time on the upper Potomac is what brought that belief to conviction.

In the sense that nature is a talisman or charm, I believe it has mystical properties. In the sense that wildness inspires and instructs in ways that cannot be explained, I believe it is a kind of magic. I believe that the river weaves spells, and I believe this is no mere metaphor but a concrete and palpable fact. The river is nothing so vague as a dream, but rather, it leads us to dream ourselves, and that is a potent reality. If you went, sick at heart and in pain, to a doctor to cure your ills, and he gave you something that cured them, you would surely call it real and respect it equally as science. Yet I tell you that such things once ailed *me,* and I went not to a doctor, but adventuring on the Potomac, and by that I was largely healed. The river does not set broken legs or remove malignant tumors, but it saves one from going off the deep end, if that is respectable medicine.

So I keep its option available, keep the chance to pay it a visit always near at hand, store its fetish against blues and angst in some readily accessed place, and apply its charm as needed. There is nothing trivial about this, nor is it mere tongue in cheek. The ability to get down to bankside, the reality of that "treatment" and its equally real effect, is a critical part of my life. And I've come to think it is spirit, not science, which brings the eventual improvement. The agent cannot be verified; there are no measurable results. I merely put faith in this amulet and the fact that it casts healing spells. In today's world this makes me a madman or a fool, but in my world it makes me sane.

I also believe I am woven there, interlaced somehow with the river, knotted with its winding streams, spliced to its margins and mysteries, pitched down the warp of its main stem flow each time I launch *Testubo. Testubo*—the small rubber shuttle that the river flings its length or works back and forth on its tributary strands in lateral woofs and wefts. But the metaphor isn't important, only the sense of linkage, a linkage I feel when I take boat and car and make my way down to the river.

It is autumn on the upper Potomac. The river is low and easy. At Lock 22, where Ma Pennyfield once skinned eels for a president, her old house stands deserted, its crooked porch roof sagging. The pasture is dappled with hazy sun, a rotten-apple fragrance pervades; there are walnuts scattered by the cracked board fence, tennis-ball-big and green. There is cricket-quiet by the towpath, which is layered with fallen leaves, and down I go to the river, past the drab young migrant warblers, the spicebush and sassafras yellowing, the black silt and flood wrack at bankside, the worm cartons, beer cans, hook packets, the bobbers hung in trees.

*Testubo* is getting old. Her gunnels are faded and scratched, her blue bottom scarred, her ropes showing signs of decay. She has started to take on water. But down she drifts regardless, no complaints or grumbles from this silent friend—bouncing off ledges, scraping bars, maintaining balloon elevation above the submerged bottom landscape. The smallmouth bass are finicky; they seem to get more so each year. Too much fishing pressure from the new suburban masses. Maybe Seneca Creek carries too much local silt, or Goose Creek or the Monocacy. But I don't merely come for the fishing. I'm down here for the drift, for autumnal ripeness, for the quiet submarine gardens, for my unfailing dose of solace. Yet I now must fight my way down here. The roads are plagued by gridlock, and Potomac, that once sleepy town, is now the hip pocket of D.C. This used to be a hidden corner. Now I hear trucks on River Road; planes and jet copters buzz overhead; there is too much traffic on the towpath. Even the Goodyear Blimp has showed up, high above the downstream trees, to cover some upcoming ballgame. A kind of fussiness nags me and a sense of being pursued. Is the modern world closing in? Is the charm at last going to fail me? Maybe I should get upriver, spend more than an afternoon. Maybe I just need time and room—to be passed along the garment's length and shuttled among the weave.

Up then, to Frederick County, as soon as we find the time. *Testubo*'s bottom has been patched and glued; my car has a new set of tires. The riverside ripens like a long vine of grapes, and the Middletown Valley shimmers after dawn, lifts its fog from the treetops, spills its leaves in the creeks.

Here is pawpaw country, the old weirs and campsites of Catoctin Creek, the ghosts of hobo jungles upstream, the leaf-embowered towpath, the train horns, the freights rumbling out from the tunnel. By the banks bloom mist-flower and aster, gray lichens cover the rocks like so much peeling paint, herons leave fried-egg droppings, sunfish throw shadows in the tinted pools and black snails comb the ledges. The smallmouth rise early, slaughter wounded minnows, sink back in amber holes.

Up again, to Brunswick, past the switchyard and roundhouse, Horine's and the B & O Museum, into Knoxville, then Weverton, to the lot off Keep Tryst Road, wading the glides off the vanished sluice where stone walls still rise at bankside, Round Hill looming gold against blue, the rapids gurgling without letup, the runt bass schooling off ledges, pecking the blue-green surface, leaping like tarpon when hooked.

Lunch at Cindy Dee's, the meatloaf and mashed potatoes, the cornball slogans on the tractor caps, the counter peppered with regulars at every other stool.

To Taylor's Landing by the back door now, past the Kennedy farmstead where John Brown plotted, and Antietam Creek, which once ran with blood below Burnside's Bridge and now slips past the ironworks, anemic, under the limestone aqueduct, out to its fishy confluence with the low bronze-backed river. Sharpsburg is a yuppified relic these days yet redolent of charm, of graystone rural quiet and small-town friendly manners. The wan echo of conflict still spreads out beyond the streets, in the parchment sunlight, the cicada stillness of afternoon, as I thread Mondell Road to the river, across from the monument to Patrick's Brigade who made their stand for the Union.

Taylor's Landing is a sepia ghost, a heartbreak throb of autumn, the sycamores past the river all dull brass and copper and dusty palpitation, the breeze carrying fust and leaf-reek, the water a smoky bottle full of blue and gray and glints of steel, the current contrasting with the rigid bank, the ripeness a kind of mourning. Dogs bark from nearby yards. I head upstream on the towpath to the campsite called Big Woods. It is faced by a limestone cliff that stares out from West Virginia and the place known as Terrapin Neck, a fitting location for *Testubo.*

We play together in the pools, my boat and I, all that afternoon, tugging fish out of fossil-resin holes, dropping them back like golden pippins when the tug-of-war is through. We stay above the fast-water ledge where the river is shallow and placid; we beach ourselves on a rocky spit beyond which the water deepens; we drop below the rapid and fish along the cliff, catching hungry 10-inch bass and a tiger-striped two-pounder.

Afternoon dozes, dusk seeps in, fish are filleted and eaten, a sleeping bag is flattened on the down of floodplain leaf-fall, a gap is reserved in the canopy above for staring at pale constellations.

Breakfast is served at Jeanne's after a predawn charge to Williamsport: fifty-cent hotcake, egg and toast for six bits, triple refill of coffee beneath the mural of the mule while watching the girl at the stainless steel grill, who hand-slices spuds into home-fries in her bright pink smock and bow. Then a stroll by the river, past the rubble of limestone canal blocks, the teenager drinking in his car by the bridge, the Cushwa Coal and Brick sign mirrored in the stagnant basin, the New York aster and stinging nettle, the box elders, maples, and half-bare walnuts gone tallow above the roadway. Cloudy now, the river's sky reflections like a stream of gray milk afloat on a long spill of 30-weight. Quickly, to

Wolfe's On the Square, to buy a Snickers for later and ogle the trophy snapshots that cover half the wall: a 10-pound musky on a minnow; a 4-pound walleye on a grub; a brown trout taken from Antietam Creek which was 2 ounces short of 4 pounds.

Now swiftly into Virginia, through Winchester down to Millville, to a stretch of the Shenandoah, the Potomac's strong right arm. *Testubo* launched by a farm road, near a pasture, the riverbanks thick with sycamore, the sky soon turning bright and blue, igniting drab leaves to chartreuse and polishing twisted boughs. A shallow, meandering float, setting nicely the tone of the season: pools caked entirely with fallen leaves, bluejays screaming as they go, limestone ledges that gurgle and foam and challenge *Testubo*'s patched bottom. I sit on the bow to probe each pool, view the drowned, outstretched snags, white as cadavers, and the young bass that chase my offerings. Fish fling themselves up from eddies when they strike, as if trying to reach hanging branches, then splash down and spit out my crawdad. The pace, after time, is so lulling and sweet that I lose all sense of my bearings. The delight becomes generic: I am at that daydream location, that place with no map coordinates, that imagined autumn float trip that is a lifetime's composite reverie. Perhaps a whole day has passed, perhaps only an hour. My take-out point meets the bend in a road, a bankside gallery of sunlight, of maples, sycamores, suffusions, smoke settling like gold-dust from some local barnyard bonfire.

I rest beneath a hickory, break off a staff, gather my things for the hike. No towpath here, just a hilly backcountry farm road, sunken in places to form earthen walls that are woven with grapevine and creeper and scarlet poison ivy, all dulled by a dusty pumice. Stunted locusts double as fenceposts; ash and hackberry lean; wrens and cardinals stutter. The air is wood-smoke pungent, the light hazy; the pastures above the banks ring with heifer-bleat and cowbell and the slow-busy sounds of farmwork, and I am Ichabod Crane, pounding the road-dust with a hickory staff, gangling, carefree, with an unbalanced pack, a distant scholarly appointment, a head full of foolish dreams.

It is roundabout to my car on these roads. I crest a hill between white board fences, between donkeys, beef calves, sycamores even here, and a sign reading *Angus-Aberdeen,* flanked by a giant black bull. The river comes back into view below, looking honey brown in the radiance between the far-off trees.

Back I go into Berryville for lunch, to the Town House Restaurant and its chuckwagon steaks, country ham and eggs, and a lettered promotion for the "Texburger," trailed by the curious epigram: "That's Big Son." Lacquered signs and arrowheads dot the knotty-pine walls; old women gossip among empty booths about who is dying at the hospital.

Down, then, to Front Royal, junction of the North and South Fork, dusty heel of Skyline Drive, long-ago frontier outpost still fitted with a few rough nails, with pawnshops and tattoo parlors mixing at its gentrified hub. Then to Limeton and Luray and down to the mellow South Fork for some long casts under a bridge. Thread the needle to New Market, through the gap in Massanutten Mountain. Up from there, in the shadow of Mount Jackson. Stopping to wade the North Fork a few miles downstream from Edinburg. Little bass beside old Route 11 and drifts of coppery leaves. Next, People's Drugstore in Edinburg itself, with its gnome-sized lunch-counter stools in back, and where big Harry Murray, redheaded fly-fishing legend, jumps from behind his pharmacist's nook to help sell one of his books, or a Murray's Strimp or Hellgremite, which resemble your father's mustache, set out in bins among fly rods and vests, across from the Dr. Scholl's footpads.

Now north again, loping in the late afternoon, up Route 522 to Hancock, coffee there at the Park 'N Dine, with its view of the sycamores and river, a stop by the parched canal, a drink in the old Town Tavern. Then up on cemetery hill in the crickety dusk, a harvest moon on the rise, above the cramped little crossroads, above St. Patrick's Church where the Union repelled Stonewall Jackson, where Irish navvies were laid to rest, where traders and trappers and nomads before them looked down on this natural junction, above the Tonoloway creeks, the amber wooded hills, the big sky and fish-barred clouds, persimmon in the failing light as they have been for uncounted ages, at just this time of year, from just this spot on the ridges.

Supper is again at the Park 'N Dine, beneath photos of the icy river, a head-on CSX engine, a poplar gnawed by a beaver. Sleep is the Hancock Motel, the tidiest place in town, as tidy as an old aunt's bedroom.

Come morning the sky has gone pewter; the river is a slab of lead. I take back roads to Little Orleans, beside the old traces of the Royal Road, the colonial bypass of Sideling Hill, the ghosts of Braddock's marchers. I float down from the mouth of Fifteen Mile Creek, hook smallmouth and fallfish in a quarter-mile pool that was angled by Herbert Hoover, unwitting architect of Brunswick's hobo jungles. A somber morning with a chilly wind, the mountains tinged with sadness, the water dull and cold. It is a day that tests believers, weeds out the summer soldiers: cold hands and feet, the fatigue of aimless travel, the fishing generally slow, chainsaws buzzing from a bankside yard, sprinkles of icy rain, memories of loss and failure, sprays of low-grade depression with every bite of the breeze. The inevitable low point, this: the wanderer's mid-journey crucible, the hump that must be surmounted. A candy bar brings some solace, a cup of coffee some warmth. I beach *Testubo* at Indigo Neck in a hopelessly overgrown tangle, have trouble breaking trail to the towpath, retreat to the windblown bank, deflate *Testubo* in disgust, lie down against a sycamore, full of nameless aches.

I eat my soggy sandwich and watch maples just downstream, their leaves going light, then lighter, whenever the breeze twists their stems. A root beer foam rides the river, my pack is drying in the wind, rapids purl, chickadees chatter overhead. Then again the sudden flicker and flash of the silver maples downstream, and the soughing music of their leaves. I close my eyes, erase my thoughts, listen only to the spinning concert. Once more the sense of a dream song, a shimmering hinge, a kind of rhythmic lifting. "Be wary," said an unknown Christian mystic, "that thou conceive not bodily that which is meant ghostly, although it be spoken bodily in bodily words as be these, up or down, in or out, behind or before."

Up now, feeling lighter, grabbing my pack, fighting out to the hidden towpath. Up the trail toward Fifteen Mile Creek, the black gum and creeper gone scarlet in the woods, a pileated woodpecker calling. The clouds are starting to break here, showing little lakes of blue, and before long I'm back at my car. Now up the road past Paw Paw, lacing west to Oldtown, called of old King Opessa's Town, home to Shawnees and Senecas, whose path I then follow southward. An ancient human trace, its margins now lead me in the clearing day, in the old gold afternoon, as I skirt the nomad graveyards, called Blue's Rocks and Slim Bottom by white men, toward the junction of the frontier meat fork, the three-pronged Wappacomo. The wind is dying, the sky has cleared, it will frost tonight in the valleys. I keep my heading for Seneca Rocks, for the North Fork up near Spruce Knob, and will spend the night in the Smoke Hole by some caves beneath the ridge brows, companioned by the natural magic that brings solace to my time on earth.

The spell is holding up. I know I'm not some madman, but a creature sound and sane. I know that nothing can unravel me as long as the river winds, weaves among the valleys and hills and flows beside the floodplains. Somewhere on the edge of my reason I grasp this thread of reckoning: that this is the charm that all rivers wield, everywhere on the planet. And if this is not real magic, then no real magic exists.

# Bibliography


Alderton, Jan P. "Old Store Attracts Tourists." *Cumberland News,* June 5, 1975.

Baker, Peter. "Maryland Deer Hunting Is Suddenly Wide Open." *Baltimore Sun,* November 23, 1992.

Barrat, John. "Startling Harbingers of Spring." *Smithsonian News Service,* April 1991.

Benson, Adolph B., ed. *Peter Kalm's Travels in North America.* New York: Dover Publications, 1966.

Benton, Michael. *The Dinosaur Encyclopedia.* New York: Simon and Schuster, 1984.

Birch, Doug. "Natural Maryland: The Way It Was." *Baltimore Sun,* August 22, 1993.

Borland, Hal. *A Countryman's Woods.* New York: Alfred A. Knopf, 1983.

Borror, Donald J., and Richard E. White. *A Field Guide to the Insects.* Boston: Houghton Mifflin, 1970.

Brown, Melvin L. "Floristics of Shale Barren Endangered Species." MS.

Brown, Melvin L., and Russell G. Brown. *Herbaceous Plants of Maryland.* Baltimore: Port City Press, 1984.

Burt, William H., and Richard P. Grossenheider. *A Field Guide to the Mammals of America North of Mexico.* Boston: Houghton Mifflin, 1976.

Carr, Archie. *The Reptiles.* Alexandria, Va.: Time-Life Books, 1979.

*Chesapeake and Ohio Canal: Handbook 142*. Washington, D.C.: Division of Publications, National Park Service, U.S. Department of the Interior, 1991.

Clark, Ella E., and Thomas F. Hahn, eds. *Life on the Chesapeake and Ohio Canal 1859*. Shepherdstown, W.V.: American Canal and Transportation Center, 1975.

Cohn, D'Vera. "High Dioxin Levels Measured in Fish in W. Maryland." *Washington Post,* November 19, 1988.

———. "Is Bambi Hogging the Forest?" *Washington Post,* December 1, 1992.

Conant, Roger. *A Field Guide to Reptiles and Amphibians of Eastern and Central North America.* Boston: Houghton Mifflin, 1975.

Core, Earl L. *Spring Wildflowers of West Virginia.* Morgantown: West Virginia University Press, 1981.

"Destructive Floods Hit D.C., Richmond." *Washington Post,* November 7, 1985.

Engelman, Robert. "Washington before Washington." *Washington Post Magazine,* July 13, 1986.

*Field Guide to the Birds of North America.* Washington, D.C.: National Geographic Society, 1983.

Franz, Richard, and Dennis Slifer. *Caves of Maryland.* Educational Series no. 3. *Maryland Geological Survey* (1971).

Fuller, Harry J. *The Plant World.* New York: Henry Holt, 1951.

Garrett, Wilbur E. "George Washington's Patowmack Canal." *National Geographic,* June 1987.

"Geologic Map of Maryland." *Maryland Geologic Survey* (1968).

Gude, Gilbert. *Small Town Destiny.* Mt. Airy, Md.: Lomond Publishers, 1989.

———. *Where the Potomac Begins: A History of the North Branch Valley.* Cabin John, Md.: Seven Locks Press, 1984.

Gutheim, Frederick. *The Potomac.* New York: Rinehart and Co., 1949.

Hahn, Thomas F. *Towpath Guide to the Chesapeake and Ohio Canal.* Shepherdstown, W.V.: American Canal and Transportation Center, 1982.

Henshall, James A. *Book of the Black Bass.* Cincinnati: Robert Clarke and Co., 1881.

Hesser, Robert B. "Water Pollution." MS. Pennsylvania Fish Commission.

Ingalls, Edgar T. *The Discovery of Gold at Great Falls, Maryland.* N.p.: Edgar T. Ingalls, 1960.

Johnson, Edgar. *Charles Dickens: His Tragedy and Triumph.* New York: Simon and Schuster, 1952.

Johnson, Michael G. *American Woodland Indians.* London: Osprey Publishing, 1990.

Kelly, Howard. *Snakes of Maryland.* Baltimore: Natural History Society of Maryland, 1936.

Lawson, John. *A New Voyage to Carolina.* Chapel Hill; University of North Carolina Press, 1967.

Laycock, George. "Games Otters Play." *Audubon* (January 1981).

Lee, David S. "Aquatic Zoogeography of Maryland." *Atlantic Naturalist* (Winter 1976).

Marshall, N. B. *The Life of Fishes.* New York: Universe Books, 1970.

Marye, William B. "Notes on the Primitive History of Western Maryland." *Maryland Historical Magazine* 38 (1943).

———. "Patowmeck above Ye Inhabitants." *Maryland Historical Magazine* 30 (1935).

———. "Warriors' Paths." *Pennsylvania Archeologist.* Harrisburg, Pa.: Society for Pennsylvania Archeology, 1943.

*Maryland Birdlife: Bulletin of the Maryland Ornithological Society.* Vols. 46–48. Baltimore: M.O.S., 1990–92.

*Maryland Historical Records.* Stokes File, box 42, folder 36.

McCauley, Robert H., Jr. *Reptiles of Maryland and the District of Columbia.* Hagerstown, Md.: Robert H. McCauley, Jr., 1945.

McClane, A. J. *McClane's Field Guide to Freshwater Fishes of North America.* New York: Holt, Rinehart, and Winston, 1965.

McClane, A. J., and Keith Gardner. *McClane's Game Fish of North America.* New York: Times Books, 1984.

McClinton, Arthur T., ed. *The Fairfax Line: A Historic Landmark.* Edinburg, Va.: Shenandoah County Historical Society, 1990.

Meredith, Dennis. "Tweet Mystery of Life." *Duke Magazine* (July–August 1994).

Merritt, Richard W., and Kenneth W. Cummins. *An Introduction to Aquatic Insects of North America.* Dubuque, Ia.: Kendall-Hunt Publications Corp., 1978.

Miller, Dorcas. *Track Finder: A Guide to Mammal Tracks of Eastern North America.* Berkeley, Calif.: Dorcas Miller, 1981.

Mitchell, John G. "Soft Skins and Sprung Steel." *Audubon* (July 1982).

*Mountains to Marshes: The Nature Conservancy Preserves in Maryland.* Chevy Chase: Maryland Chapter of the Nature Conservancy, 1991.

Newcombe, Lawrence. *Newcombe's Widlflower Guide.* Boston: Little, Brown, 1977.

Nicholls, Richard E. *The Running Press Book of Turtles.* Philadelphia: The Running Press, 1977.

Niering, William A. *Wetlands.* New York: Alfred A. Knopf, 1985.

Oglesby, Ray T. et al. *River Ecology and Man.* Academic Press, 1972.

Page, Lawrence M., and Brooks M. Burr. *A Field Guide to Freshwater Fishes.* Boston: Houghton Mifflin, 1991.

Parker, Arthur C. *Seneca Myths and Folk Tales.* Lincoln: University of Nebraska Press, 1989.

Pavol, Ken. "Rebirth of the Potomac." MS. Maryland Department of Natural Resources.

Peattie, Donald Culross. *A Natural History of Trees.* Boston: Houghton Mifflin, 1966.

Peterson, Roger Tory. *A Field Guide to the Birds East of the Rockies.* Boston: Houghton Mifflin, 1968.

Peterson, Roger Tory, and Margaret McKenny. *A Field Guide to Widlflowers of Northeastern and North-Central North America.* Boston: Houghton Mifflin, 1968.

Platt, Rutherford. *1001 Questions Answered about Trees.* New York: Dodd, Mead, 1959.

Pousson, John F. *Archeological Excavations at the Moore Village Site, C & O Canal National Historical Park, Allegheny County, Maryland.* Washington, D.C.: National Park Service, U.S. Department of the Interior, 1983.

Powell, Terry. "Mud and Fire—Tools of the Dugout Canoe Maker." *Bulletin of Primitive Technology* 1, no. 6 (1993).

Rafinesque, Constantine. *Ichthyologia Ohiensis.* Lexington, Ky.: W. G. Hunt, 1820.

Reid, George K. *Pond Life.* New York: Western Publishing Co., 1967.

"Revitalizing the North Branch." *Potomac Basin Reporter* (Interstate Commission on the Potomac River Basin [ICPRB]) (March 1991).

Rhodes, Richard. *The Ozarks.* New York: Time-Life Books, 1975.

Richards, Keith. *Rivers: Form and Process in Alluvial Channels.* London: Methuen, 1982.

Riechmann, Deb. "Shore Otters Transported to Populate Western Maryland." *Baltimore Sun,* April 19, 1992.

"The River's Vital Statistics." *Washington Post,* February 16, 1984.

Rue, Leonard Lee, III. *The World of the Beaver.* New York: J. B. Lippincott, 1964.

———. *The World of the White-tailed Deer.* New York: J. B. Lippincott, 1962.

Ryden, Hope. *Lily Pond: Four Years with a Family of Beavers.* New York: William Morrow, 1989.

Rzoska, Julian. *On the Nature of Rivers.* N.p.: Dr. W. Junk Publishers, 1978.

Schwartz, Frank J. "Several Maryland Fishes Are Close to Extinction." *Maryland Conservationist* 39, no. 3 (1964).

Shaffer, Larry L. "The Limestone Streams of Pennsylvania." MS. Pennsylvania Fish Commission.

Shiffer, Clark N. "Snakes in Pennsylvania." MS. Pennsylvania Fish Commission.

Shosteck, Robert. *The Potomac Trail Book.* Boston: Appalachian Trail Club, 1973.

Smith, J. Lawrence. *The Potomac Naturalist.* Parsons, W. Va.: McClain Printing, 1968.

Spence, Lewis. *The Myths of North American Indians.* New York: Dover Publications, 1989.

Springer, Ethel M., and Thomas F. Hahn. *Canal Boat Children.* Shepherdstown, W.V.: American Canal and Transportation Center, 1977.

Stanton, Richard L. *Potomac Journey: Fairfax Stone to Tidewater.* Washington, D.C.: Smithsonian Institution Press, 1993.

Stranahan, Susan Q. *Susquehanna: River of Dreams.* Baltimore: Johns Hopkins University Press, 1993.

Tasker, Greg. "Dose of Lime May Revive Dead River." *Baltimore Sun,* October 5, 1993.

——. "Pawpaws Ripe for Return to Glory." *Baltimore Sun,* September 12, 1993.

Terres, John K. *The Audubon Society Encyclopedia of North American Birds.* New York: Alfred A. Knopf, 1987.

Vance, Joel M. "The Tortoise and the Pair." *Audubon* (July 1985).

Wayland, John W., ed. *The Fairfax Line: Thomas Lewis' Journal of 1746.* New Market, Va.: Henkel Press, 1925.

# Index

## Index

## Index

Jack Wennerstrom is a writer and naturalist who lives in Randallstown, Maryland. He is the author of *Soldiers Delight Journal: Exploring a Globally Rare Ecosystem* and is a contributing editor to *Bird Watcher's Digest.*

Library of Congress Cataloging-in-Publication Data

Wennerstrom, Jack, 1948–
Leaning sycamores : natural worlds of the upper Potomac / Jack Wennerstrom.
p. cm.
Includes bibliographical references and index.
ISBN 0-8018-5189-0 (alk. paper)
1. Natural history—Potomac River Valley. 2. Potomac River Valley. I. Title.
QH104.5.P67W46 1996
508.752—dc20 95-19839
CIP

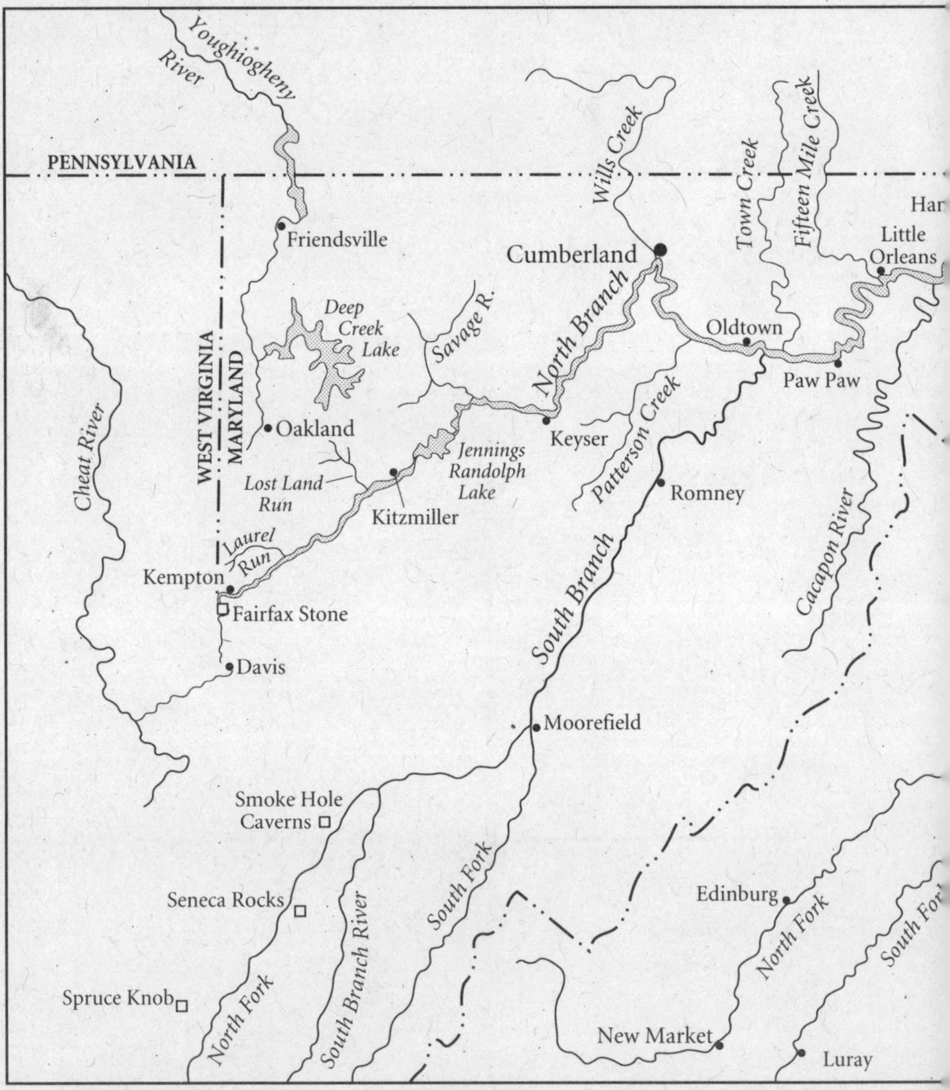
Youghiogheny
River
PENNSYLVANIA
Friendsville
Wills Creek
Town Creek
Fifteen Mile Creek
Little
Orleans
Cumberland
Deep
Creek
Lake
Savage R.
North Branch
Oldtown
Paw Paw
WEST VIRGINIA
MARYLAND
Cheat River
Oakland
Keyser
Patterson Creek
Jennings
Randolph
Lake
Lost Land
Run
Kitzmiller
Romney
Laurel
Run
Kempton
Fairfax Stone
South Branch
Cacapon River
Davis
Moorefield
Smoke Hole
Caverns
Seneca Rocks
South Fork
South Branch River
Edinburg
North Fork
Spruce Knob
North Fork
New Market
Luray